AN INTRODUCTION
TO FUNDAMENTAL
RIGHTS IN EUROPE

CW01474858

AN INTRODUCTION TO FUNDAMENTAL RIGHTS IN EUROPE

HISTORY, THEORY, CASES

ALESSANDRA FACCHI

SILVIA FALCETTA

NICOLA RIVA

EE Edward Elgar
PUBLISHING

Cheltenham, UK • Northampton, MA, USA

© Alessandra Facchi, Silvia Falcetta and
  Nicola Riva 2022

Cover image: Tullio Pericoli, *Terre fragili*, 2018,
oil on plaster on canvas

All rights reserved. No part of this publication
may be reproduced, stored in a retrieval system
or transmitted in any form or by any means,
electronic, mechanical or photocopying,
recording, or otherwise without the prior
permission of the publisher.

Published by
Edward Elgar Publishing Limited
The Lypiatts
15 Lansdown Road
Cheltenham
Glos GL50 2JA
UK

Edward Elgar Publishing, Inc.
William Pratt House
9 Dewey Court
Northampton
Massachusetts 01060
USA

A catalogue record for this book
is available from the British Library

Library of Congress Control Number:
2022931152

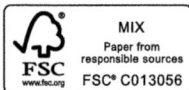

FSC
www.fsc.org
MIX
Paper from
responsible sources
FSC® C013056

ISBN 978 1 78811 702 9 (cased)
ISBN 978 1 78811 704 3 (paperback)
ISBN 978 1 78811 703 6 (eBook)

Printed and bound in Great Britain by TJ Books Limited, Padstow, Cornwall

CONTENTS IN BRIEF

FULL CONTENTS

PREFACE

The idea that all human beings are endowed with some fundamental rights has been with us for almost five centuries now, having first been expounded in the natural rights theories of the sixteenth and seventeenth centuries. Throughout that time this idea has served as a powerful tool with which to criticize the conduct of actors both private and public—governments, international and transnational organizations, corporations, and persons—as well as to justify demands for legal and social reform. Even more important was the development that came in the late eighteenth century, when human rights began to gain a legal status proper, gradually becoming a central institution in contemporary legal systems at different levels: national, regional, and—in the form of global human rights—international.

At the national level, fundamental rights come in the form of constitutional rights, often secured through mechanisms of judicial review. As such, they are a distinctive institution of constitutional democracy, a form of government that over the last two centuries—not without ruptures and temporary regressions—has developed to establish itself as the dominant form of government across the world.

In 1948, with the adoption of the Universal Declaration of Human Rights by the General Assembly of the United Nations, fundamental rights gained full international recognition. International charters and treaties affirming and specifying those rights have since multiplied, and new international and transnational organizations, public and private alike, have been established with the aim of protecting fundamental rights.

Especially significant in this respect is the emergence of continental or 'regional' regimes for the protection of fundamental rights, the most advanced and effective of which is the European regime, set up in 1950 with the adoption of the European Convention on Human Rights, establishing the European Court of Human Rights (ECtHR), and reinforced at the level of the European Union with the creation of the Charter of Fundamental Rights in 2000.

On the contemporary understanding of fundamental rights, these rights are conditions of political legitimacy. They set limits and goals around the exercise of political authority and around the use of public resources. Fundamental rights establish the ways in which political authority *cannot* be exercised and public resources used—in ways that frustrate important individual interests—and the ways in which that authority *should* be exercised and those resources used, namely, to protect those interests from public and private violations and to enable them to be fulfilled.

This volume provides an introduction to fundamental rights from a multidisciplinary perspective. It is primarily addressed to students of law, philosophy, and political science but can also appeal to a nonacademic public of readers interested in understanding the basics of such an important institution.

The book is organized into three parts. Part I—'History'—traces the historical development through which fundamental rights, starting out as social aspirations, mature into legal institutions, in a reconstruction that takes into account the role played by philosophical and legal theories as well as by political mobilization. Part II—'Theory'—deals with issues, both analytical and normative, relating to the definition and classification of fundamental rights, their implementation, and their justification. Finally, Part III—'Cases'—analyses some key fundamental rights cases selected from the jurisprudence of the ECtHR and the Court of Justice of the European Union (CJEU). Opening each of the three parts is an introduction providing a more detailed description of its aims and contents.

Although the three parts may present some stylistic differences, owing to the fact that they are written by three different authors, we have made sure that their terminology is consistent throughout, and where a topic is discussed from different angles in different parts, cross-references help the reader make the connection.[1]

Throughout this book we adopt a European perspective. This is evident in Part III, which focuses on the jurisprudence of the ECtHR and of the CJEU. In selecting the themes to be analysed in that part, we had to make some difficult choices. Since the aim in Part III is to illustrate how courts approach conflicts between fundamental rights and contribute to the evolution of fundamental rights themselves, we decided to focus on some themes that are particularly debated in contemporary society and on which the European courts have developed significant jurisprudence.

The need to condense a rich literature and jurisprudence into a volume of reasonable size has led us to some inevitable simplifications and choices that some readers may disagree with. Conceiving this work as an introductory textbook, we decided to reduce the bibliography to a minimum, with a focus on primary sources.

Alessandra Facchi, Silvia Falcetta, Nicola Riva

---

[1]   Alessandra Facchi is the author of Part I, Nicola Riva the author of Part II, and Silvia Falcetta the author of Part III. The authors would like to thank Filippo Valente for the linguistic revision of the manuscript and for his assistance in uniforming the different parts of the text.

ABBREVIATIONS

CEDAW	Convention on the Elimination of All Forms of Discrimination against Women
CJEU	Court of Justice of the European Union
CoE	Council of Europe
ECHR	European Convention on Human Rights
ECmHR	European Commission of Human Rights
ECtHR	European Court of Human Rights
EEC	European Economic Community
EU	European Union
EU Charter	Charter of Fundamental Rights of the European Union
EU law	The law of the European Union
FGM	Female genital mutilation
HRBA	Human Rights-Based Approach
ICCPR	International Covenant on Civil and Political Rights
ICESCR	International Covenant on Economic, Social and Cultural Rights
IP rights	Intellectual property rights
ISP	Internet service provider
NGO	Nongovernmental organization
P1-1	Article 1 of Protocol 1 to the ECHR
P1-2	Article 2 of Protocol 1 to the ECHR
TFEU	Treaty on the Functioning of the European Union
UDHR	Universal Declaration of Human Rights
UN	United Nations

PART I
HISTORY

Alessandra Facchi

INTRODUCTION

The contemporary landscape of fundamental rights could scarcely be understood without looking at the history of these rights, and that history is in large part a European history.[1]

Fundamental rights trace their origins to the Middle Ages, and the process through which they evolved can be described as a layering and mutual feedback of ideas, facts, and norms, and more specifically of theories, social movements, and legal documents.

Before fundamental rights took form as norms and principles across the territories of Europe, they expressed themselves as socially widespread needs and demands asserted through social struggles: the legal order heeded some of these demands, and in so doing it also helped to call attention to them. The formation of fundamental rights can indeed be viewed as a process that develops from the grassroots: needs that are widely felt across a section of society gradually come to be perceived as a matter of 'justice', thus taking the form of moral rights; increasingly, as these moral rights gain consensus as legitimate social demands, pressure is exerted so that political and legal authorities will recognize them, and along the way the demands so asserted sometimes take the form of legal rights, set forth and guaranteed in national and/or supranational law.

The formation of different fundamental rights thus bears a direct connection to transformations in the economic structures of society and in the power relations among different components in the population, as well as to the emergence of various political visions and to the new possibilities broached by scientific and technological discoveries.

Social movements, groups, and organizations played an essential role in the past—and continue to play to this day—not only in claiming new rights but also in extending established rights to previously excluded groups, as well as in denouncing violations of fundamental rights. Consider, for example, the social groups that fought for religious and political independence in the Middle Ages, the great movements that led to American independence and

---

[1]   I write 'in large part', because significant contributions to that history have come from all over the world. Some authors have considered some ancient texts, belonging to different civilizations, as first expressions of human rights. While those texts express values similar to those underlying human rights, I do not think that referring to them we can properly speak of human rights, insofar as there is no trace in them of the concept of subjective, individual, and universal rights.

to the French Revolution, the struggles to abolish slavery and gain universal suffrage, the workers' and women's movements, and the movements that in our own day all over the world fill the streets and spread through the Internet, along with the activities of nongovernmental and other organizations, including the reporting and advocacy of various social networks and media outlets and organizations.

In some cases, social demands have been asserted that subsequently found expression in theoretical statements; in others it was instead the theories that paved the way, expressing in the form of natural or fundamental rights the basic needs of groups of people who might otherwise have lacked the language needed to demand that those needs be met.

Once fundamental rights have established a foothold in society, they will also establish themselves as law and as theoretical principles, and in this lies one of their strengths: the tension and mutually reinforcing energy that flows between the two planes acts as a decisive factor in bringing about the transformations that have shaped the history of rights.

In the historical development outlined in the following pages the greater emphasis in the discussion falls on theories and declarations of rights, not excluding some hints to the social conditions that have made it possible for different fundamental rights to take hold.

The three chapters making up this first part cover three main phases in the history of fundamental rights.

Chapter 1 focuses on the idea of universal natural rights: looking at the origins of this idea in the natural law school of the sixteenth century and its development in the subsequent social contract theories and the Enlightenment reform proposals, and then considering how the same idea informs the declarations of rights issued at the end of the eighteenth century.

Chapter 2 is devoted to the processes of codification of citizen's rights in the nineteenth and twentieth centuries in the context of the liberal state, focusing on the institutionalization of civil and political rights and on the rise of social rights in Europe.

Chapter 3 deals with the refoundation of fundamental rights after World War II and their recent developments at both the national and supranational levels. The discussion devotes special attention to the main features of the European system of fundamental rights, thus introducing the contents of Part III.

'Women's rights are human rights': this statement, first issued on the occasion of the World Conference on Women held in Beijing in 1995, sums up a narrative arc that spans three centuries of history. Across all three chapters the history of women's rights forms a through line. Indeed, although this history overlaps and intersects with that of the rights of man, it also charts its own distinctive path: not only does it follow a different timeline, but it lays its own foundations and introduces its own set of guarantees.

The literature on the history of fundamental rights is vast, addressing a whole range of contentious and intensely debated issues. Having to fit five centuries into a confined space, it has been necessary to simplify, all the while attempting to convey a sense of the complexity of the history of rights. Choices had to be made: this meant leaving out a string of significant authors, currents, and documents; portraying complex historical developments in silhouette;

and setting the secondary literature entirely aside. Inevitably, then, this part of the book offers only one of several snapshots that can be taken of the history of fundamental rights.[2]

---

[2] Given the didactic and introductory character of this book, bibliographic references have been limited to the works of the authors whose contribution to the history of fundamental rights is considered, avoiding references to the critical literature. For some general works see Alessandra Facchi, *Breve storia dei diritti umani: Dai diritti dell'uomo ai diritti delle donne* (Il Mulino 2013); Marcello Flores, *Storia dei diritti umani* (Il Mulino 2008); Micheline Ishay, *The History of Human Rights: From Ancient Times to the Globalization Era* (University of California Press 2008); John M Kelly, *A Short History of Western Legal Theory* (OUP 1992); Gerhard Oestreich, *Geschichte der Menschenrechte und Grundfreiheiten im Umriß* (Duncker & Humblot 1978); Gregorio Peces-Barba Martínez, Eusebio Fernández García, Rafael de Asís Roig, and Francisco Javier Ansuátegui Roig (eds), *Historia de los derechos fundamentals*, 22 vols (Dykinson 1998–2014).

1
Origins: from the sixteenth to the eighteenth century

1.1 THE 'FREE MAN' AND HIS NATURAL RIGHTS

1.1.1 The first claims to those personal liberties that would then develop into fundamental rights came from groups and communities that sought to fight back the oppression of the religious and political authorities in medieval Europe.

The resistance mounted against the power of the Catholic Church gave shape to the first assertions of religious freedom on the part of minority religious movements, as well as on the part of individuals who in word and deed rebelled against the dogmas and abuses of the papacy and the clergy. It is only with the Protestant Reformation and its spread in the sixteenth century that it proved possible to break the dominance of the Catholic Church, providing a firm foothold for a religion with its own clergy and institutions—a religion that, while invoking the common Christian roots, set itself up against Catholicism. It is to the reformers' efforts and doctrines, to the struggles that pit them first against the Catholics and then against one another, to the intersection of religious and political conflicts, to the ability to conceive values that could assert themselves over political authority by virtue of their superiority to it, that we can trace the establishment of those principles which from religious freedom would, in the modern age, lead to freedom of conscience and opinion—the seminal core in which lay the foundation for the rights of man.

Over the long period that set into motion the construction of the modern state with the corresponding centralization of absolute sovereign authority, there also sprang up an intensifying effort to fight back the absolute sovereigns' authoritarianism and to reclaim autonomy on the part of the aristocracy, the clergy, the professional and craft guilds, the corporations, and even entire cities, as in the case of the Italian communes. These demands and struggles made it possible to gain spaces of personal freedom, *in concreto* guarantees against arbitrary provisions that might compel persons to pay in life and limb or might target their goods and activities.

Numerous writs and charters offer evidence of how spaces of autonomy and particular safeguards across the territories of medieval Europe were carved out affording protection against sovereigns: these were the so-called *jura et libertates*.

Most notable among these was the Magna Charta Libertatum—issued in 1215, and then reissued in a definitive version in 1225—which contained the principle of habeas corpus, providing for an intangible personal sphere that cannot be encroached on except under due process of law:

> No free man shall be seized or imprisoned, or stripped of his rights or possessions, or out-lawed or exiled, or deprived of his standing in any other way, nor will we proceed with force against him, or send others to do so, except by the lawful judgement of his equals or by the law of the land. (Article 39 of the Magna Charta)

The Magna Charta also contains other principles that are constitutive of the modern funda-mental rights, among which are the proportionality between offence and punishment (Article 20); access to a fair trial, which cannot be sold, denied, or delayed (Article 40); and freedom of movement, enabling merchants to enter or leave England and travel within it to ply their trade 'free from all illegal exactions' (Article 41).

However, like many other documents issued in the European territories in subsequent centuries, the Magna Charta did not apply to all persons, but only to so-called freemen, and so only to those belonging to specific social groups.

Rights, by contrast, come into being with the requisite of universality, resting as they do on the idea of natural equality among all men. They presuppose a revolution at once conceptual and social: freedoms and protections are no longer conceived as privileges conferred on this or that social group, but as rights recognized for all men or citizens, regardless of what other group they may belong to, whether by birth or by subsequent admittance.

The idea that all men are born equal, regardless of what this may be taken to mean, was revolutionary for ancient societies: an idea first introduced into Western culture by the Stoic philosophers in the third century BC and then reasserted by the Church Fathers, for whom all men have equal dignity before God, and for whom the fruits of the earth are held in common.

Liberty and equality, understood as original attributes of all men, are coupled with the idea of natural rights, meaning rights that all men enjoy in the state of nature.[1] According to the natural law tradition, there exist norms, precepts, and principles qualified in precisely that way—as 'natural'—by virtue of their being founded on divine will and revelation. Positive law, or man-made law, must be in keeping with these precepts, which, being natural, are thereby 'just' and tend towards universality.

1.1.2 The first statement of the idea of *natural rights*, understood as claims that one may assert on the basis of natural law, has been found in William of Ockham (1290–1359), who in defending the Franciscan order against the papacy mentions natural rights to liberty: these rights, conferred on mortals by God, prevail on the law posited by man. But for a full theory of universal natural rights of man we have to look to Francisco de Vitoria (1483?–1546), the jurist and theologian who founded the School of Salamanca, or Second Scholastic. In two lectures (*relectiones*) delivered in Salamanca, *De Indis* (On the American Indians) and the *De Jure Belli*

---

[1] See Brian Tierney, *The Idea of Natural Rights: Studies on Natural Rights, Natural Law, and Church Law, 1150–625* (Scholars Press 1997); Richard Tuck, *Natural Rights Theories: Their Origin and Development* (CUP 1979); Michel Villey, *Le droit et les droits de l'homme* (PUF 1983).

(On the Law of War) he intervenes in the debate that originated out of the Spanish conquest of Latin America, discussing what actions are legitimate in dealing with the native populations and laying the foundations of 'just' war. In so doing, he makes an argument in favour of universal rights, thus setting out the first theory of human rights.

For Vitoria, it is not just Christians who are right-holders but any human being endowed with reason, regardless of geographic location, political organization, religious faith, or usage and custom. Even the natives are rational beings, and so they each have a right to preserve their own life, land, and property. On the basis of these rights, Vitoria argues that the native peoples should not be enslaved, subjugated, or plundered. However, he also affirms that all men have a right of travel (*ius peregrinandi*), sojourn (*ius degendi*), and occupation (*ius occupationis*) in unclaimed lands and property and these rights justify migrating to foreign lands, as well as conquering and colonizing them.[2] In this list of rights Vitoria also includes the natives' own right to life in cases involving cannibalism and ritual human sacrifice. It was in order to defend these natural rights—both of the settlers and the natives—that the Spaniards were justified in the use of force: Vitoria thus formulates the first 'just war' theory.

At the root of the idea of a right is that of *dominium*, a Latin term that can be translated as 'property'. In the sixteenth century the idea of property—a person's *dominium*—pointed to a broad power of exclusive disposition, a power to exclude others from disposing not only of one's own goods but also of one's personal liberties and life and limb, all of which were understood as an extension of the individual. For Vitoria, to enjoy *dominium* is to have 'the right to use a thing for one's own benefit (*ius utendi re in usum suum*)'.[3]

The idea of natural rights took hold in European theological and legal culture, and did so finding application well beyond the historical circumstances that had prompted Vitoria to theorize it. The notion of *ius* as a right of the person already forms the kernel of the theory expounded by Hugo Grotius (1583–1685), regarded as the founder of modern natural law, which he characterizes as the complex of precepts which all men may learn from natural reason.[4] What through this process gets honed to perfection in the modern natural law school, then, is the idea of natural rights of man which can be discovered by reason, and which pre-exist political society and stand independently of what anyone may will or may attempt to enact into law on that basis.

The natural rights of man then get folded into the contract theories of the seventeenth century, becoming a constitutive element of modern constitutionalism. In these theories, the idea of a state of nature in which all persons are free and equal, enjoying the same innate rights, is welded into the tradition according to which the authority of the sovereign rests on a covenant with his subjects, a tradition that was already firmly lodged in European culture, going back to the end of the Middle Ages.

---

[2]   Francisco de Vitoria, 'On the American Indians (*De Indis*)' in *Political Writings* (Anthony Pagden and Jeremy Lawrance eds, CUP 1991) 231–92, at 283. Lecture originally delivered in Salamanca in 1539 and first published in Latin in 1557.

[3]   Vitoria (n 2) q 1, art 4, para 20, 247.

[4]   Hugo Grotius, *On the Law of War and Peace* (first published in Latin 1625; Stephen C Neff ed, CUP 2012).

The theoretical framework for modern fundamental rights can thus be said to have originated from a merging of two traditions: the legal natural law tradition and the philosophical social contract tradition.

The initial premise shared by all seventeenth-century contract traditions is the condition of liberty and equality of all men in the state of nature. Why should they give up that condition? How is it that sovereigns hold all the powers that by nature rest with persons? How to legitimize sovereign power after the idea of divine or hereditary investiture has gone into demise? Social contract theories attempt to answer these questions through a two-pronged account by which to rationally explain both society, or the reasons why men should live together, and obedience to a ruler—and the account needs to ultimately go back to an act of will, considering that men in the state of nature are born free. Political power comes into being when men renounce exacting their own justice and entrust their protection to an authority acting under a set of rules enacted by an apparatus of persons so authorized.

The concern to legitimize the concentration of powers in a single sovereign, in such a way as to ward off the scourge of civil war, finds its highest expression in Thomas Hobbes (1588–1679), and in particular in *Leviathan*, in which we also find a clear distinction between the concept of *ius* (right) and that of *lex* (law).[5]

1.1.3 But it is not until the *Second Treatise of Government*, by John Locke (1632–1704), that natural rights are theorized both as a limit and as a source of commitment for governments, thereby giving us the first form of constitutionalism. Locke's *Treatise* is inextricably bound up with the history of England in the seventeenth century, and in particular with the Glorious Revolution, which put an end to a period of civil strife and culminated in the passage of the Bill of Rights of 1689. This act expressly sets out some basic civil liberties of British subjects and providing that the crown is subordinate to the laws of Parliament, thereby putting an end to its absolute power.

The *Second Treatise of Government* marks a key turning point in the theory of fundamental rights. The state of nature, as described by Locke, affords all men with an equal distribution of power, freedoms, and property, in 'a *State of perfect Freedom* to order their Actions, and dispose of their Possessions, and Persons as they think fit, within the bounds of the Law of Nature'.[6]

In this condition, however, the natural rights of individuals are always hanging in the balance, under constant threat from the abuses and usurpations that any individual may visit on any other. Hence the function of the political authority established through the social contract, which is to guarantee the protection of the rights with which every human being is endowed by nature: liberty, life, bodily integrity, and property. If the sovereign should fail to honour the pact, the people, whose will is expressed through the voice of the majority, have the

---

[5]   Thomas Hobbes, *Leviathan* (first published 1651; Richard Tuck ed, CUP 1991).

[6]   John Locke, 'The Second Treatise of Government' in *Two Treatises of Government* (first published 1689; Peter Laslett ed, CUP 1988) ch 2, para 4, 265–428, at 269 (italics in the original).

right to rebel, take back their liberty, and institute a new government. In this way Locke provides a justification for popular revolution, thereby theorizing the so-called right to resistance.

Life, liberty, and estate form the well-known triad of natural rights that will then become the fundamental rights protected in modern constitutional systems, and a necessary complement to that triad is therefore the right to security: it becomes a basic responsibility of the state to guarantee that everyone is secure in their persons, property, and liberty.

It takes centuries to construct a right to property understood as *ius excludendi alios*, the right to exclude others from the use of real (immovable) and personal (movable) property. Although in the Middle Ages the institution of private property is recognized, it is discussed in terms of its foundations in Christian doctrine. The description of the state of nature as a situation in which goods are owned in common can be found in a variety of authors, among whom Grotius and Hobbes, who locate the formation of property in the birth of civil society by effect of the social covenant. The right to property thus presents itself as a right established, governed, and guaranteed by the sovereign. In Locke's work, by contrast, property is elevated to the status of natural right par excellence, making its protection the primary task of political authority.

On Locke's conception, man holds a natural right not only over his own life and person but also over the fruits of his own labour: 'Though the Earth [...] be common to all Men, yet every Man has a *Property* in his own *Person*. This no Body has any Right to but himself. The *Labour* of his Body, and the *Work* of his Hands [...] are properly his'.[7]

Personal liberty, and the self-ownership on which it rests, acts as the basis for all other rights, and this makes them inalienable: 'For a Man, not having the Power of his own Life, *cannot*, by Compact, or his own Consent, *enslave himself* to any one, nor put himself under the Absolute, Arbitrary Power of another, to take away his Life, when he pleases'.[8]

In Locke, rights are natural rights in the sense that they belong to man by nature, before the birth of society, and so before the formation of a political authority bound to recognize, guarantee, and protect them. They are personal and individual, meaning that they belong to the individual simply by virtue of his being a person. All men are in this sense right-holders, regardless of birth, class, or affiliation. The state is brought into existence in order to protect the fundamental rights of citizens, which rights at the same time form the *basis* of the state's legitimate power and define the *limits* of that authority.

The proprietary vision of one's self and one's own rights establishes itself in modern natural law. Life, liberty, and estate—the original triad from which spring the natural rights of man—are based on a common understanding of a person's relation to his own goods, over which he is lord and master, and which he can accordingly freely dispose of. For Locke, man is free insofar as he has ownership over himself, his body, and his actions.

The right-holder is the *dominus*, owner of his own body, liberty, and goods, through which he will bring his life to fruition. He is an autonomous subject, for he is not dependent on anyone else, and insofar as he is autonomous he is also responsible, having the ability to freely

---

[7]   ibid ch 5, para 27, 287–8 (italics in the original).

[8]   ibid ch 4, para 23, 284 (italics in the original).

choose and to answer for those choices. He is also a rational subject, and in fact in reason lies the universal foundation of human rights—that which all men in the world share in common. Insofar as he is rational he also has the capacity to distinguish good from evil and to calculate his own interest, and so a capacity for moral judgement and for economic reasoning. It is therefore not coincidental that the new order of civil society should rest on the social contract: the contract is the quintessential expression of individual autonomy, for it presupposes a free individual, capable of judging good from evil by his own lights, as well as of binding himself, that is, of making and honouring a commitment. At the same time, the contract expresses an instrumental rationality, calculating costs and benefits: it signifies man's exercise of free will, but a self-limiting exercise held in check by the use of reason.

The anthropological traits associated with the ideal right-holder painted an image that excludes women, and that exclusion would last for almost two centuries in the European legal systems.

The 'free man' endowed with reason is quintessentially what the expression itself suggests, a man: in women, the dominant note is instead the emotive one of feeling, which is ill-suited to economic and political decision-making, to the responsibility which comes with the assumption of a public trust or office, to contractual relationships, to the legal professions. The exclusion of women from a variety of trades, professions, roles, positions, and rights has long been justified on the basis of their 'natural' differences from man—a complex of traits that predispose them to certain activities and make them inept at others.

Woman is not regarded as autonomous or independent, either morally or culturally: her decision-making is dependent on those who exercise power over her. As a matter of both fact and law, women are precluded from receiving an education—or rather, the education they do receive is specifically tailored to a future role as wife, mother, governess, mistress of the household. Nor is she economically independent: most women depend economically on some male within the family (the husband or father, a brother or son). It is for the man to enter the labour market and act as the breadwinner. Women are confined within the realm of domestic work: tending family members, raising the children, caring for the elderly. If they belong to the upper ranks of society, they will accordingly be entrusted with social roles. None of these activities are paid, and the value that attaches to them is a judgement that falls to the discretion of the men who stand to benefit from them. If women are considered irrational and irresponsible, and are therefore unpropertied, then it should not come as a surprise that the holder of the rights of man will accordingly be 'man'.

1.2 THE ENLIGHTENMENT: RIGHTS, REASON, AND LEGAL REFORM

1.2.1 Natural law and social contract theory brought into the common store of European political culture two ideas that to this day stand as fundamental principles: that of individual rights, innate and equal for all, and that of popular sovereignty. Key to the spread of these ideas—making it possible to deepen and apply them in putting forward proposals for legal reform—was Enlightenment thought. The Enlightenment philosophers distinguished themselves for their effort to gauge their theoretical positions in light of their civil commitment as they sought to transform society, political authority, and the law. For all the variety of the positions they held, their ideas, analyses, and proposals marked a turning point in European culture, a moment that we still go back to.

The Enlightenment thinkers gave currency to the idea of the natural rights of man by building on this idea in such a way as to expand its political and social import: for the people to gain rights is for them to make economic, social, and cultural headway, with the abolition of entrenched class privileges and the protection of individuals from abuses of power, ancient and new alike, as well as from superstition and from exposure to the consequences of deviating from the standard of supposedly universal reason. Indeed, rights are recognized for every person as such, regardless of birth: they are based on the principle of equality before the law, and as such they do away with privilege.

The idea of the rights of man cannot be understood to have emerged if not in connection with the revolution that in European history placed the individual at the centre of the world as an interlocutor which political authority must reckon with. Only once individuals gain an independent moral standing is it possible to conceive of them as bearers of rights *as individuals*, that is, apart from the group, community, or station into which they are born.

In the eighteenth century, alongside the march of the universal rights of man, a parallel development was taking place that was driving the rise of a social morality built on the keynote value of the autonomy of individuals, equipped with personal freedom and a capacity for economic and social advancement. Whereas in English and American history, religious freedom established itself through the struggle to gain recognition for the demands asserted by Protestant movements, in continental Europe the same freedom advanced on the strength of the ideas of toleration and freedom of conscience—ideas whose roots are not Christian (neither Protestant nor Catholic) but rather secular and civic, being predicated on the principle of the separation of church and state.

The idea of toleration comes into form against the backdrop of Europe's interchange with non-European civilizations, but in its paradigmatic statement—most famously expressed in Voltaire's (1694–1778) *Traité sur la tolérance* (Treatise on Tolerance)—it is recognized as a principle calling for coexistence between Catholics and non-Catholics, while requiring the state to hold itself neutral with regard to such plurality of faiths and affiliations. Although Voltaire appealed to God in advocating for toleration, his view of the relation among the clergy, the state, and the people was clear:

> No Ecclesiastical Law should ever be in force till it has formally received the express sanction of the government. [...] To permit or prohibit working on holidays, should only be in the magistrate's power [...]. Every thing relating to marriages should depend solely on the magistrate [...]. All Ecclesiastics whatever should, as the State's subjects, in all cases be

under the controul and animadversion of the government. [...] Magistrates, farmers, and priests, are alike to contribute to the expenses of the State, as alike belonging to the State.[9]

Freedom of conscience and the separation of church and state are two principles that, while operating on two different planes, are closely interconnected in the secularist French Enlightenment model. What also flows from this model is the criticism directed at obscurantism, religious fanaticism, the church's encroachment on public affairs and individual liberty, the privileges based on church hierarchy, and the intolerance of minority religions.

Religious freedom—the freedom to believe in and profess any religion or none at all—stems from a single root: freedom of conscience. This latter freedom is understood as the faculty to make a choice that is not necessarily based on faith but is rather grounded in reason and in the human will—a choice that ultimately hinges on each individual's sphere of autonomy.

The reform spirit that animated the eighteenth century also called into question the forms of serfdom that had become culturally established and legally sanctioned. Various Enlightenment thinkers took a public stand against slavery, working to abolish the institution and undercut the interests of slave traders.

But to achieve the ideal of the natural rights of man it was necessary to effect a deep transformation of current institutions and law. The Enlightenment project to reform the law—an effort that would lead to concrete change in the nineteenth century—sought to bring certainty and clarity to the law, as well as to unify the law across the national territory, thereby eliminating legal fragmentation and particularism, and to ensure the equality of all citizens before the law, which in turn meant abolishing hereditary privilege.

The area in which the Enlightenment had the greatest impact was that of law and criminal procedure. On the basis of a utilitarian and humanized vision of punishment, some fundamental reforms were introduced whose aims included re-envisioning the function of punishment, no longer understood as retribution for the crime committed but geared towards social protection and crime prevention; ensuring proportionality between crime and punishment; abolishing capital punishment, and generally establishing a standard of humanization of punishment, without corporal punishments; and instituting due process—all innovations that in the centuries to come would concretize into fundamental rights for the accused and the imprisoned.

Of great significance in this regard was the contribution that came out of the Italian Enlightenment, with the immediate and wide resonance achieved by Cesare Beccaria's (1738–1794) *Dei delitti e delle pene* (On Crimes and Punishments) as well as Pietro Verri's (1728–1797) *Osservazioni sulla tortura* (Observations on Torture), making arguments, as yet unsurpassed, that not only underscore the inhumanity and injustice of torture and the death penalty but also, in so doing, point out how useless and ineffective these practices are.

The assertion of rights to liberty and property also provides the framework out of which sprang reform initiatives like the push to abolish unfair inheritance laws and to liberalize trade

---

[9]   Voltaire (François-Marie Arouet), 'Civil and Ecclesiastical Laws' in *The Philosophical Dictionary* (first published in French 1764; John Morley and Tobias Smollett eds, Bernard Dornin 1793) 206–7.

and commerce. From the movement launched by the physiocrats, the first 'economists', came the principles asserting the right to work and the ability to choose one's own trade, while also offering a novel way to think about the right to property, freedom of economic activity and enterprise, and the role of the state in the economy.

In French eighteenth-century culture, private property was generally extolled as a natural right, to be guaranteed almost without restriction. But next to this view a critical tradition was being revived whose most significant statement came from Jean-Jacques Rousseau (1712–1778). In his *Discours sur l'origine et les fondements de l'inégalité parmi les hommes* (Discourse on the Origin and Foundations of Inequality among Mankind), Rousseau argues that the institution of private property, to which we must trace the very origin of society and the civil laws, itself originates from a power grab:

> The first man who, having enclosed a piece of ground, to whom it occurred to say *this is mine*, and found people sufficiently simple to believe him, was the true founder of civil society. [...] Beware of listening to this impostor; You are lost, if you forget that the fruits are everyone's and the Earth no one's [...].[10]

Rousseau was not a lone voice: next to the concern with protecting the property and economic freedoms of the bourgeoisie, there also arose a concern to fight poverty and to redistribute the national wealth. This sensitivity to social problems began to translate into a vision of the state as a promoter of greater economic equality and equal opportunity among citizens, and often presented as a necessary step in that direction was public education—free, open to all, and compulsory.

1.2.2 Enlightenment culture also gave some women the opportunity to express their individuality and talent by taking up artistic and philosophical pursuits, participating in literary salons, and engaging in the cultural and political debates of the day, thereby freeing themselves from the roles previously allotted to them as wife or mother. The idea of moral and rational equality between the sexes was put forward, to take issue with the restrictions and discriminations to which women were subject, and to call for legal reform aimed at reinstating their natural rights, in such a way that women could be guaranteed access to public life, as well as an education, suffrage, and an equal legal status within the family.[11]

The first fully fleshed out statement of women's rights came from a woman, Olympe de Gouges (1748–1793), whose political tracts and plays and whose activism, particularly aimed at abolishing slavery, saw her play an active part in the French Revolution. In the *Déclaration des droits de la femme e de la citoyenne* (Declaration of the Rights of Woman and of the Female Citizen), penned in 1791, she recast the 1789 Declaration of the Rights of Man and of the Citizen in the feminine, bringing the woman's point of view front and centre in pronouncing

---

[10]   Jean-Jacques Rousseau, 'Discourse on the Origin and Foundations of Inequality among Men' (first published in French 1755) in *The Discourses and Other Early Political Writings* (Victor Gourevitch ed, CUP 1991) 111–222, at 161.

[11]   See Marie Jean Antoine de Condorcet, *Oeuvres*, 12 vols (Frommann 1968) vol 10, 119–30.

that 'the only limit to the exercise of the natural rights of woman is the perpetual tyranny that man opposes to it' (Article 4).[12]

The effort to recognize woman as an autonomous and responsible person did not exhaust itself in a push for equal rights and unrestricted access to all positions, titles, public offices, and political functions but also included an assertion of equal *duties*: equal payments into the public treasury and equal punishments for the same crimes.

A new alertness to the question of women and their subordination, and to the demand for equal rights between the sexes, began to take hold across many parts of Europe, and particularly in England with the philosophical radicalism advanced by reformist thinkers like Thomas Paine (1737–1809), Jeremy Bentham (1748–1832), and James Mill (1773–1836), and later John Stuart Mill (1806–1873) (s 2.2.2). In 1792 one member of this group, Mary Wollstonecraft (1759–1797), wrote *A Vindication of the Rights of Woman*, which would come to be considered the first text in feminist theory. Wollstonecraft defended the equal power of reasoning and moral judgement between the sexes and argued that the first objective women needed to aim for was that of education—but a 'masculine education' entirely different from the kind they had 'hitherto received', which 'only tended, with the constitution of civil society, to render them insignificant objects of desire' thereby feeding their oppression.[13] Wollstonecraft was speaking to middle-class women, urging them to act so as to change the image branded onto them in a male-dominated society: she was thus infusing women with a sense of agency, underscoring the central role they can play in wresting themselves from their position of subordination.

1.3   DECLARATIONS OF RIGHTS IN THE EIGHTEENTH CENTURY

1.3.1   The process through which the natural rights spilled over from theoretical discourse into the arena of law and politics was punctuated by moments of great social and political upheaval that reached a climax with the Glorious Revolution of 1688 in England, then with American independence from British rule, and then with the French Revolution of 1789.

Out of the latter two events came the eighteenth-century declarations of rights, the first legal documents to solemnly proclaim the existence of fundamental rights, recognizing some rights as natural and universal—rights which any man or citizen enjoys, and which everyone is bound to respect, even governments.

In mid-eighteenth-century America, the process of unifying the colonies under a single legal framework began to advance in tandem with the colonies' push to gain independence from Great Britain. The colonies' protest initially took the form of a demand for representation in Parliament (this was the context out of which came the slogan 'no taxation without representa-

---

[12]   See 'Declaration of the Rights of Woman and the Female Citizen' at <https://www.olympedegouges.eu/rights_of_women.php> accessed 16 January 2022.

[13]   Mary Wollstonecraft, 'A Vindication of the Rights of Woman' (first published 1792) in *A Vindication of the Rights of Man—A Vindication of the Rights of Woman—An Historical and Moral View of the French Revolution* (OUP 1999) 63–284, at 149 and 74.

tion'), as well as a demand that the rights and liberties of British subjects be extended to the colonists. When the discontent boiled over into the proclamation of independence, the colonies formed themselves into states by enacting constitutions, starting with the Constitution of the Commonwealth of Virginia, of 1776, followed by a stream of other constitutions, leading up to the United States Constitution of 1787 and then, in 1791, to the federal Bill of Rights, with the passage of the first ten amendments to the Constitution. In these events we have the first historical manifestations of modern constitutionalism, a current of thought that in the constitution sees a state's founding document, which in turn contains the basic rules and principles framing the legal order and governing the institutions of the state, and which sets forth the rights of citizens.

About a decade later in France the crisis of the absolute monarchy came to a head with the revolution of 1789. This is the historical event that abolished feudal rights in France and spelled the end of a social, economic, and political organization that had persisted for centuries—an event that would send shock waves rippling across territory well beyond France.

The first phase of the revolution unfolded without violent conflict. When in May of 1789 the Estates General met, having been convened by King Louis XVI in a bid to resolve his conflict with the aristocracy, representatives of the Third Estate from all over France descended on Paris, and in the upshot the body turned into the National Constituent Assembly. In the Assembly, it would soon be resolved that a declaration of rights needed to be issued as a basis on which to set up a new social and political order. The final text was approved on 26 August 1789. The drafting committee, chaired by Mirabeau, had set itself a specific objective of clarity: the declaration needed to be universal in the sense (among others) that it was to apply to everyone and be easy for all to understand, considering 'that ignorance, forgetfulness or contempt of the rights of man are the sole causes of the public miseries and of the corruption of governments'.[14] Hence the drafters took it as their aim 'to set forth, in a solemn declaration, the natural, inalienable, and sacred rights of man, in order that this declaration, being ever present to all members of the social body, may unceasingly remind them of their rights and duties'. In this way, 'the acts of the legislative power and those of the executive power may be each moment compared with the aim of any political institution and thereby may be more respected', at the same time enabling 'the demands of the citizens' to be 'grounded henceforth upon simple and incontestable principles' (Preamble).

1.3.2 The 1789 Déclaration des droits de l'homme et du citoyen would go down in history as the first charter of universal rights, the document that marked a watershed in Western civilization, proclaiming rights incompatible with the Ancien Régime and ushering in a radically different set of political and social structures.

This document gave political and legal effect to those revolutionary advances that had previously been expressed only as a matter of theoretical principle: the body politic, previously

---

[14]   All quotations from the 1789 Declaration are from the following English translation: 'Declaration of the Rights of Man and Citizen' in *The Constitutions and Other Select Documents Illustrative of the History of France, 1789–1901* (Frank Maloy Anderson ed, The HW Wilson Company 1904) 58–60.

made up of subjects, and hence bearers of duties, was henceforth to be made up of citizens, bearers of rights; and the people, previously subject to the sovereign, now became the foundation of sovereignty.

The true protagonist of the 1789 Declaration was the individual. The relationship of direct access that is set up between individuals and the state also entails a political and ideological nullification of other groups and institutions (corporations, the clergy, local and church authorities), as well as of their privileges and the powers through which they could act in place of or next to the state. The new order is premised on a radical individualism that exalts a single affiliation, namely, the nation, and the equality of all citizens before the law (equal laws protecting equal rights).

Thus, next to the three principles asserted by the French Revolution—*liberté, egalité,* and *fraternité*—we have the three ideological foundations underpinning the Declaration— universalism, rationalism, and individualism: rights belong to all individuals—and to individuals alone, without regard to their membership in this or that group—and are based on a common human reason.

The intellectual bases informing the 1789 Declaration are mainly Locke's theory of rights and the state, the theory of popular sovereignty developed by Rousseau and the theory of the separation of powers associated with Montesquieu (1689–1755). More broadly, the document expresses the vision of law and politics which the Enlightenment philosophers have most importantly helped to shape.

The only legitimate source of authority and sovereignty is the nation, the bulk of which is made up by the Third Estate, meaning the people (the commoners). The basic task of the state is to respect and guarantee the 'natural, inalienable, and sacred rights of man': these rights offer the guarantee of peaceful coexistence among citizens; they are the linchpin of political organization, legitimizing the state and its function.

Liberty and equality are declared to be the natural condition of man. But equality understood as a status that does not admit of any exception implies the equality of rights under equal laws; social inequality, by contrast, is allowed, but it needs to be justified, and this can be done only if shown to serve the interests of the collectivity: 'Men are born and remain free and equal in rights. Social distinctions can be based only upon public utility' (Article 1 of the Declaration). Legal equality means that the law 'must be the same for all, whether it protects or punishes' and that all 'are equally eligible to all public dignities, places, and employments, according to their capacities, and without other distinction than that of their virtues and their talents' (Article 6).

Under Article 4 freedom is defined as 'the power to do anything that does not injure others', which in turn means that 'the exercise of the natural rights of each man has for its only limits those that secure for the other members of society the enjoyment of these same rights. These limits can be determined only by law'. This conception—establishing a connection between personal liberty and the law—can be found in Montesquieu and Rousseau but is most clearly stated in Locke: '*Freedom of Men under Government*, is, to have a standing Rule to live by […];

A Liberty to follow my own Will in all things, where the Rule prescribes not; and not to be subject to the inconstant, uncertain, unknown, Arbitrary Will of another Man'.[15]

As much as the enjoyment of individual liberty is brought directly into connection with the need to respect the law, the first rights to liberty set forth in the Declaration are those that secure personal freedom vis-à-vis the state's power and coercive apparatus. Thus we have due process rights in Article 7, under which 'no man can be accused, arrested, or detained except in the cases determined by the law and according to the forms that it has prescribed'; the principle of nonretroactivity in criminal law in Article 8, providing that 'no one can be punished except in virtue of a law established and promulgated prior to the offence'; and the presumption of innocence in Article 9, stating that 'every man being presumed innocent until he has been pronounced guilty'. These are the principles which had been forged out of the Enlightenment debate on reform of the criminal law, and out of which emerged the framework for the modern justice system based on the safeguards afforded under the rule of law.

Freedom of religion appears in Article 10 under the broader rubric of freedom of expression, while Article 11, devoted to the 'free communication of ideas and opinions', describes this as 'one of the most precious of the rights of man'. On the opposite face of the rights to life and to liberty—what makes them possible in the first place—is the right to security, even if this latter right is only indirectly called into play by providing for a 'public force' (*force publique*) to be paid for by way of taxes 'equally apportioned among all the citizens according to their means' (Article 13). At the same time, however, citizens have the right to know and determine what use such public resources are being put to and how much ought to be spent (Article 14), and generally to hold government and its officials accountable for their administration (Article 15). The right to property that in Article 2 figures among the natural and inalienable rights is reprised in the closing article, where in similar language it is recognized as 'sacred and inviolable' (Article 17).

Keeping watch over all the provisions in the Declaration of the Rights of Man and of the Citizen is the vigil eye of the principle of legality, under which the law alone can limit the exercise of rights. In the sovereignty of law lies the limit of the state's authority as well as of individual liberty (Article 4); likewise, the law is the only source of prohibitions and permissions (Article 5), and so the only basis for the use of public force, detention, and punishment (Articles 7 and 8). The primacy and supremacy of law is owed to its origin, its ultimate source being the general will, to which 'all citizens have the right to take part' (Article 6). As Rousseau writes in the *Du contrat social* (Of the Social Contract): 'The People subject to the laws ought to be their author'.[16] In the French tradition, legalism is the foundation of the state under the rule of law: in the scheme governing the separation of powers, the legislative power carries greater weight, for it is understood as the expression of the nation's will. As the people's representative, the Parliament alone can be the author of rules limiting the freedoms of the people themselves and stating how these freedoms are to be exercised.

---

[15]　Locke (n 6) ch 4, para 22, 284 (italics in the original).

[16]　Jean-Jacques Rousseau, 'Of the Social Contract' (first published in French 1762) in *The Social Contract and Other Later Political Writings* (Victor Gourevitch ed, CUP 1997) bk 2, ch 6, 39–152, at 68.

Above the laws there only stands the Constitution. This is recognized in Article 16 of the Declaration, regarded as the first normative statement of constitutionalism, even if the language is admittedly generic: 'Any society in which the guarantee of the rights is not secured or the separation of powers not determined, has no constitution at all'. The Constitution—with the rights and separation of powers that are essential to it—is thus implicitly laid at the foundation of the new legal order.

This makes the 1791 Constitution a necessary complement to the 1789 Declaration of Rights, and indeed in that Constitution we find a further set of rights, like freedom of the press, freedom of association, and freedom of movement.

After the 1789 Declaration, two others would follow that mark the different phases in the transition from revolutionary France to the Bourbon Restoration. The 1793 Déclaration des droits de l'homme et du citoyen, also known as the Jacobin Declaration, lays emphasis on social and economic equality in a way that the earlier 1789 Declaration does not. The spirit of greater substantive equality with which the Jacobin Declaration is imbued brings not only the bourgeoisie into the new order but also the other groups making up the people: peasants, artisans and tradesmen, factory workers. The Jacobin Declaration also explicitly abolishes slavery and serfdom, thereby asserting the principle that no person may be bought or sold or be held to service or labour: 'Every man can contract his services and his time, but he cannot sell himself nor be sold: his person is not an alienable property' (Article 18).[17] This declaration, however, never came into force, having been immediately overtaken by the events of the Reign of Terror. It was followed by the 1795 Declaration already foreshadowing the Bourbon Restoration, a text that keeps vigil over a new order.

---

[17] 'Declaration of the Rights of Man and Citizen' in *The Constitutions and Other Select Documents Illustrative of the History of France, 1789–1901* (n 14) 170–74.

2
From man's natural rights to citizens' fundamental rights

2.1 THE POSITIVIZATION OF RIGHTS

2.1.1 The eighteenth-century declarations of rights marked the early stages in the process through which rights would come to be positivized, a process moving from the theorizing of the natural rights of man to the enactment of the rights of the citizen into positive law. Indeed the nineteenth century ushered in a new phase in the history of rights, a phase in which they transitioned from natural to positive rights, from rights of man to rights of the citizen, from universal rights to national rights. Civil and political rights thus became prerogatives of citizens, applying within national boundaries and within the framework of each state's legal system.

The constitutional charters that throughout the century came in succession across continental Europe gradually expanded the catalogue of personal rights and liberties, thereby establishing themselves as a necessary element for a liberal and democratic state. However, even if the fundamental rights became enshrined in constitutions and declarations of rights, this was not, and still is not, enough to guarantee an actual enjoyment of them. In order to give effect to these rights, such that they might mean something in the lives of those who are entitled to them, they need to be backed by safeguards and guarantees, and so by an additional set of legal provisions (ss 5.2.1 and 5.2.2). It is also necessary for them to be justiciable; that is, there need to be institutions that could intervene when those provisions were infringed, and the remedy needed to be administered according to rules and procedures themselves constructed in keeping with the fundamental rights (s 4.2.4).

The process through which such citizens' rights were written into positive law in each national system, and so were judicially guaranteed, overlapped with another sweeping historical change that shaped the course of European law: the codification of law. This latter process began with the Prussian code of 1794, but it was the French Code Napoléon of 1804 that had the greatest resonance and influence across Europe and beyond. Previously, the law in force had come from a patchwork of different sources: countrywide and local laws; customs; case law; rules deriving from Roman, Germanic, and Canon law; usages tied to specific areas of activity or established by specific guilds; local ordinances; and so on. The central idea underpinning the codification process was that the entire nation should come under a single body of law, set forth in a single text containing clearly stated, accessible, systematically connected provisions that apply equally to all citizens across the national territory. In this way the standard of equality before the law and of the certainty of law was pursued by way of general and abstract rules issuing from a single source—the legislator, the expression of popular sovereignty—and applied by a single judiciary trained to uniformity.

Reflected more or less extensively in the criminal codes was the need previously underscored by Enlightenment thinkers to humanize punishment and revisit its function. Expressed in these codes were principles such as the nonretroactivity of criminal law, the presumption of innocence, the *ex ante* principle of legality requiring fair notice of punishment stated in clear and unambiguous language (*lex certa*), and the proportionality between crime and punishment. Helping to consolidate the safeguards put in place to protect the accused was the construction of a tiered judicial system, affording the ability to appeal any conviction. Likewise, the civil codes, proceeding from the notion of the individual as an autonomous and rational economic agent, protected private property, real and personal alike, and freedom of enterprise, as well as succession rights, and they regulated relationships within the family.

In the Napoleonic Code, civil rights made up a broad and heterogeneous class that looks like a derivation of the Lockean triad of life, liberty, and estate: they included the fundamental freedoms, the rights to private autonomy, habeas corpus rights protecting individuals against arbitrary detention, marriage and succession rights, and property rights. In the category of civil rights personal freedoms overlap with property rights.

The increasing specification of the fundamental freedoms ended up multiplying the provisions needed to protect them, covering areas such as freedom of thought and conscience, freedom of speech, freedom of the press, freedom of movement, secrecy of correspondence, freedom of association, the inviolability of the person and of the home, economic freedoms (including freedom of enterprise), and due process. Another matter was that of the political rights, covering the right to vote and to hold office, as well as any other form of participation in the running of government: for the most part, these rights fall within the purview of administrative law, in a succession of provisions enacted all through the century and in every country, modifying the criteria—and hence the classes of citizens—who enjoy political rights.

As rights moved from the sphere of theoretical discussion to that of constitutional protection and then to that of public policy and legal enactment, the process not only brought technical and political challenges but also significantly changed the very conceptions of rights.

2.1.2 In the theory of law, the idea of rights engaged the efforts of legal positivism, the dominant current of thought in jurisprudence in Europe in the nineteenth century and the early twentieth century. Legal positivism holds that positive law—the law in force at any particular time and place—is independent of natural law, and in so doing it restricts the ambit of legal science to the former: the only proper object of study for jurists is the law in force, while natural law becomes a matter for philosophical and religious speculation.

Even rights need to adapt to the new framework: no longer understood as founded on nature, religion, or reason, and so as prior to posited law and as a benchmark against which to assess the legitimacy of governments and their legal system, rights become 'positive' in the sense that they now find their basis exclusively in the legal provisions through which they are put on the books.

In German legal science the distinction is drawn between private and public rights. Rights are par excellence those that citizens enjoy in their private affairs: they are alienable rights governed by statute. The natural rights of man become public rights, that is, rights which citizens can assert against the state: they are generally inalienable but are valid only insofar as they are part of the state's legal system, within its national boundaries, and they apply only to those who fall under its sovereignty, and hence to citizens. Rights are no longer conceived as pre-existing limits on state power, and so as untouchable, but as creations of the state, things the state itself brings into being in its commitment to self-limiting government. Thus the idea takes shape that the fundamental rights—a term first introduced in the Imperial Act concerning the Basic Rights of the German People, of 27 December 1848—are to be understood as deriving from a limit the state places on its own sovereignty.

In legal positivist theory, rights drift gradually away from their foundation in natural law and find themselves being enfolded in the law in force, ultimately to be conceived as no more than the correlatives of duties, that is, of the legal obligations needed to guarantee those rights, ensuring that they are given effect to (s 4.1.2). In this sense, the explicit element in any legal provision lies in the obligation it sets forth for someone—be it a private person or entity or the state—to do or abstain from doing something: the correlative right is thus reduced to an abstraction, an idea. Even the fundamental rights to liberty are looked at primarily through the lens of the statutory nonintervention limits placed on public power. What comes into form, then, is a conception of rights under which they no longer enjoy any autonomy from law.

At the same time that, in legal positivist theory, rights are sapped of their power and cut down to size, in other nineteenth-century streams of thought they are called into question on account of their presuppositions and underpinnings. Auguste Comte (1798–1854) considers them a metaphysical conceit, an idea lacking any empirical backing, and lays emphasis on duties and social solidarity: sociology would henceforth, for a long time to come, cast a leery eye on rights.

But the most radical criticism comes from Karl Marx (1818–1883), who considers rights an idea conceived in liberal thought, serving to maintain the social, economic, and political hegemony of capitalism. Rights, for Marx, will never be serviceable as instruments by which to effect any deep transformation of society and achieve real equality among all its classes, for they rather serve the interests of only a segment of society. He calls out the ostensible universalism of rights as spurious: the right-holder is not some Universal Man but a particular kind of man, the propertied bourgeois citizen. It is around this kind of man that the rights declared by the French Revolution are wrapped, for which reason they can specifically be traced to a well-defined historical foundation and set of material interests: those that lie beneath the formation of the capitalist economic system. Another sharp criticism is levelled at the foundations on which rights rest. These foundations can be detected even in the 1789 Declaration of the Rights of Man and of the Citizen, in which Marx sees an individualistic conception of society, focused on 'the liberty of man regarded as an isolated monad, withdrawn into himself'.[1] The

---

[1]   Karl Marx, 'On the Jewish Question' (first published in German, under the title 'Zur Judenfrage', 1844) in *The Marx-Engels Reader* (Robert C Tucker ed, 2nd edn, Norton 1978) 26–52, at 42.

highest expression of this individualistic conception of liberty—liberty understood as 'the right to do everything which does not harm others'[2]—is 'the right of property', characterized by Marx as 'the right to enjoy one's fortune and to dispose of it as one will; without regard for other men and independently of society. It is the right of self-interest'.[3]

2.1.3 What instead emerges out of political philosophy and the nascent constitutional theory is an effort to set out new foundations for political and civil rights. On the one hand—through an inquiry into the different forms of popular participation, into the electoral and administrative machinery, into the relation among the powers of the state, into the protection of minorities—a theory of democracy is built. On the other hand—in the face of the process that is consolidating the nation-state, centralizing and expanding the functions entrusted to its organs—liberal thought concerns itself with the problem of protecting individuals and their ability to assert themselves in relation to the public powers, in a context in which they can no longer rely on community networks.

Beginning in the late eighteenth century, a 'liberal' conception of liberty takes shape that posits a sphere of individual autonomy which no power can encroach on except in specific cases set out by law. The greatest threat to this liberty therefore comes from the state, the very entity on which its protection depends. On the basis of this liberal liberty the fundamental rights to liberty are defined, conceived as the ability of individuals to express their opinions and to act without having to be concerned about government interference in their affairs or about any form of control except as provided by law.

In 1819, in a lecture titled *De la liberté des Anciens comparée à celle des Modernes* (The Liberty of the Ancients Compared with That of the Moderns) Benjamin Constant (1767–1830) distinguishes liberty understood as the ability of the individual to participate in the public sphere from liberty understood as the individual's ability to act in the private sphere. The first liberty was typical of ancient Greek societies, where it distinguished the freeman (the citizen of the *polis*) from the slave or barbarian; the second one was instead typical of modern societies from the French Revolution onward, and it presents us with the other face of the process through which the state came to monopolize power and the law. In broad outline, Constant's statement of how liberty was understood in his own time comports with our own understanding of it. Liberty, he writes,

> it is the right to be subjected only to the laws, and to be neither arrested, detained, put to death or maltreated in any way by the arbitrary will of one or more individuals. It is the right of everyone to express their opinion, choose a profession and practice it, to dispose of property, and even to abuse it; to come and go without permission, and without having to account for their motives or undertakings. It is everyone's right to associate with other individuals, either to discuss their interests, or to profess the religion which they and their associates prefer, or even simply to occupy their days or hours in a way which is most compatible with their inclinations or whims. Finally it is everyone's right to exercise some

---

[2]   ibid.

[3]   ibid.

influence on the administration of the government, either by electing all or particular officials, or through representations, petitions, demands to which the authorities are more or
less compelled to pay heed.[4]

2.2   CIVIL AND POLITICAL RIGHTS: PEOPLE INCLUDED AND PEOPLE EXCLUDED

2.2.1 Despite the constitutional proclamations of equality and liberty, there have been
throughout the nineteenth century, and in some cases even into the twentieth century,
classes of persons that have been denied access to citizens' rights. Citizenship thus shapes
up as a boundary of inclusion and exclusion: only those who check off the appropriate boxes
can be recognized as having the rights protected by the modern state. When the natural and
inalienable rights of man get written into positive law, they end up excluding a whole range
of human beings, either wholly or in part. This exclusion extends to the fundamental rights to
liberty. One need only consider in this regard the example of slavery in the French colonies,
an institution which, though abolished in 1794, was reinstated by Napoleon and ran through
much of the nineteenth century.

Formally, anyone who was a male citizen and legally competent qualified as a right-holder,
but to actually benefit from the powers and protections afforded by civil rights was something
that only the well-off could do: much of the population lacked the time and resources needed
to do so, nor did they have much interest in doing so. Even if the popular classes created by
the Industrial Revolution played an essential role in the economy, they were excluded from
the national political process and, even more insurmountably, they were excluded from the
increasing economic prosperity, living a threadbare existence scarcely at the level of subsistence, in conditions of social insecurity and cultural marginalization.

As for the political rights, meaning the right to vote and run for office these were reserved by
law for select constituencies within the male population until the latter half of the nineteenth
century, and in some cases into the twentieth century. It was on the basis of income and sex
that the dividing line between full and formal citizenship was most immediately drawn.

In the early decades of the nineteenth century the distinction took hold between 'active
citizens', meaning male citizens who paid taxes above a given threshold, and 'passive citizens':
only the former enjoyed the right to vote or serve in a public capacity. Only property holders—
as freemen, not dependent on others, and generally educated to some extent—were deemed
to have the requisite capacity for independent judgement without falling under the sway of
a master.

The debate on the requisites for exercising the right to vote was already well under way in
seventeenth-century England, but only in the nineteenth century did universal suffrage come
to the forefront of the working class's demands.

---

[4]   Benjamin Constant, 'The Liberty of the Ancients Compared with That of the Moderns' in *Political Writings*
(Biancamaria Fontana ed, CUP 1988) 309–28, at 310–11. Lecture originally delivered in Paris in 1819.

In all European countries, the extension of political rights to all male citizens came gradually, in a process that took in broader and broader swaths of the population, reaching completion after World War I.

2.2.2 Women continued to be excluded. In many European countries, women's suffrage was introduced after World War I, but in others it had to wait until after World War II.

Indeed, under the law of the European states, to be a woman was to be denied access to political rights and have diminished civil rights. It was indeed common for the law to prevent women from exercising property rights, enjoying basic freedoms, and gaining access to education and the professions, or at least the law would restrict their ability to do so.

The exclusion of women from rights was often justified by pointing to their lack of education and their economic dependence on men, and so on the basis of the very criteria of income and education that were being used to exclude much of the male population from access to political rights. With women, however, this was not just a *de facto* condition but a *de jure* status, considering that they were prevented by law from attending the same schools and finding the same employment as men, and likewise codified was their lack of autonomy from men within the household. The most widespread argument rested on the idea of a 'natural' difference from men: the idea of certain traits distinctive to women, explaining why they ought to be treated differently under the law. The different sets of rights recognized for men and women corresponded to two neatly distinguished spheres of human action and morality: on the one hand was the public sphere of economic activity; income-generating employment; and political office; on the other hand was the private sphere of the home, family, motherhood, affection, and care. The public sphere was mostly reserved for men, while the private sphere was a woman's domain. The two were distinct but complementary: the entrepreneurship and paid work of men would not have been possible without the unpaid work that women devoted to homemaking. Rights to liberty, property, and political participation fell almost exclusively within the public sphere, having next to no bearing on the private and familial sphere.

By the end of the nineteenth century, compulsory schooling had become standard across Europe, and yet women were still discriminated against in education. In fact the prevailing view was that women should learn a different set of skills from men, all geared towards managing the household (a skill taught as 'home economics') and tending to the family. Training women for the skilled trades, professions, and public offices reserved for men was not only regarded as wasteful but was also thought to undermine social and family harmony. Access to education was thus essential if women were to exit their condition of economic and cultural subjugation, and so it is that education remained a focus for Western feminist thought for almost two centuries.

A seminal work in liberal feminist theory was *The Subjection of Women*, by John Stuart Mill.[5] In this essay, whose stated purpose is to end the legalized subordination of women, Mill challenges the presumption of women's inferiority and puts forward various arguments

---

[5]   John Stuart Mill, 'The Subjection of Women' (first published 1869) in *'On Liberty', with 'The Subjection of Women' and 'Chapters on Socialism'* (Stefan Collini ed, CUP 1989) 117–217.

blocked out in earlier essays written with his wife, Harriett Taylor (1807–1858). As Mill contends, if the differences between men and women are to be distilled down to a 'natural' or inborn essence, it will first be necessary to strip away all those traits that can be explained by way of education or circumstance: this path has never been pursued, and so it has never been demonstrated that what separates the sexes is a difference by virtue of which women are inherently inferior to men. Likewise, the purported superiority of men is ultimately based on the law of the strongest: this superiority is called 'natural', and likewise, any power deriving from custom is called 'natural'.

So the law should not make unequal what nature has created equal. What most fundamentally needs to happen if the subjection of women is to come to an end is that women need to have the legal power to participate in writing the rules that apply to them: they should therefore have an opportunity to vote for their representatives and put themselves forward as representatives. In the pages that in various writings Mill and Taylor devote to this question, they do not confine themselves to demanding equal rights: they insist throughout on economic independence, access to education, free choice as to motherhood and divorce, and generally the ability not to be materially and culturally dependent on men.

Apart from a few theoretical discussions, nineteenth-century feminism most prominently expressed itself as a social movement. And in mid-century, particularly in the United States, Great Britain, and France, a new political subject came onto the scene: the suffragette, and they were so called because they made it their primary aim to gain universal suffrage, meaning the right to vote. For almost two centuries, feminist theories and movements were essentially devoted to fighting for citizenship rights, abolishing all rules designed to exclude women, and doing away with all differential treatment between men and women. Equality of rights meant not only the right to vote but also access to all professions and public offices and the ability to freely choose how to manage one's own life and assets, as well as equal status within the family and in the workplace. The main goal of first-wave feminism was to ensure that women could act as independent subjects, responsible, with ownership over their own lives, free to make their own decisions about their own bodies, lives, and property.

Next to liberal feminism, asserting equal rights against male power, there emerged a socialist strain in feminism, arguing that men and women alike had a common enemy in the capitalist economic system: there was little that the formal conquest of equal rights could do for women without any change in the material conditions and structures of society. It was therefore the task of the socialist revolution to free women from these forms of capture, along with the rest of the proletariat.

2.3   THE RISE OF ECONOMIC AND SOCIAL RIGHTS

2.3.1 The nineteenth-century workers' movements demanded not only that the franchise be extended to all but also that protections be afforded to everyone in their social and economic situation: this meant freedom of association and the right to strike and unionize, as well as a minimum wage and a range of other guarantees and economic benefits, contractual or otherwise (like unemployment and worker's compensation).

The needs of the growing working classes put increasing pressure on European governments. Economic and social rights can be characterized as having a grassroots origin, and so, unlike rights to liberty, they did not start out as political theories translated into constitutional principles and provisions but rather came in the form of statutory and administrative law and court rulings.

The first significant social welfare measures packaged into a comprehensive programme came in Great Britain with the 1834 Poor Law and the labour laws enacted in the same period, particularly with a view to protecting women and children. In Germany, similar initiatives came from Otto von Bismarck, the 'Iron Chancellor', under whose leadership a sweeping and innovative social security scheme was introduced in 1883.

These and other reforms adopted by European governments initially presented themselves as a matter of social duty towards the working class, as measures designed to improve its standards of living, and also to enable workers and their children to access services and entitlements the middle class could secure for itself privately in areas such as education, healthcare, and housing. These were demands for which the workers' movement had to struggle hard, igniting social conflict, but they also found a basis in liberal thought and were consistent with widely held values about meritocracy and individual self-reliance and enterprise, while also finding support in the idea of the national interest (ss 6.3.4 and 6.3.5).

The first achievements of wageworkers came with the introduction of standard working hours, the weekly rest, protections specifically tailored to women and especially children, unemployment benefits for those no longer able to work, healthcare, and aid for pensioners and the disabled. These measures would often take the form of labour protections designed so that contractually weak parties were not subject to exploitation, as well as of legislation providing a social safety net. Labour and social security were also the first areas to see the enactment of maternity protections.

Although social rights originated primarily out of the struggle for labour protections and social security, it is also worth devoting a few words to the right to education. In fact compulsory primary education was the first public service to have been demanded for all citizens, male and female alike, with pressure for it coming from several quarters throughout the nineteenth century. In the context of the century's socioeconomic structure, the introduction of compulsory public education paid for by the state broke the nexus between income and education that had acted as requisites for gaining access to political rights, and it made social mobility possible, enabling persons to advance their social station on the basis of merit, as opposed to being born into wealth and status.

A common frame of reference for the early workers' movements was the 1793 Jacobin Declaration (s 1.3.2), for in this document equality is no longer just a formal concept (the idea that the law applies equally to everyone) but also begins to take on the contours of a substantive aim requiring government action and wealth redistribution. This emerges in particular in a couple of provisions, harbingers of social rights, that speak the language of the duties owed by society, which needs to provide for its 'unfortunate citizens'—those who are unable or no longer able to work (Article 21)—and to 'put education at the door of every citizen' (Article 22).

The 'social question' comes particularly into focus in the constitutions enacted in the wake of the mid-nineteenth-century upheavals. In France, the 1848 Constitution puts a new emphasis on solidarity and work, couples rights with duties, individual liberties with the need to support workers and the most vulnerable citizens, and states that all citizens are entitled to social protections and to an education:

> The Constitution guarantees to citizens liberty of labor and of industry. Society favors and encourages the development of labor by gratuitous primary education, professional educa-tion, equality of relations between the employer and the workingman, institutions of savings and of credit, agricultural institutions, voluntary associations, and the establishment by the State, the departments and the communes of public works suitable for the employment of unemployed hands; it furnishes assistance to abandoned children, the infirm, and the aged that are without resources and whose families cannot relieve them. (Article 13)[6]

In Germany, in 1848, the Imperial Act concerning the Basic Rights of the German People not only enshrined the personal liberties, citizenship rights, and those relating to the inviolability of the person but also abolished the privileges associated with the estate system, declaring that all German citizens are equal before the law. Like the French Constitution of 1848, it provided for compulsory primary education and, correspondingly, free access to education for children in the poorer classes.

But these were not yet conceived as personal rights proper: the idea of a personal right to entitlements is extraneous to the overall scheme of nineteenth-century liberalism. Indeed the idea of social rights originates from the politico-economic doctrines that sought to steer a middle course between the free-market approach and that of socialist revolution: these were reformist doctrines that saw a role for the state in levelling out social inequalities and providing aid for the most disadvantaged. While Marx cast a critical eye on the rights of man, that was not the case with the majority of workers' movements and the proponents of reformist social-ism. Out of these currents came projects for new declarations of rights founded on the values of social solidarity, looking to achieve an 'economic democracy' next to political democracy, or substantive equality next to formal equality.

Social legislation became widespread in the early twentieth century, often introducing services either funded by the state or delivered directly by it. Services providing healthcare, education, public housing, and social security and pension schemes were generally turned over to the state. In the decades bestriding the nineteenth and twentieth centuries, public services were introduced to address other basic aspects of citizens' lives as well, especially by way of infrastructure (transportation, the road system, the power grid, water supply) and poverty relief. There was, then, a significant expansion in the scope of government action, increasing the size of the administrative apparatus and its network of officials and civil servants.

With the state taking social services directly into its own hands, its role in the economy began to look like that of a business firm, even if not one strictly subject to the dynamics of the

---

[6]   'Constitution of 1848' in *The Constitutions and Other Select Documents Illustrative of the History of France, 1789–1901* (Frank Maloy Anderson ed, The HW Wilson Company 1904) 522–38, at 525.

market economy. If ever the state had been a mere 'night watchman', in the first decades of the twentieth century that description could no longer apply, with the state being asked not only to guarantee security and liberty, but also to intervene directly in citizens' social and economic lives—a new role requiring new resources and projects, as well as persons and institutions devoted to them.

The construction of public apparatuses through which to deliver social services did not happen under a unitary scheme. The formation of the social state did not generally follow a linear course but rather came about through an accretion of various and sundry overlapping provisions, contingent and diversified, dictated by different political interests and social concerns.

The emergence of socioeconomic rights can be described as a work of compromise necessitated by a confluence of demands: these came from social movements and from business firms seeking to shift costs and risks, and on top of that was the interest of the administrative state in maintaining social control so as to prevent the outbreak of conflict. The guarantees and protections introduced for those most at risk gradually morphed into duties of society, into workers' rights, and ultimately into rights accorded to all citizens, male and female alike: the rights previously designed to protect only certain segments of the population now became rights recognized for everyone.

2.3.2 While the Mexican Constitution of 1917 already incorporated social principles and reforms, the first constitutional document containing an extended list of social rights understood as rights of all citizens complementing the traditional rights to liberty was the Weimar Constitution of 1919,[7] enacted during the brief moment in German history that lasted until the rise of Nazism. The Weimar Constitution parts with the individualistic and atomistic view of society and of rights typical of the nineteenth century and brings back the social value of fraternity (*Vereinigung*), inflected in such a way that the state is entrusted with the function of guarantor of social solidarity and guardian of collective values. The text's underpinnings and provisions are nothing short of innovative:

> The organization of economic life must accord with the principles of justice and aim at securing for all conditions of existence worthy of human beings. Within these limits the individual is to be secured the enjoyment of economic freedom. (Article 151)

Property is a source not only of rights but also of social obligations aimed at realizing the 'common good' (*Allgemeinheit*) (Article 153). On this basis the subsequent articles give the state forms of control over landed property, the resources of the soil, businesses, and economic activities (Articles 155–6) and give every German citizen a right to housing, authors' rights, the right to gainful employment, and the right to unemployment benefits for those unable to work. The text also provides for a social security system 'for the maintenance of health and capacity to work, for the protection of maternity, and for provision against the economic consequences of age, infirmity, and the vicissitudes of life' (Article 161).

---

[7]   *The Constitution of the German Republic* (Heinrich Oppenheimer ed, Stevens and Sons 1923).

Freedom of association is expressly guaranteed as necessary to ensure wholesome working and economic conditions (Article 159).

Detailed provisions (Articles 143–7) are devoted to education and schooling, providing for free compulsory education until the age of 18 on the basis of a single comprehensive plan under which teacher training is standardized across the German territory and needy families are eligible for aid.

Even when it comes to women's rights the Weimar Constitution marks a turning point: 'All Germans are equal before the law. Men and women fundamentally have the same civil rights and duties' (Article 109). In subsequent articles it is stated that marriage rests on legal equality between the sexes, and all rules containing discriminatory exceptions putting women at a disadvantage in the workplace are suppressed.

Reflected in this Constitution—still focal to an important legal and political debate—was an attempt to build a social public law adequate to a liberal democracy, in part against the background of the 1917 October Revolution in Russia, with the forces it set in motion. Indeed the Soviet Russia Constitution of 1918[8] had introduced a fundamentally new paradigm, for in it the central subject of rights was no longer man or the citizen but the 'labouring and exploited people', meaning the entire body of workers and peasants, with the explicit exclusion of capital, the exploiting class. Under Article 3, 'all private property in land is abolished', and 'all factories, mills, mines, railways, and other means of production and transportation' are nationalized. The 1936 Constitution of the Soviet Union[9] reiterated the right and duty to work, but this was coupled with social rights: the right to rest and leisure, to fair pay, to social insurance, to education, and to healthcare, all at government expense (Articles 118–21). The document also proclaimed equal rights for men and women 'in all spheres of economic, state, cultural, social and political life' (Article 122). Freedom of speech; freedom of the press; freedom of assembly, including the holding of mass meetings; and freedom of street processions and demonstrations were all guaranteed (Article 125), but only so long as they were exercised 'in conformity with the interests of the working people, and in order to develop the organizational initiative and political activity of the masses of the people' (Article 126). So even rights to liberty found their realization through the state, which was entrusted with ensuring that the people had the tools needed to exercise these rights.[10]

Even the Constitution of the Second Spanish Republic of 1931 contained some significantly innovative provisions: these included a list of social and economic rights, legal equality between the sexes, and the introduction of a constitutional court. But this would be a short-lived constitution, done away with under the Franco regime.

After World War II social rights found their place in every new national constitution and in the United Nations' 1948 Universal Declaration of Human Rights (UDHR). Accompanying this development, and consistent with these guarantees, was an expanding economic role

---

[8]   *The Russian Constitution, adopted July 10, 1918* (The Nation 1919).

[9]   *Constitution (fundamental law) of the Union of Soviet Socialist Republics* (State Publishing House of Political Literature 1938).

[10]   See József Decsényi, Gábor Pulay, Jòzsef Halász, *Socialist Concept of Human Rights* (Akadémiai kiadó 1966).

which the state saw for itself in the effort to meet social needs. Although in different ways and to different degrees, Western governments looked to these values in shaping a vision of their own role in society: thus next to the liberal liberties came freedom from want; the notion of human dignity was expanded to include a decent life; formal equality before the law was buttressed with equality of opportunity.

2.3.3 Despite the earlier work done in developing socialist and solidaristic doctrines, it was not until the mid-twentieth century that a proper theory of social rights took shape: prominent among the first works to offer a full-fledged vision and a universalizable foundation was *La déclaration des droits sociaux* (The Bill of Social Rights) by Georges Gurvitch (1894–1965), which came out in New York immediately after France was liberated from Nazism. In it Gurvitch envisions a new French Revolution, arguing that 'liberty, equality, and fraternity have to be realized with all energy and force in the economic field',[11] and on the basis of a renewed connection among these values he advocates the development of social rights.

In Gurvitch's vision, however, social rights are not yet qualified as essential attributes of the citizen. This is something that would happen only a few years later in a book by Thomas Marshall (1893–1981) titled *Citizenship and Social Class*, where citizenship is defined as 'a status bestowed on those who are full members of a community. All who possess the status are equal with respect to the rights and duties with which the status is endowed'.[12] It is this equal-rights status, Marshall observes, that essentially distinguishes the modern age from feudal society, in which 'status was the hall-mark of class and the measure of inequality'.[13]

To Marshall we owe the tripartite distinction that places rights into three buckets—civil, political, and social—understood as constructs that historically have developed in successive stages, in an evolutionary scheme that posits an incremental march towards greater and greater equality (s 5.1.2). In this scheme social rights figure as the contribution the twentieth century made to the process of consolidating a single citizenship status within the nation-state, a process that had begun in the eighteenth century with the introduction of civil rights and continued in the nineteenth century with political rights.

Whereas, in Marshall's reconstruction, civil and social rights merge into the status of citizenship, in the public and scholarly debate they have long been viewed as being at loggerheads. The problem first surfaced in the clash that pit workers' rights against the right to property, the latter understood in the broad, hallowed, and inviolable sense in which it figures in nineteenth-century constitutions and legal systems. In fact the first measures introduced to protect workers were challenged, citing the need to protect the rights of property holders and economic freedoms, including freedom of contract between worker and employer. Proponents of the 'hands-off' view of the government's role in the economy—the so-called

---

[11] Georges Gurvitch, *The Bill of Social Rights* (first published in French 1944; International Universities Press 1946) 10.

[12] Thomas H Marshall, *Citizenship and Social Class and Other Essays* (CUP 1950) 28–9.

[13] ibid 12.

laissez-faire philosophy—objected to the government intervening in the economy and society with costly regulations that would place burdens on private enterprise.

Rights to liberty and social rights owe their historical ascension to two profoundly different conceptions of the role of government: the former a conception of *limited* government, the latter one of *expanded* government. Whether social rights translate into government-provided services or into provisions regulating the private sector, and employers in particular, they entail choices that have an impact on economic activity, on the allocation of resources, and on several fundamental aspects of the lives of citizens. This goes in precisely the opposite direction from the laissez-faire conception: on the interventionist conception of the state's role, the state intervenes directly in social and economic relationships and redistributes the national wealth.

The scepticism towards an expanding menu of public functions is driven by various factors: in the first place is the concern about the taxes that need to be levied in order to ensure those functions, but there is also the fear of wasteful government spending, of the mission creep relative to the stated objectives of government programmes, and of the curtailment of individual liberties that may occur when functions previously left to the market are entrusted to the state's central planning. In fact the expansion of public powers needed to implement social rights often translates into a regulatory and administrative apparatus that intrudes on many spheres of citizens' private lives: one need only mention here education and healthcare—essential services that require standardized, 'cookie-cutter' delivery. Even if such standards are shaped within a democratic political system, and so broadly reflect the will of the majority, they can translate into impositions for those who do not feel part of the majority.

Even if social rights are widely recognized in the West in its twentieth-century constitutions, case law, and legal scholarship, they are not unanimously seen as standing on the same footing as rights to liberty. Starting with the Weimar Constitution, the provisions setting forth social rights are considered 'programmatic provisions', meaning that they are goal-oriented, setting out an objective of government action rather than introducing legally binding requirements. Although social and economic rights are amenable to implementation in a wide range of different ways, with much discretionary policy latitude, and are not easily justiciable, some legal systems contain social rights, like the rights to education and healthcare, that through constitutional legal precedent and scholarship have gained the status of inalienable rights that are binding on the legislature. In the law of the European Union, social rights have gained increasing significance and binding force for member states.

3
Fundamental human rights and their multilevel protection

3.1   THE REFOUNDATION OF FUNDAMENTAL RIGHTS AND CONSTITUTIONAL SYSTEMS

3.1.1 In twentieth-century Europe the experience of Nazism and Fascism revealed just how fragile a construction fundamental rights were, just how easily they can crumble at the hands of government: the most basic rights saw an official, systematic, brutal clampdown. The very idea of humanity was denied under a methodically planned-out annihilation of a whole swath of it. The mainstream legal thinking in both regimes did away with fundamental rights altogether: the idea that individuals should be recognized as having inalienable rights they can assert against the state's authority was incompatible with the totalitarian regimes' ideology and policies. Likewise, individual autonomy was depleted of its public bearing under a conception of the national population as a homogeneous unit organized into corporations and social groups of which the individual is an organic and integral part.

World War II thus drove a wedge into the history of rights: the Western nations felt the inadequacy of the tools that qualified the rule of law and called on the international community to make itself responsible for the future.

The need arose to anchor the positive law and the action of governments to principles of justice whose violation would justify citizens in engaging in civil disobedience and the international community in responding to address such violations. In the Nuremberg trials, the Nazi criminals were charged on the basis of universal values and norms translated into new principles of international law.

Fundamental rights were put back into the toolkit needed to protect the liberties of individuals, even those who do not identify with the majority, by binding governments to new limits and commitments. In fact, if rights were to perform these functions, they certainly could not have as their only basis the laws enacted or applied by those very governments.

Legal positivism drew criticism for its enabling role in having made it possible for any law to pass as valid and legitimate regardless of its content. The 'crisis of legal positivism'—a theoretical approach that, in the eyes of many, had helped to justify the Nazi and Fascist laws—refashioned itself and splintered into a variety of orientations, among which was a revived natural law theory. Having gone into demise in the nineteenth and early twentieth centuries, natural law theory re-emerged in the post-war period as a theoretical foundation on which to address concerns about justice that reasserted the idea of natural human rights. Even Christianity found a renewed interest in the rights of man, which had been called into question by the churches, Catholic and Protestant alike, since the time of the French Revolution. The post-war period also injected new life into constitutionalism as both a political and a legal current of thought: constitutions were no longer limited to serving as the form through which fundamental rights are declared but also acted as their basis.

A new theoretical and social debate sprang up on the question of the foundations of rights and the role that constitutions should play in liberal and democratic legal systems. Apart from the conceptions that developed out of this debate, it became a primary concern to construct legal institutions that would enable the fundamental rights to establish themselves as necessary and binding elements of liberal and democratic states. In this effort to guarantee and protect rights, a two-pronged approach was adopted that took both the domestic and the international scenario into account, in the former case looking to rigid constitutions and constitutional courts, in the latter to human rights declarations and international conventions.

3.1.2 National legal systems were redesigned on the basis of new constitutions shaping the basic framework of the rule-of-law state. On this model, the constitution acts as the founding document for the national community, defining a common set of principles that, as the highest law of the land, are binding on the government. The premise behind the constitution so conceived is that a democracy cannot stand on popular sovereignty alone: even if governmental powers are exercised on the basis of popular mandate, the government itself is bound by some fundamental principles and must uphold and protect the rights of all citizens.

Rigid constitutions contain procedures that make amendment more difficult than is the case with ordinary laws: larger majorities and greater hurdles that need to be overcome if governments are to be able to untether themselves from what the constitution requires. A necessary complement to the system is judicial review, be it *ex ante* (before law is enacted) or *ex post* (afterward). As much as the legislature may be the embodiment of the popular will, it is no longer an absolute sovereign but is itself subject to limits. It is no longer only the law that ultimately establishes the framework and boundaries within which the government and citizens must act but the constitution, and this happens through the reading of it provided by the constitutional courts. Over the decades, these courts would come to play an increasingly expanded role, both in clarifying the content of rights and the forms of their implementation and in defining the relation between the powers of government.

Constitutions also play a key role as a source of new rights. In fact rarely are new rights introduced legislatively from the top down: they rather tend to come into being through a gradual bottom-up process driven by the pressure of social needs and demands, a process that then moves into the public debate and makes its way to the courts, whose case law is repackaged into the restatements of legal scholarship and provides a basis for interpreting the constitution. And then out of this process come recommendations which the courts make to parliaments, urging them to fill the gap by enacting new law. In this way, rights gain new significance as tools with which to convey and give shape to the demands of citizens, advocacy groups, and movements, over time increasingly assuming a social and political role.

In recent decades the warp and woof of constitutional rights has grown more complex, in part because the institutional framework has begun to come apart in a process of attrition involving the crisis of the nation-state, whose legislative sovereignty has shrunk in ceding ground to supranational interests; the breakup of citizenship understood as a single status applying to all right-holders; and a growing array of institutions that assert and define rights at the local and global levels. Although neoconstitutionalism foregrounds the role of the constitution within each democratic state's national system, this current of thought has increasingly been turning its attention to the supranational, regional, and global arenas.

By the time of the post-war constitutions, it was common for social and economic rights to have found their place next to civil rights. But there was also another fundamental development that came with these documents: women gained legal equality. Even so, it would take some time for this constitutionally protected equality of rights between men and women to translate into law, through a process of legislative reform and constitutional interpretation. Then, too, legal reform based on formal equality soon revealed itself to be inadequate, especially in the areas of family and labour law. It became apparent that, precisely by virtue of the statutorily mandated equal treatment, the new laws could even put women at a disadvantage unless they took account of motherhood, women's actual living conditions, the economic resources available to them, the cultural conditioning they are subject to, the power dynamics and division of labour that exist within the family, or simply the distinctiveness, needs, and lifestyles of women. The women's movements of the latter half of the twentieth century thus came to a new realization: legal equality before the law is not enough when systemic discrimination and oppression are structurally baked into the culture and into society. Access to the labour market and to politics brought out into the open the real challenges that women face in the context of institutional and cultural structures that over the course of centuries have been built by men, with the costs these structures entail for women when equality means that they are expected to adapt to male models.

3.2 INTERNATIONAL HUMAN RIGHTS: LAW, THEORIES, AND PRACTICE

3.2.1 After World War II, it was not so much from national societies as from the international community, led by the winning powers, that there came a push to tie the states' sovereignty to their respect for universal principles and rights. The states that joined the United Nations (UN) committed themselves to 'promoting and encouraging respect for human rights and for fundamental freedoms for all without distinction as to race, sex, language, or religion'.[1]

Once more, then, rights came to be conceived as human rights, expressing universal principles, values, and needs recognized by everyone in the world.[2] They accordingly entered

---

[1]   UN Charter (1945), Article 1(3).

[2]   See Antonio Cassese, *Human Rights in a Changing World* (Polity 1990); Michael Freeman, *Human Rights: An Interdisciplinary Approach* (Polity 2002; 2nd edn, Polity 2011); Mary Ann Glendon, *A World Made New: Eleanor Roosevelt and the Universal Declaration of Human Rights* (Random House 2001); David Kinley, Wojchiec Sadurski,

a process of internationalization, and through this process—inaugurated by the UDHR, adopted by 48 states in 1948—the rights of individuals and of peoples gained formal primacy over the sovereignty and interests of states. The Universal Declaration marked the start of a new era, one in which *individuals*, and not just states, become subjects of international law, such that they can also assert their rights against governments by appealing to supranational documents and institutions. Fundamental human rights are recognized for persons *qua* persons rather than as citizens, and in this way the status of right-holder is enjoyed independently of the three classic elements of the state: sovereignty, a people, and a territory.

In a form that recalls the preamble to the 1789 French Declaration of Rights, the preamble to the UDHR introduces the values the document is founded on and guided by. These require, in the first place, a 'recognition of the inherent dignity and of the equal and inalienable rights of all members of the human family', understood as 'the foundation of freedom, justice and peace in the world', which need to be legally protected against the kinds of 'barbarous acts which have outraged the conscience of mankind'. In a similar vein, the UN and its member states reaffirm 'their faith in [...] the equal rights of men and women' and make a pledge to 'promote social progress and better standards of life in larger freedom'. Thus the protection of freedom is coupled with a public commitment to improving the lives of all peoples.

The natural law foundation and the values of the French Revolution can also be found in Article 1, stating that 'all human beings are born free and equal in dignity and rights. They are endowed with reason and conscience and should act towards one another in a spirit of brotherhood'. The following Article 2 sets out the principle just mentioned that rights belong to everyone regardless of their recognition by any state:

> Everyone is entitled to all the rights and freedoms set forth in this Declaration, without distinction of any kind, such as race, colour, sex, language, religion, political or other opinion, national or social origin, property, birth or other status. Furthermore, no distinction shall be made on the basis of the political, jurisdictional or international status of the country or territory to which a person belongs, whether it be independent, trust, non-self-governing or under any other limitation of sovereignty.

Article 3 establishes the right to life, liberty, and security of the person, with an extended catalogue of protections in Articles 4–20 specifying the content of these rights. Article 21 establishes the political rights: the right to take part in governing one's own country, the right of equal access to public service, and the right to 'genuine elections [...] by universal and equal suffrage and [...] held by secret vote'. And Articles 22–7 list the economic, social, and cultural rights deemed to be indispensable to human dignity and flourishing.

There ensued among nations a dialogue aimed at specifying what duties and obligations the UN member states have in relation to the rights enshrined in the UDHR. Out of this dialogue came two covenants: the International Covenant on Civil and Political Rights (ICCPR) and the

---

Kevin Walton (eds), Human Rights: Old Problems, New Possibilities (Edward Elgar 2013); Samuel Moyn, *The Last Utopia: Human Rights in History* (Harvard UP 2010); James Nickel, *Making Sense of Human Rights* (University of California Press 1987; 2nd edn, Blackwell 2007).

International Covenant on Economic, Social and Cultural Rights (ICESCR), both adopted in 1966 and entered into force only ten years later.

The ICCPR, more prominently reflecting the concerns of Western Europe and the United States, contains an extensive list of rights having immediate binding force on the ratifying states. The ICESCR instead more emphatically reflects the concerns of socialist and non-Western states: it commits the ratifying states to the goal of achieving greater social and economic equality not only among citizens within each state but also among people in different parts of the world. As much as the ICESCR may mark an advance in specifying rights to benefits and services, the document is still programmatic, setting forth no more than a duty of best efforts under which each states party is to commit itself 'to the maximum of its available resources'. The two covenants also contain a new right to self-determination of peoples, with which the international community closes the historical chapter of past colonial ventures and declares the illegitimacy of any and all such ventures in the future.

Unlike the UDHR, the two 1966 Covenants are binding on the ratifying states, in the sense that they become law within each state. The same holds for the many international treaties and conventions that have followed, whether they are aimed at protecting specific classes of persons—as with the 1951 Convention Relating to the Status of Refugees or the Convention on the Rights of the Child or the Indigenous and Tribal Peoples Convention, both ratified in 1989—or whether they are aimed at responding to violations of specific classes of rights, as with the 1984 UN Convention against Torture, the 1965 International Convention on the Elimination of All Forms of Racial Discrimination, or the 1990 International Convention on the Protection of the Rights of All Migrant Workers and Members of Their Families.

However, ratification is not enough to ensure that fundamental rights are respected within each state: there need to be enabling acts and institutions charged with guaranteeing those rights. From the start, the main challenge in the process of internationalizing rights has been that of making them effective: more than 70 years since the 1948 Declaration, the rights contained in it are still by and large ineffectual.

Without institutions having enforcement powers, without a system of pre-established penalties, without international tribunals—making exception for the International Criminal Court, whose judgments are binding on the parties concerned, even if its jurisdiction is limited to extreme cases, such as genocide and other war crimes and crimes against humanity—we find ourselves in a situation where the response to human rights violations still relies in large part on the domestic law enforceable within each national legal system. As is evidenced by the reports put out by international organizations (such as Amnesty International and Human Rights Watch), it is often governments themselves or the great supranational economic and political powers that violate the human rights of populations or allow their violation to take place. Many gaps and flaws have come to light in the implementation system designed by the UN.

3.2.2 Women's rights have developed along independent paths on the international plane as well.[3] Equality of rights under the law between men and women is provided for in the UDHR and figures as an explicit commitment of governments in the 1966 Covenants. But the text that crucially set women's rights on a path to internationalization is the 1979 Convention on the Elimination of All Forms of Discrimination against Women (CEDAW), which indeed proceeds from the premise that even if international law already recognizes equal rights between the sexes, 'extensive discrimination against women continues to exist'. The achievement of women's rights, an integral part of human rights, cannot rely solely on a formal extension of existing rights to women: it also requires states parties 'to take all appropriate measures to eliminate discrimination against women'. This means both *de jure* and *de facto* discrimination against women, accordingly defined as

> any distinction, exclusion or restriction made on the basis of sex which has the effect or purpose of impairing or nullifying the recognition, enjoyment or exercise by women, irrespective of their marital status, on a basis of equality of men and women, of human rights and fundamental freedoms in the political, economic, social, cultural, civil or any other field. (Article 1 CEDAW)

From the CEDAW onward, women's access to rights becomes an objective to achieve where it no longer suffices to reform the law: there also need to be economic, social, and cultural transformations. In part, this requires states parties to

> modify the social and cultural patterns of conduct of men and women, with a view to achieving the elimination of prejudices and customary and all other practices which are based on the idea of the inferiority or the superiority of either of the sexes or on stereotyped roles for men and women. (Article 5 CEDAW)

Particularly significant among the world conferences on women's rights that would follow is the World Conference on Women held in Beijing in 1995. Two key principles are laid out in the Beijing Platform for Action adopted on that occasion: that of women's empowerment, with the objective of enabling women to achieve self-determination and full participation in all institutions and spheres of society, and that of gender mainstreaming, understood as

> the process of assessing the implications for women and men of any planned action, including legislation, policies or programmes, in all areas and at all levels. It is a strategy for making women's as well as men's concerns and experiences an integral dimension of the design, implementation, monitoring and evaluation of policies and programmes in all

---

[3]   See Charlotte Bunch, 'Women's Rights as Human Rights: Toward a Re-Vision of Human Rights' (1990) 12 *Human Rights Quarterly* 486; Martha C Nussbaum, *Women and Human Development: The Capabilities Approach* (CUP 2000); Julie Peters and Andrea Wolper (eds), *Women's Rights, Human Rights: International Feminist Perspectives* (Routledge 1995).

political, economic and societal spheres so that women and men benefit equally, and inequality is not perpetuated. The ultimate goal is to achieve gender equality.[4]

By comparison with human rights broadly, the implementation of women's rights in the world raises challenges that are specific to them. These challenges concern their violation at the hands not only of public powers but also of private powers, specifically within the family and the community. In fact, it is within this private sphere that most violence and discrimination against women takes place, and the protections needed to deal with this problem often cut against the grain of traditions, religions, and personal ties. In much of the world, it is women's lives that stand to be most profoundly regulated by traditional, community, and religious norms: the friction between the universality of rights and the particularity of cultures becomes especially apparent when it comes to women's rights.

3.2.3 In fact, while the class of right-holders may be universal, the rights accorded to them are not universal in content, nor do they rest on universal foundations, having been conceived in a Western mould. Therefore, the moment those same rights are declared to be universal, the legacy that ties them to European history and culture becomes apparent. From the start it proved a challenge to apply human rights law universally across the world in areas whose populations are foreign to the Western canon,[5] and this all came to the surface in the UN's World Conference on Human Rights held in Vienna in 1993.

In countries marked by a strong communitarian tradition and an overlap between government and religious institutions, particularly in Asia and Africa, internationally codified rights are felt to be foreign, and difficult to reconcile with these countries' social mores and with their theoretical understandings of rights, significantly compounding the problem of implementation. The human rights system has also faced criticism for its perceived role as a tool of neocolonialism and cultural imperialism, reflecting a Euro-centric and paternalist evolutional paradigm. It has even been criticized as a thinly veiled pretext which the Western powers have used to justify their own aggrandizement, with policies of foreign interference so intrusive as to reach the point of 'humanitarian' war.

As a result of this opposition and criticism, the universality of rights has increasingly positioned itself no longer as a starting point but as an objective that can only be achieved through an interchange and dialogue among cultures and by way of mutual feedback between theories and practices, societies and institutions, and rules at the local, national, and supranational levels.

Despite the difficulties tied to implementation and universalization, human rights have increasingly been expanding their footprint across the world. Human rights language is no longer the special preserve of politics, lawyers, national and international institutions, and can no longer be described as having been conceived in high quarters but has become a medium of popular protest and action, a way for people across almost all of the world to put forward social

---

[4]   UN, *Report of the Economic and Social Council for 1997* (UN Doc A/52/3, 18 September 1997) ch 4, at 28.

[5]   See The Executive Board of the American Anthropological Association, 'Statement on Human Rights' (1947) 49 *American Anthropologist* 539.

demands. Human rights have become a powerful tool enabling social movements, communities, and organizations in every continent to address unanswered needs and gain legitimacy: witness the emergence of 'new rights' like the right to water, the rights of indigenous people, and environmental rights, but also the popular uprisings that have taken place in the name of the traditional rights to liberty. As it turns out, the very idea of having a right and being able to claim it is a powerful idea that outpaces the institutional culture within which that idea was conceived.

Decisively contributing to this spread is the 'practice of human rights', understood as the set of actions undertaken to implement rights not only on the part of international agencies and organizations but also on the part of national and transnational social movements, organizations and associations, minorities, media campaigns, and the like.[6]

More to the point, this activity has in recent decades become the primary focus of nongovernmental organizations (NGOs), with an emphasis on direct implementation of rights, as well as on monitoring and denouncing their violation and on advocacy, while putting pressure on national and international institutions. Despite many contradictions and hurdles, the work that so-called human rights activists have been doing across the world is having the effect of translating the language of human rights into forms that people can understand, carrying human rights over from the world of institutions to that of social life.

Starting in the 1990s, UN agencies, NGOs, and national and international organizations have been adopting what is known as the Human Rights-Based Approach (HRBA), 'a conceptual framework that is normatively based on international human rights standards and operationally directed to promoting and protecting human rights'.[7] Under HRBA, all development programmes and humanitarian actions need to be aimed at implementing human rights in keeping with the standards set by international human rights law. The approach sets out three types of human rights obligations that states are to meet: respecting, protecting, and fulfilling these rights. The first obligation is to not interfere with their enjoyment, the second to take measures aimed at preventing others from interfering, and the third to undertake actions aimed at enabling human rights to be progressively achieved. In conjunction with two other approaches—'leave no one behind' and 'gender equality and women's empowerment'—HRBA also forms the basis for the 2030 Agenda for Sustainable Development.

Despite the impressive headway made by the international human rights system, it is still nation-states that play a pre-eminent role in the realization of human rights, considering that these states are responsible for enforcing the laws needed to apply and protect human rights, as well as for the bulk of the investments needed to that end.

---

[6]   See Mark Goodale and Sally Engle Merry (eds), *The Practice of Human Rights: Tracking Law between the Global and the Local* (CUP 2007).

[7]   See UN Sustainable Development Group, *Human Rights-Based Approach* <https://unsdg.un.org/2030-agenda/universal-values/human-rights-based-approach> accessed 14 July 2021.

3.3   THE EUROPE OF RIGHTS

3.3.1 The supranational process towards a greater range of human rights and protections also moves through regional human rights systems whose formulations of rights and implementing measures are more closely aligned with the needs and cultures of the areas of the world in which they operate. In this regard, specific declarations and conventions have been adopted in Europe, the Americas, and Africa.

Immediately after World War II in Europe, human rights were introduced as fundamental values on which basis to construct a union of states founded on common values and principles. Within the Council of Europe (CoE)—established in 1949 based on the need to protect human rights, the rule of law, and democracy—negotiations were undertaken that in 1950 would lead to the adoption of the European Convention on Human Rights (ECHR). This was the first supranational treaty to subject states to both negative and positive obligations relating to civil and political rights, on the one hand requiring states not to violate these rights, and on the other requiring them to adopt rules and measures with which to guarantee their enjoyment and prevent or punish violations, even if committed by private entities.

This founding document also established two supranational organs charged with protecting the human rights set forth in it: the (now defunct) European Commission of Human Rights (ECmHR) and the European Court of Human Rights (ECtHR), established in 1959 and head-quartered in Strasbourg. Allaying the states' fears about the prospect of diminished national sovereignty, the Court gradually consolidated its jurisdictional authority and increasingly assumed a central role not only in ensuring judicial protection of human rights but also in interpreting these rights and bringing uniformity to the variety of national provisions. The ECtHR is now competent to hear cases involving states but also cases brought by individuals, and herein lies its most innovative aspect. It means that anyone, regardless of citizenship, has standing before the Court in actions involving a human rights violation by any of the signatory states, including the state of which the individual is a citizen. The ECtHR is limited in its action, however, in that it cannot directly require states to correct their domestic law, to which end it must ultimately rely on whatever initiative may be taken by the states, which in many cases have confined themselves to compensating the victims.

Other conventions were subsequently adopted by the CoE. Most important among these was the European Social Charter, signed in 1961, revised in 1996, and entered into force in 1999: it protects social and economic rights, including the rights to work, housing, health, education, social protection, and welfare; it provides a legal frame of reference for each ratifying state as well as for the law of the European Union (EU law). Social and economic rights are another area in which the European institutions have played an increasingly important harmonizing role. In the twenty-first century, the protection of fundamental rights has been addressed in a range of conventions and additional protocols, including, most recently, ones dealing with data protection, extradition, trafficking in human beings and organs, biomedical research, and the protection of minors against exploitation. In 2011 came the CoE Convention on Preventing and Combating Violence against Women and Domestic Violence (also known as the Istanbul Convention), the first international binding instrument providing a legal framework, along with monitoring mechanisms, aimed at eradicating violence against women in any form, protecting women from such violence, and prosecuting all cases when they arise (s 7.1.3).

Another pillar of the European legal system is the Court of Justice of the European Union (CJEU), established in 1952 and headquartered in Luxembourg, with jurisdiction over EU law and its application by member states. The CJEU also renders judgments involving fundamental rights, but does so less frequently and directly than the ECtHR, considering that the European Union (EU) was initially conceived primarily as an economic union and would retain that focus for a long time thereafter. Over the years the two courts, each acting within its own jurisdiction, have been playing an increasingly robust role in protecting and redefining fundamental rights, helping to establish the European system as the one equipped with the strongest supranational framework for enforcing them.

Throughout the twentieth century, whenever the question of fundamental rights came up before the CJEU, it was addressed by looking to the member states' constitutional traditions, the ECHR, and EU and international treaties. But the need was felt for a charter of rights specific to the EU. And so in 2000, following a broad political, theoretical, and social debate, came the adoption of the Charter of Fundamental Rights of the European Union (EU Charter), though it did not become legally binding until the Treaty of Lisbon made it so in 2009. The rights contained in the EU Charter are structured by reference to six values/principles: dignity, liberty (freedoms), equality, solidarity, citizenship (citizens' rights), and justice, in an innovative setup that advances beyond the classic distinction among civil, political, and socioeconomic rights.

The EU Charter rests on values common to the European populations and rooted in their history. At the same time, however, the EU Charter underscores in its preamble the need 'to strengthen the protection of fundamental rights in the light of changes in society, social progress and scientific and technological developments by making those rights more visible in a Charter'.

3.3.2 The drafters of the EU Charter thus carried forward a process, generally referred to as 'multiplication of rights', that had begun in the latter half of the twentieth century on both the national and the international stage.

By way of simplification, three lines of development can be identified in this process, under which (a) rights are extended to subjects (both individual and collective) different from natural persons (so as to include the family, the embryo, minorities, populations, future generations, animals, and so on); (b) the range of right-holders is extended, being no longer limited to man or the citizen but also made to include persons on the basis of membership in a group defined by characteristics such as age, a birth condition, or a life choice (this includes, for example, workers, children, women, the elderly, the sick, people who identify as lesbian, gay, bisexual, transgender, queer, or consumers); and (c) the range of goods worthy of protection is broadened (so as to include the environment, water, the commons, and so on).

In the public debate, the multiplication of rights has taken on the contours of a proliferation of rights: every social demand or protest tends to put itself forward as a right—a new right being claimed or an old right that has been violated.[8] Rights are invoked to both oppose and advocate public policies, to call for new action, to protect and build support for values, interests, and principles.

The very act of packaging a claim as a right lends greater force to it, suggesting that it finds its foundation in an entire group of people understood to share a common, unaddressed grievance. In this way, the claim turns into something that is 'owed', into a corresponding duty borne by others: a claim that manages to establish itself as a right gains social legitimacy in a way that is then difficult to roll back. Furthermore, rights advance a moral claim, acting as a bulwark against the special interests that make it into policy, protecting the fundamental values essential to the person and to society.

For some decades now, the traditional rights have been sharing the stage with a new crop of rights. These 'new rights' are a heterogeneous bunch that runs the full gamut from civil and political rights to socioeconomic and cultural rights and includes individual and group rights, often simply offering new interpretations or applications of an old right. These rights are often tied to scientific discoveries or technological transformations that have significantly expanded the range of individual choices. Especially in bioethics and biolaw, new rights have been fashioned that include, for example, the right to genetic identity, the rights of the embryo, the various rights tied to assisted reproductive technology, or the right to make one's own end-of-life choices (s 7.3.3). With the Internet and the various forms of communication it has spawned, radical transformations have taken place that cut across national borders in such a way as to elude traditional means of governmental oversight and control. The right to privacy has grown to such complexity that a dedicated, constantly evolving area of law has developed around it, and the same goes for the right to identity. Resource exploitation, pollution, and deterioration of the natural heritage and of heritage assets are all the concern of the environmental rights claimed for present and future generations (s 8.3).

Sex and gender differences are becoming increasingly significant in many areas where rights are being defined and protected, areas such as marriage, the family, education, labour policy, medicine, and reproduction (ss 7.1 and 7.2).

Sexual orientation survives as a long-neglected and culturally rooted cause of discrimination, calling for a specific effort aimed at achieving genuine equality of access to rights in every social sphere.

Although female citizens in the EU outnumber male citizens, and *de jure* equality has been achieved for some time now, there continue to be areas of significant *de facto* discrimination coupled with difficult access to rights. We can see this, for example, in the underrepresentation of women in politics, in the gender pay gap, in the greater burden that falls on women when it comes to domestic work and caregiving, in the smaller share of leisure time afforded to women, in the persistent scarcity of women in leadership positions (in both the private and public sectors), in the subordination that women continue to face in various aspects of social

---

[8]   See Norberto Bobbio, *The Age of Rights* (Allan Cameron tr, Polity 1996); Carl Wellman, *The Proliferation of Rights: Moral Progress or Empty Rhetoric?* (Westview Press 1999).

life, and in the violence that women are subjected to as women. Gender equality figures among the main objectives to which EU institutions have committed themselves.[9]

The migrations that began in the second half of the twentieth century have wrought deep change in European societies, with wide repercussions in the area of fundamental rights. The most significant 'new right' that comes fraught with a full array of problems is one of the first ones to have been theorized as a universal right of man: *ius migrandi*, the right to freedom of movement, the right of every person to travel to any part of the world for survival or in search of better life prospects. Migrants, asylum seekers, and their offspring invoke a series of other rights as well—the right to life, to healthcare; the rights of minors and workers; political and social rights—each configured in various ways considering the status of presence in European territories (ss 7.2.1, 8.2.3, and 9.3.3).

Freedom of religion—protected as both a spiritual commitment and a ritual and practice—requires a broad understanding of citizenship rights under which people are allowed to observe religious and cultural practices in settings such as schools, the workplace, hospitals, and prisons. But sometimes freedom of religion claims the ability to carve out spaces of legal autonomy, particularly in the personal and familial spheres. The experience of coming into contact with European legal and political traditions has also brought into relief the fault lines along which secular thinking about public spaces, basic freedoms, and gender equality clashes with some freedoms and protections claimed by groups or individuals by virtue of their religion or cultural background. Rights are thus inflected in different ways depending on the moral and religious norms they fall under, whether these are majority norms or those espoused by various minorities.

With the multiplication of rights inevitably comes a multiplication of conflicts. The rights of some can collide with those of others: economic freedoms clashing with the workers' and environmental rights, consumer rights with the rights of manufacturers, privacy protections with freedom of expression, the rights of the embryo with those of the mother, the rights of the traditional family with those of nontraditional ones, animal rights with freedom of enterprise and scientific research, the rights of future generations with those of the present, cultural rights with women's rights, religious freedoms with the principle of the separation of church and state, and, more in general, collective rights with individual rights, and so on.

Science has changed the configuration and possible interpretations of many rights, including the right to life, increasingly pitting two competing views against each other: on the one hand is the view that ties rights to individual choice, underscoring the individual's self-determination; on the other is the view that ties rights to an inalienable interest or value that can override the individual's exercise of free will.

In the public debate and in political language conflicts are always emerging between different rights, between the rights of different groups or persons, or between divergent interpretations of the same right. Moral rights claim legal recognition and protections, sometimes

---

[9]   See European Commission, *Gender Equality Strategy: Achievements and Key Areas for Action* <https://ec .europa.eu/info/policies/justice-and-fundamental-rights/gender-equality/gender-equality-strategy_en> accessed 14 July 2021.

making it necessary for legislative and judicial organs, national and supranational alike, to address the issues raised.

In this context, the European courts find themselves playing an increasingly crucial role, not only in ensuring that government bodies are respecting and protecting the classic personal rights and liberties, but also in striking a workable balance between different kinds of rights, in interpreting rights in light of the changing circumstances of the present, and in making it possible for new rights to be recognized.

PART II
THEORY

Nicola Riva

INTRODUCTION

Following the reconstruction of the history of fundamental rights provided in Part I, Part II will be devoted to some theoretical questions arising in connection with fundamental rights.

Chapter 4 will analyse the concept of fundamental rights. If we want to establish which fundamental rights individuals or collectives living under a specific normative system have—for example, which fundamental rights persons have under the ECHR—we need a preliminary understanding of what fundamental rights are, of what kind of 'entity' we are looking for. Contributing to such an understanding is one of the central tasks of legal philosophy understood as general jurisprudence, whose aim is to analyse those fundamental legal concepts that may then be used to describe specific legal systems. In our analysis of the concept of fundamental rights, we will start from the general concept of rights (s 4.1); we will then introduce some distinctions relating to rights in general (s 4.2), at which point the discussion will hone in on two concepts of fundamental rights and on their implications as regards the responsibility for respecting and enforcing those rights (s 4.3). The chapter closes by arguing that the 'political concept' of fundamental rights—under which they are understood as rights that individuals and collectives have primarily against governments—is the concept that better accounts for the contemporary reality of those rights.

On that concept, it is governments that have primary responsibility for respecting and enforcing those rights. Starting from such an assumption, Chapter 5 will tackle some issues concerning the reality of fundamental rights. The discussion will not be specific to any single legal system but is rather meant to generally apply to all legal systems that include some fundamental rights. We will start by analysing some categories standardly used to classify established fundamental rights (s 5.1). We will then address some questions regarding the implementation of fundamental rights, paying special attention to questions specifically concerning social rights (s 5.2). In that context, we will also discuss a third concept—the 'cluster-concept'—of fundamental rights, different from the ones distinguished in Chapter 4, and the relation between fundamental rights and constitutional rights. As observed in Chapter 3 (s 3.3.2), a distinctive feature of the contemporary reality of fundamental rights is the multiplication of those rights. This inevitably creates the possibility for conflicts between fundamental rights and between those rights and general interests. Chapter 5 closes by outlining these conflicts and considering how they are or may be dealt with (s 5.3).

Finally, Chapter 6 addresses questions regarding the justification of fundamental rights understood—according to their political concept—as limits on the exercise of political authority and on the use of public resources. As illustrated in Part I, the history of fundamental rights is in large part a history of the arguments and theories that have been advanced in an attempt to justify those rights, and that remains a primary task of ethics in connection with fundamental rights, or of those branches of political and legal philosophy that may be considered an application of ethics to matters of political and legal concern. The discussion is not aimed at justifying any particular account of fundamental rights, specifying which rights should be included among fundamental rights and what such an inclusion would require of governments: such a discussion would fall far beyond the scope of this book. Instead, Chapter 6 will consider what it might mean to look for a justification of fundamental rights and how the validity of such a justification may be understood (s 6.1), and then a rough overview will be provided of the kinds of arguments that may be and have been offered in justifying the general idea of fundamental rights (s 6.2) and specific classes of those rights (s 6.3).

4
The idea of fundamental rights

4.1   THE CONCEPT OF RIGHTS

4.1.1 Fundamental rights are rights. In order to define fundamental rights, then, we should first of all clarify the concept of rights. Rights are normative properties. They are 'properties' in that they belong to a subject—a person or some other entity. As regards normativity, they are normative in two different senses. First, they are normative because their existence depends on norms. When we think of rights, we typically think of either moral or legal rights, dependent on moral or legal norms respectively, but it will be a mistake to think that those rights exhaust the class of rights. Any kind of norm can confer rights: thus, for example, the rules of a board game, while neither moral nor legal, confer rights on each player, and that is true of many other conventional norms, such as linguistic norms or the norms of etiquette. Second, rights are normative in the sense that they can justify prescriptions, normative judgements— especially judgements qualifying some behaviour, practice, or institution as morally, legally, or in some other way good or bad—and normative expectations, that is, expectations about how other subjects should behave, as opposed to expectations about how they will behave.

Once we have defined rights as normative properties, we need to consider what kind of normative properties they are. A classical starting point in analysing the concept of rights is the work of the American legal theorist Wesley Newcomb Hohfeld (1879–1918), who in a famous article of 1913 analysed how the term 'right' was used in judicial reasoning and distinguished four different uses of that term.[1] According to Hohfeld the term 'right' can refer to four different legal positions: liberties,[2] claims, powers, and immunities.

Persons have a *liberty* to do (or not do) something if they have no duty not to do (or do) that thing. For example, persons have the liberty to criticize the government if they have no duty not to criticize the government. Having the liberty to do something does not imply having the

---

[1]   Wesley Newcomb Hohfeld, 'Some Fundamental Legal Conceptions as Applied in Judicial Reasoning' (1913) 23 *The Yale Law Journal* 16.

[2]   While he himself recognizes the two terms as synonyms, Hohfeld prefers the term 'privilege' to denote what is more commonly referred to as a 'liberty'. Following the example of many other theorists who have referred to Hohfeld's analysis, I will use the more common term, because the term 'privilege' may be misleading. Cf Hiller Steiner, *An Essay on Rights* (Blackwell 1994); Matthew H Kramer, NE Simmonds, and Hillel Steiner, *A Debate over Rights: Philosophical Enquiries* (OUP 1998).

liberty not to do that thing. Indeed, having that liberty is consistent with having a duty to do that thing. Of course, persons may have both the liberty to do something and the liberty not to do that thing: in that case, they are permitted to choose whether or not to do that thing. Nor does the fact that one has a liberty to do something imply that others have a duty to allow or help that person to do that thing. The fact that persons have a liberty to criticize the government does not imply that, if they decide to exercise that liberty, other persons have a duty not to try to prevent their criticism from being heard, as by speaking over them or by refusing to publish or circulate their pamphlets criticizing the government.

Persons have a *claim* (or 'claim-right') against other persons that the latter do (or not do) something if the latter have a duty to do (or not do) that thing. For example, persons have a claim against the police not to be arrested for having criticized the government if police officers have a duty not to arrest them for having done so. Claims can be negative, if they refer to an act of noninterference, or they can be positive, if they refer to an act of assistance or remuneration. Thus, under parliamentary rules, members of a parliament may have a claim against the entire parliament or against its president to be given an opportunity to publicly express their criticism of some act of the executive during a parliamentary session.

Having a *power*—in the legal sense of 'power'—means having the ability to do any of the following: changing one's own legal position towards others or changing some other person's legal position towards either oneself or third parties. Powers, then, can be held in relation to oneself or in relation to some other persons. Persons change their own or other persons' legal position when they create, cancel, suspend, or transfer their own rights (ie liberties, claims, powers, or immunities) or duties or the rights or duties of those other persons. For example, the author of a pamphlet criticizing the government may grant a publisher the exclusive liberty to publish that pamphlet and, by doing so, will incur a duty not to grant the same liberty to another publisher; a parliament may have the power to cancel the liberty to criticize the government of persons subject to its authority, exercising that power by enacting a law laying down a duty not to criticize the government.

Finally, persons have an *immunity* protecting some of their rights (ie liberties, claims, powers, immunities) against other persons' attempt to deprive them of those specific rights if the latter lack the power to deprive them of those specific rights. To the extent that persons lack the power to change their own legal positions, they can be said to have an immunity against themselves. For example, in securing persons' liberty to criticize the government against parliamentary attempts to deprive them of that liberty, a constitution may protect the same liberty with an immunity, that is, it may deny the parliament the power to enact a law depriving persons of that liberty. A constitution can also grant that immunity only to some persons, such as members of parliament: in that case, the parliament may deprive the ordinary citizen—but not its own members—of the liberty to criticize the government. In both cases, the authority of parliament is limited by the immunity.

Hohfeld's account of the concept of rights refers to the legal uses of the term 'right', but other authors have suggested that his analysis also applies to the moral uses of that term.[3]

According to Hohfeld, only claims, or claim-rights, are properly rights. The other normative positions—liberties, powers, immunities—are rights only in a loose sense. In what follows, assuming that Hohfeld is correct, I will follow the suggestions of those authors who recommend using the term 'right' to refer only to claim-rights, that is, to rights proper.[4] I will use the term 'prerogatives' to refer to the full set of the four normative positions identified by Hohfeld.

Notice that rights are often not isolated prerogatives but are combined with other prerogatives, including other rights, into complex normative positions, that is, into 'aggregations' or 'clusters' of prerogatives. These complex normative positions may themselves be referred to as 'rights' or as 'cluster-rights' (s 5.2.3).[5]

4.1.2 According to Hohfeld rights (proper) are correlative to duties. This is the thesis of the *correlativity of rights and duties*: if a person has a right, another person has a corresponding duty. The person that has the right is the *right-holder*, while the one that has the correlative duty is the (correlative) *duty-bearer*. A right provides the right-holder a valid reason to claim something from the (correlative) duty-bearer. According to the thesis of the correlativity of rights and duties, if a right exists, a corresponding duty should also exist. Is the reverse also true? Is it enough that a duty exists in order for a right to exist? It seems not. Under many complex normative systems, either moral or legal, persons have duties that do not clearly correspond to the rights of some identifiable person. Consider, for example, moral or legal norms forbidding cases of harmless wrongdoing, that is, behaviour that, while not harmful, is considered so wrong that any person must (ie has a duty to) abstain from it.[6] That is the case with sodomy laws, which impose a legal duty not to engage in certain sexual acts. Whose rights might correspond to the duties imposed by these provisions? Apparently, this question has no answer and any attempt to imagine rights correlative to those duties—for example, an individual right to a social environment free of immoral conduct or a collective right to the preservation of a community's positive morality—seems to misunderstand what is (or was) the point of those provisions: banning behaviour felt to be grievously immoral.[7]

Let us assume, then, that the correlation between rights and duties is univocal, that is: that it applies to all rights, not to all duties. What would follow? It would follow that Hohfeld's account of the concept of rights (proper) is incomplete. If the correlativity of rights and duties

---

[3]   See, eg, Carl Wellman, *A Theory of Rights: Persons under Laws, Institutions, and Morals* (Rowman and Allanheld 1985); Judith J Thomson, *The Realm of Rights* (Harvard UP 1990); Carl Wellman, *Real Rights* (OUP 1995).

[4]   See, eg, Kramer, Simmonds, Steiner (n 2).

[5]   See Wellman, *A Theory of Rights* (n 3); Thomson (n 3); Wellman, *Real Rights* (n 3).

[6]   On harmless wrongdoing see Joel Feinberg, *The Moral Limits of the Criminal Law* (OUP 1990) vol 4 (*Harmless Wrongdoing*).

[7]   Cf Matthew H Kramer, 'Rights without Trimmings' in Kramer, Simmonds, Steiner (n 2) 7–111, defending the idea that the correlativity of rights and duties applies not only to all rights but also to all duties.

is univocal, it would not be enough for a duty to exist to conclude that someone has a correlative right: some other condition should realize. What is that further condition?

In the philosophical debate on the concept of rights, the matter is taken up in two rival theories: the *interest theory* (of which Bentham's benefit theory is an example) and the *choice theory* (also known as 'will theory'). Sometimes the disagreement between proponents of the two theories is framed as a disagreement about the function of rights, but I think that this is a misunderstanding: while both theories have some implications regarding the function of rights, both of them are aimed at providing a structural analysis of the concept of rights, and they do so by identifying all the conditions that should realize in order for a claim that a right exists to be valid.

Proponents of the interest theory argue that for a right to exist, the existence of a duty is not enough: there should also be some person having an interest which is protected through the imposition of that duty.[8] If a person is under a duty and the point of imposing that duty is to protect another person's interest, that other person may be said to have a right. According to this theory, then, rights are protected interests. According to the interest theory the concept of rights may be broken up into two elements: a formal duty and at least one nonformal interest. The relation by which these elements are connected is not formal but justificatory: the protection of the interest is what justifies the imposition of the duty. The right-holder is the person whose interest is served by the duty. The problem for the interest theory is that sometimes it may be difficult to establish whether an existing duty is aimed at protecting some interest and, if so, which and whose interest it is aimed at protecting. It can also be the case that a single duty is aimed at protecting several different interests—independent or connected—recognized for several different persons, such that the same duty may correspond to a plurality of rights. While that is consistent with the thesis of the correlativity of rights and duties, it can make the identification of rights more controversial, because it requires investigating the reasons that may justify the imposition of a duty. That, of course, is not an argument against the interest theory. On the contrary, it could explain why the identification of rights can be a matter of deep controversy.

Proponents of the choice theory instead argue that the further elements, apart from a duty, that need to be present for a right to exist are (a) at least one power to either extinguish, alienate, waive, or enforce that duty or the duties generated by its violation (eg the duty to prosecute and punish the violator or the violator's duty to pay damages or a fine) and (b) the liberty to either exercise or not exercise that power.[9] Thus, according to the choice theory a right is a complex formal position that results from the combination of four (or more) simpler normative positions: a duty, at least one power, and the dual liberty to exercise or not exercise that power. Thus, for example, it is appropriate to say that we have rights to our property not only

---

[8]   See, eg, Neil MacCormick, 'Rights in Legislation' in *Law, Morality and Society: Essays in Honour of HLA Hart* (Peter Hacker and Joseph Raz eds, OUP 1977) 189–209; Joseph Raz, 'On the Nature of Rights' (1984) 93 *Mind* 194; Kramer (n 7) 7–111.

[9]   See, eg, HLA Hart, 'Legal Rights' in *Essays on Bentham: Jurisprudence and Political Philosophy* (OUP 1982) 162–93; Hiller Steiner, 'Working Rights' in Kramer, Simmonds, Steiner (n 2) 233–301.

because others have duties not to use our property without our permission, but also because we have some powers to dispose of our property and the liberties that allow us to exercise those powers at will: those powers may include the power to alienate (ie transfer) the rights we have over our property to other persons, the power to extinguish those rights, the power to demand the government's intervention to protect our property from violation or to punish the violation of our property by compelling the violator to pay damages. Not all these powers need to exist for a right to exist, but at least one of them needs to exist and be the object of a dual liberty. The point is that, for a right to exist, the right-holder should have some choice on others' duties. Because, according to this theory, rights reduce to a complex of formal features, and because formal features are easier to identify than interests, if we adopt this theory, it would be easier to identify rights and right-holders. This, I think, is the only significant advantage the choice theory has over the interest theory. In every other respect, the interest theory seems to provide a better account of the concept of rights. Being merely formal, the choice theory is unable to account for the justificatory relation between rights and duties, that is, for the fact that when we consider whether a given duty is correlative to a right, what we are often looking for is something that could justify that duty. But the most serious limit of the choice theory is that it is unable to account for many of the rights we consider to be more important, including many fundamental rights: many of these rights are such that the right-holders do not have any power over the correlative duties. Thus, according to the choice theory, it will not be possible to speak of a 'right not to be killed' unless we, as beneficiaries of that duty, also have the power and liberty to waive the correlative duty, by authorizing someone to kill us, or the power to waive the duties that will be generated by a violation of that duty, by establishing that the killer should not be prosecuted and/or punished: in the absence of such powers and liberties, the duty not to kill exists with no correlative right. This limit was recognized by HLA Hart (1907–1992)—one of the foremost legal theorists of the twentieth century, and himself a proponent of the choice theory—who thought that this theory could account for a wide range of rights, but at the same time he conceded that in order to account for fundamental rights a different theory of rights would be needed.[10]

4.2   SOME DISTINCTIONS ABOUT RIGHTS

4.2.1 Rights create a normative relation between the right-holder and the (correlative) duty-bearer. But who can be a right-holder and who a duty-bearer?

In the previous section I have always referred to persons' rights. The concept of a person is controversial. Not only can it refer to an ontological, moral, or legal status, but within each of these domains it is a contested concept. Confining our attention to the moral and legal uses of the concept of a person,[11] we should note that, while it partly overlaps with the concept of

---

[10]   Hart (n 9).

[11]   On moral persons see Mary Anne Warren, *Moral Status: Obligations to Persons and Other Living Things* (OUP 2000) ch 4; Christine M Korsgaard, 'Facing the Animal You See in the Mirror' (2009) 16 *The Harvard Review of Philosophy* 1; on legal persons see Neil MacCormick, *Institutions of Law: An Essay in Legal Theory* (OUP 2007) ch

a human being, it is neither identical with nor confined within the boundaries of the latter concept. On the one hand, there are beings that are biologically human but that—on reasonable, if sometimes strongly contested, grounds—are not considered persons, examples being human embryos and foetuses or brain-dead human beings. While human beings who have some cerebral capacity are considered to be persons—*natural persons*—in all existing moral and legal systems,[12] different moral and legal systems identify in different ways the criteria for moral or legal personality and the moment when human beings become or cease to be persons. On the other hand, there are *artificial* or *juristic persons*—organizations such as states, corporations, and nongovernmental organizations (NGOs)—that, while not human in themselves, are recognized as moral or legal persons.

While most right-holders are persons, it is not only persons that can be right-holders. According to some rights theorists and advocates, rights can also be recognized for nonhuman animals or for human beings who are not yet or no longer persons. These subjects, they claim, can have interests that deserve to be protected, but both of those assumptions—that they can have interests and that their interests deserve to be protected—are disputed. What is accepted in contemporary discourse about rights is that collectives that are not recognized as artificial persons—such as peoples and social groups, and especially linguistic, cultural, and religious minorities—can be right-holders. This is suggested by the common, and useful, distinction between *individual* rights and *collective* rights. There is a complex theoretical discussion about the defining features of collective rights.[13] In this context, it will suffice to say that individual rights are those rights that belong to natural persons or to collectives that have been assimilated to individuals, through fictions such as the idea of artificial persons, while collective rights are those rights that belong to collectives that have not been so recognized. It is not necessary to think that collectives such as peoples or social groups have their own interests, different from the interests of their individual members, and that collective rights protect those interests. It is enough to think of collective rights as rights protecting interests that would not deserve to be protected—that is, that could not justify the ascription of a right—if they belonged only to single individuals or to a small set of individuals, but deserve to be protected insofar as they are shared by a majority of the members of a collective having some special status.[14]

To appreciate the distinction between individual rights and collective rights consider the right to unpolluted/breathable air and the right to receive an education in one's mother tongue. On the one hand, all human beings have an interest in unpolluted/breathable air, insofar as this is needed for survival, but the fact that that interest is common to all human beings is not necessary as justification for its being qualified for protection in the form of rights: even

---

5. The concept of a person and the problem of deciding who should count as a person are central to many debates in bioethics. See Peter Singer, *Practical Ethics* (CUP 1980; 3rd edn, CUP 2011) chs 4–7; Peter Singer, *Rethinking Life & Death* (The Text Publishing Company 1994).

[12]   Article 6 UDHR states: 'Everyone has the right to recognition everywhere as a person before the law.'

[13]   See Peter Jones, 'Group Rights', *The Stanford Encyclopedia of Philosophy* (Summer edn 2016) <https://plato.stanford.edu/archives/sum2016/entries/rights-group/> accessed 14 July 2021.

[14]   Here I follow Joseph Raz, *The Morality of Freedom* (OUP 1986) 207–9.

if only a single person were to need unpolluted/breathable air to survive, that person would have a valid claim to a right to unpolluted/breathable air. On the other hand, even if it could be recognized that all persons have an interest in receiving an education in their mother tongue, we would not think that such an interest is enough to accord all persons a right to receive an education in their mother tongue: such a right is generally accorded only to the members of the linguistic community that includes the majority of persons living in a given territory, and when it is accorded to linguistic minorities as well, it is because those minorities have a relevant size and often some special claim to such a right. These examples show that an individual right is not necessarily a right to an individual good, while a collective right is not necessarily a right to a collective good: unpolluted/breathable air is a collective good, while education in one's mother tongue is an individual good.

If the identification of potential right-holders is controversial, what is uncontroversial is that duty-bearers must necessarily be persons, either individually or collectively: that is because only persons are sensitive to norms, that is, can recognize them and take them as reasons for action.

4.2.2 The content of a right and of its correlative duty is always a more or less determinate course of behaviour required of the duty-bearer. In this respect, the language of rights is some-times deceptive. It is quite common to say that someone has a right to something, where that something is a more or less abstract thing, such as life, religious freedom, education, or health. Even in these cases, however, what the right-holder has a right to is a course of behaviour from the duty-bearer. Take, for example, the right to life, considered to be among the most impor-tant of our rights. Two interpretations of this right are possible that are tied to two different concepts of fundamental rights (s 4.3.1). On the first interpretation, this is a right that each person has against every other person, corresponding to the right not to be killed or to a set of rights including the right not to be killed and maybe some other rights such as the right to be rescued from a life-threatening event (so long as no other person having a greater duty to rescue is present, and so long as that act will not expose the rescuer to significant risk). On the second interpretation, the right to life corresponds to a set of rights that persons have primarily against the government. Correlative to those rights are the government's duty not to exercise political authority or use public resources in ways that could result in the killing of persons and its duty to exercise political authority and use public resources to secure that persons' lives will be protected. As these examples show, the content of a right and of the correlative duty can be either what is conventionally described as a 'negative' course of behaviour (not killing someone) or what is conventionally described as a 'positive' one (rescuing someone, exercising political authority, using public resources). Accordingly, rights are commonly distinguished into *negative* rights and *positive* rights. And the same is true of the correlative duties.

The content of a right and of the correlative duty, that is, the behaviour they refer to, can be more or less determinate: sometimes rights are formulated in quite vague terms. This is espe-cially true of fundamental rights. Thus, for example, what the right to life requires is largely indeterminate. According to its first interpretation, it could be thought that that right corre-lates with a duty not to kill, but what about killing in self-defence or mercy-killing? And what about preventing a third party from killing the right-holder, rescuing someone, or providing them the means necessary to sustain their life? Things are not easier if we interpret the right to life as primarily a right against government: how exactly should political authority be exercised and public resources be used in order to protect persons' lives? The vagueness of a right, that is, its indeterminacy, is a matter of degree. The right to life is a much less determinate right than a right not to be killed, but the right not to be killed itself has some degree of indeterminacy: is switching off a life-support machine an act of killing? And what about administering to a suffering patient a palliative drug that will accelerate the process of dying as an unintended side effect? Many controversies about rights depend on their indeterminacy.

4.2.3 Rights can be classified according to the number of the right-holders and according to the number of the (correlative) duty-bearers. Rights belonging to all the members of a class—all persons, all citizens, all women, all workers, all peoples, and so on—are said to be *universal*, while rights belonging to specific individuals or collectives are said to be *particular*. For example, most of the rights enumerated in the Universal Declaration of Human Rights (UDHR) (s 3.2.1) are universal rights belonging to all persons, while the rights persons have to their property are particular, because they depend on specific persons being the legitimate owners of specific items of property. If we look to the number of the (correlative) duty-bearers, rights are said to be *general*, if they are held against all the members of a class, or *special*, if they are held against specific individuals or collectives. For example, under a legal system punishing murder, the right not to be killed is a general right that each person holds against every other person, while the right an unemployed person may have to receive unemployment benefits is a special right—whether it is conceived as a universal right of all unemployed persons or as the particular right of a particular unemployed person—for it can be asserted only against the specific subject that has the duty to pay out that benefit. Notice two things. First, there is no correspondence between universal and general rights on the one hand and particular and special rights on the other: both universal and particular rights may be either general or special. Second, if a person has the same right—general or special—against more than one other person, he or she has as many identical rights as are those persons: one for each of them.

4.2.4 Finally, rights can be classified on the basis of the other prerogatives—liberties, powers, immunities, and other rights—associated with them.

Considering the powers right-holders themselves or other persons have over their rights, and the liberties they have to exercise such powers, we can distinguish between *extinguishable* and *nonextinguishable* rights, *alienable* and *inalienable* rights, and *waivable* and *nonwaivable* rights.

Rights are extinguishable if they can be cancelled either by the right-holders or by other persons, and nonextinguishable if they cannot be cancelled. Thus, many of the rights deriving from marriage can be extinguished by the right-holders through divorce, while some constitutional rights are nonextinguishable insofar as governments do not have the powers to deprive the right-holders of those rights.

Rights are alienable if they can be transferred, temporarily or permanently, from the right-holders to other persons, by the right-holders or by some other persons; inalienable rights are rights that cannot be transferred. The classic example of alienable rights is property rights. When we sell some good we own (or lend or gift it) what we are transferring to another person is not that good, but rather the property rights we have over that good. By contrast, fundamental rights, as understood by most conceptions of fundamental rights, are the prime example of inalienable rights: they cannot be transferred by their right-holders nor by other persons. This is also true of the fundamental right to private property, protecting persons' interest to acquire private property and to use and dispose of their private property, as distinct from the particular property rights they may have over specific goods. Inalienable rights cannot be the object of market exchanges or of other forms of exchange.

If some of a person's rights may not be extinguished or alienated by other persons, including persons having a general power over the first person's rights—like the power that governments have over the rights of those subject to its authority or (in a more limited form) the power that parents have over their children's rights—those rights can be said to be protected by an immunity against both extinction and alienation.

As regards the distinction between waivable and nonwaivable rights, that depends on the possibility which right-holders may or may not have to allow the (correlative) duty-bearers not to comply with the duties correlative with their rights. Thus, for example, central to the debate on euthanasia is the question whether the right not to be killed is, or should be, a (partially) waivable right, permitting its holders, if special conditions realize, to authorize other persons to put an end to their lives. A right is *de facto* waivable, as well, when the right-holder has discretion over the enforcement of the correlative duty or over punishment for its violations, that is, when the right-holder has the power to demand that the correlative duty or the sanction for its violation be enforced and the liberty to decide whether or not to exercise that power.

Finally, two other very important distinctions are the distinction between enforceable and nonenforceable rights and the distinction between justiciable and nonjusticiable rights. A right is *enforceable* if compliance with the correlative duty can be coercively imposed in order to prevent violations of those rights; it is *nonenforceable* if it cannot. For a right to be enforceable there should be someone with the liberties and the powers to impose compliance with its correlative duty: typically persons having those liberties and powers are public officials or the right-holders themselves (think of cases of self-defence). Few rights are truly enforceable: they are the most important rights, protecting life, integrity, personal freedom, and property. In the normal case it is the remedies and penalties for the violation of a right that are enforceable. While most rights are not enforceable, they are *justiciable*, that is, their violations can be denounced and prosecuted, and remedies and penalties can be imposed on their violators. Justiciability is considered to be a very important characteristic of rights, to the point that *nonjusticiable* rights are often considered not to be real rights. Enforceable and justiciable rights are said to be *guaranteed* rights.

4.3   TWO CONCEPTS OF FUNDAMENTAL RIGHTS

4.3.1 In this section I distinguish two concepts of fundamental rights. A third concept will be considered later (s 5.2.3). For any concept of fundamental rights there are several specifications, often referred to as different 'conceptions' of the same concept.[15]

According to the first concept of fundamental rights—*fundamental rights as prepolitical rights*—fundamental rights are rights that each person has against every other person independently of the existence of political institutions. Natural rights theories (s 1.1) provide the best historical example of theories that undertake to specify this concept of fundamental rights. When conceived as prepolitical rights, fundamental rights are thought to create horizontal normative relations between persons, who, having rights against each other, are united by reciprocal duties. Conceptions of fundamental rights that understand them to be prepolitical rights—as is the case with many philosophical conceptions of human rights—tend to include only negative rights (ie rights to noninterference) among fundamental rights,[16] but this is not always the case: some of them include positive rights (ie rights to assistance or remuneration) as well.[17] According to the concept of fundamental rights as prepolitical rights, respect for fundamental rights is a condition of the rightness of persons' conduct.

According to the second concept of fundamental rights—*fundamental rights as political rights*[18]—fundamental rights are rights persons primarily have against governments. According to this concept, fundamental rights set limits and goals around the exercise of political authority and around the use of public resources: they do so by establishing that political authority cannot be exercised or public resources be used in certain ways and that

---

[15]   The distinction between a concept and its conceptions, where conceptions are different specifications of the concept, has become part of the contemporary philosophical lexicon, ever since John Rawls (1921–2002) used it to distinguish the concept of justice from its different conceptions. Cf John Rawls, *A Theory of Justice* (Harvard UP 1971; rev edn, Harvard UP 1999).

[16]   See, eg, Maurice Cranston, *Human Rights Today* (Ampersand 1962; 2nd edn, under the title *What Are Human Rights?*, Bodley Head 1973); Robert Nozick, *Anarchy, State, and Utopia* (Basic Books 1974); Murray N Rothbard, *The Ethics of Liberty* (Humanities Press 1982).

[17]   See, eg, Alan Gewirth, *Reason and Morality* (University of Chicago Press 1978); Alan Gewirth, *The Community of Rights* (University of Chicago Press 1996); John Finnis, *Natural Law and Natural Rights* (OUP 1980; 2nd edn, OUP 2011); Martha C Nussbaum, *Frontiers of Justice: Disability, Nationality, Species Membership* (Harvard UP 2006); James Griffin, *On Human Rights* (OUP 2008).

[18]   The idea of fundamental rights as 'political rights' refers to all fundamental rights, not only to those fundamental rights to citizenship, political participation, consultation, and representation that under the content-based classification of fundamental rights qualify as 'political rights' (s 5.1.2). The phrase 'political rights' has different meanings when used to qualify all fundamental rights and when used to refer to a class of fundamental rights. On the use of that phrase to refer to all fundamental rights see Ronald Dworkin, 'Taking Rights Seriously' (first published 1968) in *Taking Rights Seriously* (Harvard UP 1977; 2nd edn, Harvard UP 1978) 184–205.

they should be exercised and used with a view to achieving certain goals.[19] Fundamental rights, so understood, may be held against a single government, as is the case with constitutional rights within the constitutional state (s 3.1.2 and, on the relation between fundamental rights and constitutional rights, s 5.2.4); against more than one government, as is the case with the fundamental rights guaranteed by the European and the other regional systems of fundamental rights (s 3.3.1); or even against all governments, as is the case with global human rights (s 3.2.1). They create primary vertical normative relations between persons and governments and only derivatively or secondarily do they create horizontal normative relations between persons (see below). According to the concept of fundamental rights as political rights, respect for these rights by governments is a condition of political legitimacy.

While they do not implicate each other, the two concepts of fundamental rights that I have just distinguished are not necessarily at odds with each other. There is no inconsistency in thinking both that persons have rights that pre-exist political institutions and that they have rights—the same rights and/or different rights— against governments. Indeed, some political theories connect the idea of political fundamental rights to the idea of prepolitical fundamental rights, by arguing that what legitimizes the existence of governments is—uniquely or among other things—the contribution they can give to the protection and fulfilment of the prepolitical fundamental rights persons have against each other. According to those theories, the idea of prepolitical fundamental rights provides a foundation for political fundamental rights. This is the case, for example, of the natural rights theory of John Locke and of natural rights theories in general (s 1.1.3).

Almost all theories of fundamental rights as prepolitical rights include an account of how political fundamental rights may be derived from prepolitical ones. Anarchical theories constitute an exception.[20] The reverse is not true: it is possible to support a theory of fundamental rights as political rights, which does not presuppose the existence of any prepolitical fundamental rights. This is the case of theories that describe fundamental rights as the creation of a community that, subjected to a political authority and mindful of how that authority has been and may be abused, imposed some constraints on how it may be exercised.[21]

The distinction between the concept of fundamental rights as prepolitical rights and the concept of fundamental rights as political rights should not be confused with the distinction

---

[19]   See Luigi Ferrajoli, *La democrazia attraverso i diritti: Il costituzionalismo garantista come modello teorico e come progetto politico* (Laterza 2013) and Luigi Ferrajoli, *La costruzione della democrazia: Teoria del garantismo costituzionale* (Laterza 2021). Cf Rawls (n 15); John Rawls, *Political Liberalism* (Columbia UP 1993; 3rd edn, Columbia UP 2005); Jürgen Habermas, *Faktizität und Geltung: Beiträge zur Diskurstheorie des Rechts und des demokratischen Rechtsstaats* (Suhrkamp 1992; rev edn, Suhrkamp 1994) [English edn, *Between Facts and Norms: Contributions to a Discourse Theory of Law and Democracy* (tr William Rehg, Polity 1996)]. For conceptions of global human rights as political rights see John Rawls, *The Law of Peoples: With 'The Idea of Public Reason Revisited'* (Harvard UP 1999); Thomas Pogge, *World Poverty and Human Rights: Cosmopolitan Responsibilities and Reforms* (Polity 2002; 2nd edn, Polity 2008); Charles R Beitz, *The Idea of Human Rights* (OUP 2009).

[20]   See, eg, Rothbard (n 16).

[21]   See, eg, Alan Dershowitz, *Rights from Wrongs: A Secular Theory of the Origins of Rights* (Basic Books 2004).

between the conception of fundamental rights distinctive to natural rights theories and a legal positivistic conception of fundamental rights. On the one side, while all natural rights theories conceive of at least some fundamental rights as prepolitical rights, not all conceptions of fundamental rights as prepolitical rights conceive of fundamental rights as 'natural': some of these theories think of those rights as the product of historical processes that may precede the constitution of a society in a political community with specialized political institutions (a 'government'). On the other side, not all theories of fundamental rights as political rights are legal positivistic theories. The concept of fundamental rights as political rights should not be confused with the idea—distinctive to the more radical forms of legal positivism (s 2.1.2)—that the only fundamental rights that exist are those which are established as fundamental by political authorities and in positive legal systems. Consistent with the idea of fundamental rights as political rights is the idea that, whenever a government exists, persons subject to its authority have fundamental rights against it, no matter whether it recognizes those rights or not.[22]

4.3.2 While the concept of fundamental rights as prepolitical rights played a very important role in the history of fundamental rights (ch 1), and while a trace of that concept remains in the contemporary discourse on human rights (ss 3.1.1 and 3.2.1), the concept of fundamental rights as political rights seems to provide a better account of how fundamental rights are conceived today, and in particular of fundamental rights as a legal institution.[23] At present, fundamental rights are clearly considered as conditions of political legitimacy and as constraining the exercise of political authority and the use of public resources. All fundamental rights are considered as positive rights, correlative to governments' duties to exercise political authority and use public resources to guarantee certain individual or collective interests. This is true not only of economic and social rights, but also of civil and political rights: in order to guarantee those rights, governments should protect persons from a wide range of unjustifiable interferences, by private and public actors, and create the social and institutional condition for the exercise of the freedoms protected by those rights. The political nature of the contemporary understanding of fundamental rights becomes even more apparent if one considers some of the rights that are considered to be fundamental, which clearly presuppose the existence of political institutions: this is the case with the political rights to political participation, consultation, and representation, but also with those social rights that presuppose the existence of social institutions that can exist only within communities which are politically organized, such as the fundamental rights to free education, healthcare, and social security.

---

[22] Thus, for example, in debates on global justice, some theorists claim that it is the mere fact of being subject to the same political authority that generates obligations of justice between fellow citizens and entitles each citizen to some fundamental rights against government. In the absence of political institutions, it would not make sense to speak of justice and fundamental rights. See Michael Blake, 'Distributive Justice, State Coercion, and Autonomy' (2002) 30 *Philosophy & Public Affairs* 257; Thomas Nagel, 'The Problem of Global Justice' (2005) 33 *Philosophy & Public Affairs* 113. Cf Andrea Sangiovanni, 'Global Justice, Reciprocity, and the State' (2007) 35 *Philosophy & Public Affairs* 3.

[23] James Nickel, *Making Sense of Human Rights* (University of California Press 1987; 2nd edn, Blackwell 2007) argues this thesis with reference to global human rights.

4.3.3 The two concepts of fundamental rights I have distinguished have different implications when it comes to identifying who has *primary responsibility* for fundamental rights. According to the concept of fundamental rights as prepolitical rights, individual persons have primary responsibility for fundamental rights: even if the group of right-holders is not the same as the group of the duty-bearers (some persons, such as children, may be right-holders without being duty-bearers), persons are at the same time holders of fundamental rights and bearers of the duties correlative to those rights. From this perspective, fundamental rights are universal and, with a few possible exceptions (such as children's rights against their parents), general (s 4.2.3). According to the concept of fundamental rights as political rights, it is instead governments that have primary responsibility for fundamental rights. While holders of fundamental rights are persons, individually or collectively, governments are the primary bearers of the correlative duties. From this perspective, fundamental rights are universal but often special rights: rights against a specific government. Among fundamental rights, only global human rights are general in the sense that they are deemed to be rights against any government (ie against all the members of the class comprising governments).

The contrast between the implications of the two concepts of fundamental rights I have distinguished can in part be mitigated by arguing that even from the perspective of conceptions of fundamental rights as political rights it is possible to claim that persons, individually and/or collectively, have some responsibility for fundamental rights. That responsibility can be a *derivative responsibility* or a *secondary responsibility*. Derivative responsibility is the responsibility for respecting laws that governments enact in order to guarantee fundamental rights: laws imposing negative duties to abstain from harmful conduct, but also laws imposing positive duties to contribute to social cooperation schemes aimed at guaranteeing fundamental rights (this would be achieved, for example, by paying taxes). Secondary responsibility for fundamental rights is the responsibility persons have for monitoring what governments are doing to fulfil their primary responsibility to uphold fundamental rights; under this heading, persons would also be responsible for supporting good government and criticizing and opposing bad government. It may be supposed that persons' secondary responsibility for fundamental rights is stronger within a democratic community, where the people (citizens as a community) are recognized as sovereign and the government is regarded as their agent.

5
The reality of fundamental rights

5.1 CLASSES OF FUNDAMENTAL RIGHTS

Fundamental rights can be classified in different ways. Two common ways of classifying them are classifications based on their right-holders and classifications based on their content.

5.1.1 Most fundamental rights are rights that belong either to persons as *persons* or to persons as *citizens*. The concept of person has already been discussed (s 4.2.1). Here, it will suffice to remark that most of the fundamental rights that belong to persons as persons belong to natural persons. Few of them belong to juristic persons.[1]

As regards citizens, until recently the term 'citizen', understood as designating a legal status, was used to refer to natural persons considered to be full members of a sovereign political community (ss 2.2.1 and 2.3.3). This is still the prevalent use, even if, after the introduction of European citizenship, which supervenes on citizenship within each member state of the European Union (EU), it is no longer possible to identify citizenship exclusively with full membership in a sovereign political community. As the EU has created a new form of confederation of sovereign political entities, the introduction of European citizenship has transformed the institution of citizenship. What has not changed is the fact that all citizens are natural persons. Furthermore, according to Article 15 UDHR, every natural person has a fundamental right to citizenship (or 'nationality'), that is, to be recognized as a citizen by at least one state. The existence of stateless persons is a violation of such a fundamental right.

Different political communities use different criteria to identify their birthright citizens. There are two dominant models for ascribing birthright citizenship: in one model, political communities identify as their birthright citizens all natural persons who are descended from their citizens; in the other model, political communities also identify as citizens natural persons who are born in the territory over which—through the state—they exercise their sovereignty. The first model adopts the *jus sanguinis* criterion, while the second model combines that criterion with *jus soli*. No matter which model political communities adopt for ascribing birthright citizenship, almost all of them have rules that set forth procedures through which noncitizens satisfying certain conditions may be 'naturalized' as citizens.

---

[1]   The Charter of Fundamental Rights of the European Union (EU Charter) (Articles 42–4) explicitly confers fundamental rights on juristic persons.

While most fundamental rights belong either to persons qua persons or to persons qua citizens, this is not true for all fundamental rights.

Some fundamental rights belong to all permanent residents in a country's territory,[2] where permanent residency is becoming an increasingly important status as the number of persons permanently living in a country without being recognized as citizens of that country is growing as a consequence of migratory processes.

Some other fundamental rights belong to natural persons or to citizens as members of specific social groups, such as women; children; workers; members of cultural, religious, and linguistic minorities; and more.[3] Those social groups may intersect, giving rise to intersectional social statuses to which further fundamental rights may attach.[4] Some of the rights that belong to persons or citizens as members of specific groups are collective rights (s 4.2.1). That is the case, for example, with the fundamental rights of peoples;[5] of cultural, religious, or linguistic minorities; and of workers, employers, and consumers when considered as groups.[6] In some cases, these collective rights are protected through the fiction of the juristic person: organizations such as governments (in the case of peoples) or trade unions (in the case of workers) that claim to represent these collectives and are recognized in that role.

5.1.2 As regards the classification of fundamental rights based on their content, a common model sorts them into five classes: civil rights, political rights, economic rights, social rights, and cultural rights. This way of classifying fundamental rights is reflected, from their very names, in the two 1966 covenants on human rights, the ICCPR and the ICESCR (s 3.2.1). There are no uncontroversial conventional delimitations of these classes of rights. Furthermore, there could be some difficulties in classifying single rights within one of the five classes, because they may seem to slot easily into more than one class, suggesting that there may be some overlap between distinct classes. With these cautions in mind, I will provide a tentative definition of the different classes.

The first class of fundamental rights, that of *civil rights*, is the largest of them all. It includes rights protecting a plurality of interests that partly overlap but do not entirely reduce to one

---

[2]   See, eg, Articles 15(3) and 45(2) of the EU Charter, and, combining permanent residency and European citizenship, Articles 39(1) and 40.

[3]   Thus, for example, the EU Charter ascribes fundamental rights to women (Article 34(1)); children (Articles 24, 32); parents (Article 14(3)); the elderly (Articles 25, 34(1)); the disabled (Article 26); workers (Articles 27, 30–31, 32(2)); consumers (Article 38); members of cultural, religious, and linguistic minorities (Article 22); and asylum seekers and migrants (Articles 18–19).

[4]   That is the case, for example, with the rights recognized in Article 33(2) of the EU Charter, applying to persons that are at the same time parents, workers, and (for some rights) women.

[5]   See Article 1 in both the International Convenant on Civil and Political Rights (ICCPR) and the International Covenant on Economic, Social and Cultural Rights (ICESCR) or the 2007 United Nations Declaration of the Rights of Indigenous Peoples.

[6]   The EU Charter, for example, ascribes collective rights to cultural, religious, or linguistic communities (Article 22); workers (Articles 27–8); employers (Article 28); and consumers (Article 38).

another. Civil rights include, to begin with, the fundamental right to legal personality, that is, the right to be recognized as a person. This right is the most fundamental of all fundamental rights, because, as noted, all other individual fundamental rights are recognized for persons (qua persons or by virtue of some other quality). Thus, the fundamental right to legal personality is the true 'right to have rights', a phrase coined by Hannah Arendt (1906–1975) to refer not to the right to legal personality but to the right to citizenship (or nationality).[7] In the second place, civil rights include rights to life and integrity, and the fundamental rights against torture and other inhumane and degrading treatment. Third, civil rights include the fundamental rights to the basic freedoms of thought, conscience, religion, expression and information, scientific and academic research, assembly, association, movement, and residence, and the right to marry and to form a family. Fourth, civil rights include the fundamental rights to private property, protecting the freedoms to acquire private property and to use and dispose of one's private property, and to privacy. Fifth, civil rights include the fundamental rights to be free from slavery and forced labour and to enjoy the basic economic freedoms to work, to choose one's occupation, and to conduct a business. Sixth, civil rights include a series of fundamental rights that guarantee against abuses and misuses of coercive political authority: rights to personal liberty and security (including habeas corpus),[8] rights to a fair trial and to a proportionate punishment, the right not to be punished for acts that did not constitute criminal offences at the time they were committed (the principle of nonretroactivity), and the right to an effective remedy in cases involving violations of one's rights (ss 1.3.2 and 2.1.1). In this sixth group we should also include the fundamental right to 'equality before the law', excluding discrimination by government in the exercise of its functions. Seventh, and finally, civil rights include the fundamental rights to emigrate, to return to one's own country, to asylum, and to nonrefoulment.

According to the traditional understanding of the phrase 'civil rights', underpinning the distinction between civil and political rights and still prevalent in Europe, the adjective 'civil' refers to the sphere of 'civil society', where private persons go about their private affairs and pursue their personal self-realization through market interactions and other forms of private interaction. The private sphere of civil society, so understood, is distinct from the public sphere of politics, including government and the informal public forums where persons discuss political matters. From this perspective, civil rights guarantee the conditions for participating

---

[7]   See Hannah Arendt, *The Origins of Totalitarianism* (Schocken 1951; 3rd edn, Harcourt, Brace and World 1966).

[8]   Today the phrase 'habeas corpus' is sometimes used broadly to refer to all civil rights protecting personal integrity and liberty, especially in connection with one's rights to the exclusive control over one's own body. Properly understood, however, that phrase refers to a specific legal guarantee protecting persons from coercive political authority: under this principle, no one may be arbitrarily deprived of their personal liberty by a public officer—as through detention or imprisonment—and any limitation of such liberty needs to be validated by a court (s 1.1.1).

in civil society—they do so by securing, among other things, protection from arbitrary government interference—and they regulate market and private interactions within civil society.[9]

In the second class of fundamental rights—that of *political rights* in the strict sense (see ch 4, n 18)—we find, in the first place, the fundamental right to citizenship (or nationality), that is, the fundamental right to be recognized as a full member of a political community. Political rights also include the fundamental rights to political participation and consultation. They include rights enabling persons to take part, directly and indirectly, individually or collectively, in the exercise of political authority by participating in the process of electing persons who will exercise that authority, by competing for elective public offices, and by being heard by public officers. They may also include collective rights to political representation, which may justify the adoption of policies aimed at promoting the political representation of unrepresented or underrepresented social groups, and collective rights to full or partial self-government for collectives such as peoples, territorial communities, and cultural minorities. Finally, some overlap could be argued to exist between civil rights and political rights, insofar as certain civil rights protect specific forms of political participation and mobilization: consider freedom of expression, inclusive of freedom of political expression; freedom of assembly, inclusive of the freedom to organize a political event or rally; or freedom of association, inclusive of the freedom to form a political party.

The third and fourth classes—*economic* and *social rights*—are often bundled into a single class of fundamental rights under the label 'socioeconomic rights', or social rights for short. Still, in some key documents—like the 1966 ICESCR—the two classes are treated as if they were distinct classes, suggesting that there is indeed a worthwhile distinction to be made. Under one plausible criterion by which to do so, economic rights include the fundamental rights of workers and employers, while social rights form the more encompassing set of fundamental rights that guarantee access to the means by which to fulfil one's basic needs and a fair opportunity to participate in social life and compete for different social positions (ss 8.1 and 8.2). According to the distinction just suggested, economic rights would include such rights as trade union rights and the rights of employers' associations; the right to a safe workplace, inclusive of freedom from abuse; the right to a fair wage; the right to rest, implying paid holidays and limitations on daily and weekly working hours; the right to protection in the event of unjustified dismissal; and the right to maternity leave and other leaves allowing persons to take care of dependants. As regards social rights, they would include the rights to safe water and food, clothes, shelter, healthcare, and pension and social security, but also the rights to education, to fair competition in access to jobs and offices (including freedom from discrimination), and to the benefits needed to reconcile family life and social life.

---

[9]   In the United States, since the mid-twentieth century, the phrase 'civil rights' has commonly been used more broadly to also include political rights, and more generally all the fundamental rights of citizens (some of which may be recognized for noncitizens as well), which, under the US Constitution, do not include economic, social, and cultural rights. That phrase is used in that sense to refer to the civil rights movement that in the 1950s and 1960s advocated equal fundamental rights for black and white Americans and that led to the adoption of the Civil Rights Act of 1964.

Finally, the fifth class of fundamental rights—that of *cultural rights*—includes two kinds of rights. On one side are the fundamental rights to participate in the cultural life of one's own community and in the benefits deriving from cultural progress, including scientific progress.[10] On the other side, cultural rights include fundamental rights, either individual or collective, specifically aimed at protecting the interests of persons, and especially of members of cultural minorities, in being able to lead their lives in accordance with the traditional norms of their culture and in preserving that culture. These rights include parents' right to educate their children in accordance with their own cultural beliefs (s 9.1.3) and, when recognized as fundamental rights, the linguistic rights of linguistic minorities (s 9.3.1). They may also include collective rights to political participation, consultation, representation, and partial self-government for cultural communities, in which respect cultural rights overlap with political rights. This is how cultural rights are mainly understood in the debate around multiculturalism.[11]

5.2   THE IMPLEMENTATION OF FUNDAMENTAL RIGHTS

5.2.1   If fundamental rights are to be effectively guaranteed, it is not enough for governments to declare their commitment to guaranteeing them or to including them in some formal document, either in a declaration without binding legal force or in a legally binding convention or constitution: once so affirmed, fundamental rights need to be actually implemented.[12]

According to the political concept of fundamental rights, it is governments that have primary responsibility for fundamental rights (s 4.3.3). There is both a negative and a positive side to this responsibility: on the negative side, this means that governments may not exercise political authority or use public resources in ways that violate fundamental rights; on the positive side, it means that governments need to exercise political authority and put public resources to use in guaranteeing the fulfilment of the interests protected as fundamental rights. Notice that this dual responsibility applies to all the previously distinguished classes of fundamental rights—not only to those rights that are generally regarded as positive rights, that is, social rights. The guarantee of civil and political rights requires governments to enact proper legislation, such as legislation prohibiting murder and assault or legislation regulating elections, and to establish and maintain the institutions that are needed to enforce the law, to prosecute and punish its violation, and to enable persons to exercise their legal prerogatives: these are institutions like

---

[10]   This is how cultural rights are understood in the UDHR (Article 27(1)) and in the ICESCR (Article 15(1)).

[11]   See Charles Taylor, *Multiculturalism and 'The Politics of Recognition'* (Amy Gutmann ed, Princeton UP 1992; 2nd edn, under the title *Multiculturalism: Examining the Politics of Recognition*, Princeton UP 1994); Will Kymlicka, *Multicultural Citizenship: A Liberal Theory of Minority Rights* (OUP 1995); Will Kymlicka, *Multicultural Odysseys: Navigating the New International Politics of Diversity* (OUP 2007). For an overview of the debate see Sarah Song, 'Multiculturalism', *The Stanford Encyclopedia of Philosophy* (Fall edn 2020) <https://plato.stanford.edu/archives/fall2020/entries/multiculturalism/> accessed 14 July 2021.

[12]   On the implementation of fundamental rights see Véronique Champeil-Desplats, *Théorie générale des droits et libertés: Perspective analytique* (Dalloz 2019) ch 4.

the military, the police, the courts, prisons, a civil registry, and electoral offices. Although it is much less expensive to guarantee civil and political rights than it is to guarantee social rights— and we need only look at public budgets as evidence of that fact, particularly if we leave out military expenditures, whose share of the overall budget varies significantly from one country to another—it nonetheless takes a deployment of resources to maintain that guarantee: the idea of civil and political rights as negative rights is a blatant mistake.[13]

If governments have primary responsibility for fundamental rights, this does not mean that private (individual or collective) actors and private institutions have no role in fulfilling the interests covered by fundamental rights. Private actors are required to comply with the laws that governments enact to guarantee fundamental rights, but they may also contribute—and often do contribute—to this end through voluntary work, often through initiatives that are not directly aimed at guaranteeing fundamental rights but pursue other goals. Not only governments and public institutions but all members of a political community—with their beliefs, attitudes, and practices—and all of its institutions contribute to the degree to which fundamental rights are effectively guaranteed. And the role of private actors becomes especially relevant in contexts where there are no public actors with an effective capacity or willingness to guarantee fundamental rights: we can see this at the international level and in countries with authoritarian, corrupt, weak, or poorly run governments, where a significant role is played by NGOs in implementing fundamental rights, in particular those fundamental rights recognized as global human rights, even if the outcome is far from securing even minimal guarantees for these rights (ss 3.2.1 and 3.2.3).

Understanding how not only governments but also private actors may contribute to the effective guarantee of fundamental rights in a given context is important if we are to avoid a common misunderstanding regarding social rights. It is sometimes claimed that, in order to implement social rights, it is necessary that governments directly provide goods and services to the right-holders, either by delivering those goods and services themselves, or by paying for them. There is some truth to that claim, to be sure, but it needs to be qualified. It is true that, even under favourable economic conditions, some government intervention is needed to secure universal access to essential goods and services: in any real political community there will always be some persons who will not be able to access those goods and services by relying only on their private means. But that does not mean that if some good or service is needed to secure a fundamental right, all right-holders should be provided with it for free by government.

A fundamental right could be said to be effectively guaranteed if all the right-holders have effective opportunities to access to the goods and services needed to meet the interests covered by that right. Governments have a responsibility to guarantee that such a condition is realized, but they can contribute to the realization of that condition in many different ways. Which way should be chosen is a matter for political decision. In some cases—especially for some social rights, such as the rights to education and healthcare—it could be a good idea for governments to directly provide required goods and services to all the right-holders through a system of public schools and universities and a public healthcare system. This way of implementing

---

[13]   See Holmes Stephen and Cass R Sunstein, *The Cost of Rights: Why Liberty Depends on Taxes* (Norton 1999).

these rights may be judged preferable for many different reasons: it could be considered more efficient in reducing costs, and/or in enhancing the quality of the goods and services provided, and/or in promoting some other social goals. For example, it can be argued that public educational and healthcare systems reduce spending on education and healthcare because these systems will not be profit-driven—but this argument needs to be carefully evaluated in light of the available evidence about the inefficiencies which the public delivery of goods and services is liable to. It can also be argued that public systems enhance the quality of educational and healthcare services—especially for persons who will not be able to pay for the same quality in the private market—insofar as all persons or citizens, and not just the poor, could be recipients of those services and could therefore have an interest in their quality. Finally, it can be argued that public systems reduce social segregation and promote social integration between members of different social classes and groups. These arguments, if sound, would be grounds for preferring a specific solution to the problem of implementing the fundamental rights to education and healthcare, but we should not assume that this is the only possible solution or that all other solutions are going to be worse. Furthermore, a solution that works well for some rights could turn out to be less effective for others. Thus, for example, where universal educational and healthcare systems have been put in place to implement the fundamental rights to education and healthcare, it is not a foregone conclusion that the same solution will work as effectively in implementing other social rights, such as the right to the means of subsistence (safe water and food, clothes, shelter, and the like). Here, it may prove more efficient to rely on a mixed solution: a regulated market coupled with public policies designed to help the needy.

5.2.2 All governmental bodies—legislative, executive, and judicial—participate in different ways in the process of implementing fundamental rights.

Legislative bodies enact laws that, by imposing duties and conferring powers, regulate private conduct in order to prevent fundamental rights violations from taking place or to reduce their incidence, or to facilitate voluntary forms of social cooperation that could contribute to guaranteeing fundamental rights, or to establish how private persons should contribute to schemes of public cooperation aimed at guaranteeing fundamental rights, either indirectly, for example, by paying taxes to fund public expenditures, or directly, for example, by serving in the military or as members of juries. But regulating private conduct, imposing negative and positive duties, and ascribing powers to private persons does not exhaust what legislative bodies can do to implement fundamental rights. Through legislation, these bodies can establish public institutions, including executive bodies, charged with implementing fundamental rights.

Executive bodies, including the administrative apparatus and public institutions such as the educational system, the healthcare system, and law enforcement agencies, contribute to the implementation of fundamental rights by exercising their legal powers to issue regulations and by using the resources allocated to them to provide services and goods to the population (all within the constraints established by the law).

Finally, judicial bodies favour the nonviolent resolution of conflicts involving private and public actors; prosecute violations of law, including laws guaranteeing fundamental rights; and make sure that the victims of those violations will be made whole and the authors of those violations punished. They also contribute to the implementation of fundamental rights by interpreting legal texts in which these rights are recognized. Finally, and most importantly, judicial bodies such as constitutional courts and international courts of fundamental rights may have the power to scrutinize the acts of legislative and executive bodies so as to determine whether they are consistent with fundamental rights recognized as constitutional rights or as international fundamental rights, and if such acts are in fact found to be in violation of these rights, the same courts may declare them to be invalid or may impose sanctions on the governments responsible for such violations.

In implementing fundamental rights, governmental bodies invested with regulatory powers will exercise these powers in ways that will result in the enactment of laws. Thus, for example, in order to protect the fundamental right to life, governments will enact, or more likely maintain, laws prohibiting murder; they could enact laws establishing an obligation to rescue persons whose life is at risk; they will enact laws prohibiting or regulating behaviour that may result in accidental or voluntary killing, such as the buying and selling of toxic food and drugs, weapons and other dangerous artefacts, or the use of cars and motorcycles; and they will establish law enforcement agencies and courts tasked with preventing or prosecuting and punishing violations of such laws; and the list goes on. All the laws enacted to secure the fundamental right to life can be considered as the *legal guarantees* of that right. Following a suggestion by the Italian legal theorist Luigi Ferrajoli, we can distinguish two such kinds of guarantees: *primary* and *secondary*.[14] Primary guarantees of a fundamental right are those provisions that, if complied with, will prevent violations of that right or result in its fulfilment. For example, the laws against murder and those imposing a duty to rescue persons whose life is at risk are primary guarantees of the right to life. Secondary guarantees instead consist of laws under which violations of primary guarantees can be prosecuted and punished, so as to ensure that victims can effectively exercise their right to obtain justice and compensation.

5.2.3 The implementation of a fundamental right will thus result in the creation of a whole slate of legal norms—primary and secondary guarantees of those rights—that will equip the right-holders of fundamental rights with a larger set of prerogatives—further and more specific rights, liberties, powers, immunities, and liabilities—that will serve their fundamental rights. The relation between fundamental rights and the prerogatives that are ascribed to right-holders in order to guarantee those rights is a justificatory relation: fundamental rights provide a justification for the creation of their guarantees.

The moment has now come to consider a third concept of fundamental rights, different from the two concepts—the prepolitical and the political—discussed in the previous chapter (s 4.3.1). This third concept identifies a fundamental right with all the prerogatives that protect a given interest. It describes fundamental rights as *cluster-rights* (or 'molecular' rights), that is,

---

[14]   See Luigi Ferrajoli, *Principi iuris: Teoria del diritto e della democrazia* (Laterza 2007) vol 1 (*Teoria del diritto*) 668–84.

as complex sets of prerogatives: liberties, rights, powers, immunities, and liabilities (s 4.1.1).[15] This concept identifies fundamental rights with their guarantees, with the conclusion that if a fundamental right has no guarantees—if its cluster is void because governments responsible for its implementation have not yet created those guarantees—it is not simply a fundamental right which is not guaranteed as it should be but it is not a proper fundamental right.

In order to clarify this concept of fundamental rights, consider on the one side the fundamental right to private property and on the other side the institution of private property created by the laws that establish how private property of something can be acquired and lost, and which prerogatives—liberties, rights, powers, and so on—the legitimate owner of something has, as the legitimate owner of that thing. The cluster-concept of fundamental rights tends to identify the fundamental right to private property with the set of prerogatives that legitimate owners have over their property: this set will include prerogatives to use and dispose of their property, but also prerogatives preventing others from using or disposing of it without the owners' consent or even requiring others to help the owners in preventing or redressing violations of the prerogatives they have as the legitimate owners of such property.

A person concerned about the effectivity of fundamental rights may support the cluster-concept of fundamental rights and denounce rights as void or fake when they are affirmed but not properly guaranteed. Nonetheless, this concept obscures the normative dimension of fundamental rights and the justificatory relation connecting those rights and their guarantees. Ascribing to all persons a fundamental right to private property means recognizing that the interest in acquiring and using and disposing of some private property is a relevant interest deserving to be protected through the adoption of proper guarantees. This right, once recognized, may be used to criticize how governments exercise their political authority and use public resources, on the ground that they have not implemented this right through the adoption of effective guarantees. It could be argued that the worry over the effectivity of fundamental rights is better served by a concept of fundamental rights that provides a normative basis on which to criticize governments' failures to guarantee these rights.[16]

5.2.4 Among the different legal techniques that have been developed to guarantee fundamental rights, one of the most important is the constitutionalizing of fundamental rights, that is, the translation of those rights into constitutional rights through the enactment of a written constitution that includes a catalogue of rights to be protected (s 3.1.2). The constitutionalizing of fundamental rights can be considered a first step—even if not a necessary one—in the process of implementing fundamental rights and—necessary to that end—in the process of specifying them. Thus, alongside very abstract provisions referring to particular fundamental

---

[15] See Carl Wellman, *A Theory of Rights: Persons under Laws, Institutions, and Morals* (Rowman and Allanheld 1985); Judith J Thomson, *The Realm of Rights* (Harvard UP 1990); Carl Wellman, *Real Rights* (OUP 1995). Cf Giorgio Pino, *Il costituzionalismo dei diritti: Struttura e limiti del costituzionalismo contemporaneo* (Il Mulino 2017) ch 2.

[16] Luigi Ferrajoli, *La democrazia attraverso i diritti: Il costituzionalismo garantista come modello teorico e come progetto politico* (Laterza 2013) and Luigi Ferrajoli, *La costruzione della democrazia: Teoria del garantismo costituzionale* (Laterza 2021).

rights and even more abstract provisions referring to the fundamental rights included in other legal sources—for example, international declarations and conventions—constitutional texts also typically include more specific provisions that provide some specification about how given rights are to be further implemented. Consider, for example, the fundamental right to political participation. Constitutional provisions may contribute to the specification of that fundamental right, by establishing, among other things, how frequently adult citizens should be given the opportunity to exercise their voting rights. So, while constitutional rights are close to the idea of fundamental rights (more so than any other rights apart from global human rights), they need to be distinguished from the latter as a first step in their implementation.

Contemporary constitutional systems with written constitutions consider the constitution as the supreme legal source. By conferring constitutional rights, the constitution sets some limits and goals for the exercise of other governmental powers. Constitutional norms and rights are conditions for the legitimacy of other legal norms and rights. In this way the political concept of fundamental rights as rights constraining the exercise of political authority and the use of public resources is institutionalized by constitutionalizing these rights.

As a way to secure the effectivity of constitutional norms and rights as constraints on the exercise of political authority and on the use of public resources, some constitutional legal systems establish a procedure for the constitutional review of some acts of legislative and executive bodies: the power of constitutional review is commonly conferred on all judicial bodies or on special judicial bodies (constitutional courts), and less frequently on a nonjudicial body such as a constitutional council. In the first case constitutional review takes the form of judicial review. Judicial review offers the strongest guarantee for constitutional rights. From a strictly legal perspective, in legal systems that include judicial review, constitutional rights—and, through those rights, fundamental rights—may act as a condition for the validity or the legal efficacy of laws: laws that cannot pass judicial review may be declared invalid or unenforceable. More relevant for the implementation of fundamental rights is that judicial review enables courts to consider how political authority is exercised, precisely by subjecting legislation and other forms of regulation to constitutional scrutiny. To a certain extent, judicial review also enables courts to indirectly control how public resources are used. While they cannot establish how these resources are to be used, they may have the power to decide how the same resources may not be used. They can do so by declaring some forms of public expenditure to be unconstitutional—think of constitutional controversies over public funding of private schools or religious organizations—and by scrutinizing the rules that establish who can access the benefits and services funded with those resources. In exercising judicial review, courts pass judgment on the decisions that legislative and executive bodies make in the process of implementing constitutional rights, including decisions involving the resolution of conflicts between constitutional rights and other interests (s 5.3), and if these decisions are found to be unconstitutional, they will be struck down by the reviewing courts.

The institution of judicial review, which is not present in all constitutional systems, takes different forms in different countries. Insofar as it confers on a select number of judges the power to pass judgment on the conduct of democratically legitimate legislative and executive bodies, and in some cases the power to nullify their decisions, some concerns have been raised about whether this institution is compatible with the ideal of democracy. These concerns, having a normative character, will be addressed in the next chapter (s 6.2.2).

5.3 CONFLICTS INVOLVING FUNDAMENTAL RIGHTS

5.3.1 The history of fundamental rights has been marked by a tendency to expand the number of fundamental rights to cover an increasing number of human interests, and potentially also some nonhuman interests (s 3.3.2). As a consequence of this multiplication of fundamental rights, the opportunities for conflicts between fundamental rights and between fundamental rights and other interests also multiply.

Conflicts involving fundamental rights are of different types. Sometimes, they depend on the fact that, as a matter of logical impossibility, the interests they protect—at least according to some plausible interpretation of them—cannot all be fully realized at the same time. An example of this type of conflict is that between the right to freedom of expression and the right to privacy, insofar as in order to protect persons' right to privacy it is necessary to restrict their right to freedom of expression. Another example is the conflict between persons' right to life and their right to refuse life-preserving treatments, insofar as refusal of such treatments may lead to death. Other times, conflicts of fundamental rights depend on external circumstances, the more common of which is the scarcity of the resources that can be devoted to guaranteeing fundamental rights. Thus, for example, one person's right to healthcare can conflict with that of another person, insofar as there is only a limited supply of medical resources (there may not be enough drugs or organs for transplant, for example) or a limited supply of economic resources that can be devoted to healthcare: as a result, not everyone in need of healthcare may be able to receive it. Similarly, persons' right to healthcare may conflict with their or other persons' right to personal security or education, and here, too, it is the scarcity of public resources that is to blame: the resources put into hiring more physicians and nurses may well be resources that cannot be used to hire more police officers or teachers. There is, therefore, a trade-off. As these examples make clear, conflicts of fundamental rights may arise between the rights of different persons (it could be the same rights or different rights) or between different rights of the same persons.

Fundamental rights do not conflict only among themselves. Sometimes they conflict with other interests, typically collective interests that are not the direct object of some fundamental right but are nonetheless normatively relevant and deserve some consideration. It is sometimes claimed that, however relevant those interests may be, when they conflict with fundamental rights, the latter should prevail.[17] But the idea that fundamental rights always prevail over collective interests overstates the force of rights. What is true is that fundamental rights are regarded as protecting individual or collective interests so significant that they should generally prevail over other interests—individual and especially collective ones—and justify

---

[17]   This claim is often attributed to Ronald Dworkin (1931–2013) and is said to correspond to his thesis of (fundamental) rights as 'trumps' that always prevail over the pursuit of collective goals. See Ronald Dworkin, 'Taking Rights Seriously' (first published 1968) in *Taking Rights Seriously* (Harvard UP 1977; 2nd edn, Harvard UP 1978) 184–205.

sacrificing those interests to some extent. That said, it is conceded—and often established by the same documents in which fundamental rights are contained—that fundamental rights may sometimes be restricted in order to protect some especially significant collective interests, such as an interest in national security, public safety, law and order, public health, and even public morals, at least insofar as protecting these interests is a precondition for protecting fundamental rights themselves.

5.3.2 Some theorists of fundamental rights claim that, in order to reduce conflicts of fundamental rights, we should reduce the number of rights that are considered to be fundamental. This position is known as 'minimalism about fundamental rights'. Some minimalists are *normative* minimalists: they claim that many conflicts between fundamental rights depend on a mistaken identification of fundamental rights.[18] According to them, many rights that are mistakenly considered to be fundamental—in particular economic and social rights—are not fundamental or are not even rights at all: once those rights are excluded from the set of fundamental rights, we would see that the occasions for conflict between fundamental rights proper—typically identified with civil and political rights—will be significantly reduced. Other minimalists are *pragmatic* minimalists: they claim that, while many different interests would deserve the status of fundamental rights, given the scarcity of the resources that can be devoted to guaranteeing fundamental rights, it is better to limit the number of fundamental rights so as to be able to guarantee those rights appropriately. In order to select the interests that should be protected and those that should be sacrificed, pragmatic minimalists often rely on normative considerations not dissimilar from those that normative minimalists use to identify fundamental rights proper.

Critics of normative minimalism may point out that, in fact, all fundamental rights protect interests that are normatively relevant. Pragmatic minimalism is a more challenging position. Sometimes, critics of pragmatic minimalism object to its underlying view of the implementation of fundamental rights as a 'zero-sum game', where the resources devoted to guaranteeing one right are taken away from those needed to guarantee another right, such that the greater the number of rights that are considered to be fundamental, the smaller the amount of resources that can be devoted to each of those rights. Critics of pragmatic minimalism claim that this is a false assumption. For one thing, they argue, the resources devoted to guaranteeing one fundamental right sometimes actually *increase* the resources that could be devoted to other fundamental rights: thus, for example, if resources are invested to guarantee the rights to education and healthcare—figuring among the most expensive rights—we will have a more educated and healthier population, which in turn increases productivity and thus the amount of available resources. And, for another thing, investing resources to guarantee one fundamental right can reduce the need to invest resources to guarantee other fundamental rights:

---

[18]   See Maurice Cranston, *Human Rights Today* (Ampersand 1962; 2nd edn, under the title *What Are Human Rights?*, Bodley Head 1973); Robert Nozick, *Anarchy, State, and Utopia* (Basic Books 1974); FA Hayek, *Law, Legislation, and Liberty: A New Statement of the Liberal Principles of Justice and Political Economy* (Routledge and Kegan Paul 1976) vol 2 (*The Mirage of Social Justice*) 101–6; Hiller Steiner, *An Essay on Rights* (Blackwell 1994).

thus, for example, if more resources are put into social security for the poor, we will have less poverty-driven micro-criminality and therefore less need to commit resources to protecting personal integrity and property. There is something sound about both of these objections to the idea that implementing fundamental rights involves a zero-sum game. At the same time, we should be careful not to overestimate the degree to which investment in a particular fundamental right could help the implementation of other fundamental rights, whether by increasing available resources or by reducing the need for them. It is far from clear—and in the case of healthcare investment quite unlikely—that the greater productivity achieved by investing in education or healthcare would offset the costs of those investments. And it is even less likely that the costs needed to provide for social security for all will be lower than the costs needed to enhance the protection of personal integrity and property. By accepting to confront pragmatic minimalism on its own ground, its critics are accepting a quite risky game. A more promising strategy against pragmatic minimalism consists in conceding that the greater the number of fundamental rights, the greater the cost of guaranteeing those rights—even if not pound for pound, considering the virtuous circles that may be triggered by the implementation of fundamental rights—while at the same time arguing that those increased costs are nonetheless worth sustaining as far as is practicable: such is the normative force of the interests that fundamental rights guarantee. The economic costs, in other words, are outweighed by the normative gains. To this it may be added that, while it is not possible to fully resource all fundamental rights, it is preferable to slightly roll back the protection accorded to each of these rights than to entirely sacrifice some of them, considering as well that different rights benefit different persons in different ways: it is unlikely, for example, that those who stand to benefit the most from enhanced protection of personal integrity and property are the same persons as those who would stand to lose the most from cuts to social security, public education, and public healthcare.

5.3.3 If we accept that the interests deserving to be protected as fundamental rights are many, that there is no necessary harmony between them, and that, in any case, the resources that can be devoted to their guarantee are limited, we should recognize that conflicts between fundamental rights and between these rights and other relevant interests are unavoidable. It is sometimes suggested that the task of resolving these conflicts should fall to the courts, and in particular to constitutional courts (when they exist), but that is not correct: courts share that responsibility with the legislator and the executive, who have primary responsibility for implementing fundamental rights. It is primarily up to the legislator and the executive to deal with these kinds of conflicts, by deciding how to regulate conduct, such as freedom of expression, or how to invest public resources, for example, how many resources to devote to public order and safety, national security, education, or healthcare. Courts are more frequently called upon to review these decisions and determine whether, in dealing with conflicts between fundamental rights and between fundamental rights and other relevant interests, all the relevant rights and interests were duly taken into account by the legislator and the executive and whether a reasonable balance was struck between them. Only in exceptional cases do courts contribute to filling legal voids: in the most common cases, they do so indirectly, by recommending that the legislator and the executive exercise their powers to fill those voids. When courts, typically constitutional courts, have the power to nullify the decisions of the legislator or the executive, or have these decisions revised, and neither the legislator nor the executive has the power to reject the courts' decisions, the courts can be said to have the 'last word' on the resolution of conflicts between fundamental rights and between fundamental rights and other interests, but the last word is not the first word.

5.3.4 Different techniques are commonly used, more or less explicitly, to resolve conflicts involving fundamental rights at the different levels where these conflicts arise.

A first technique consists in building a hierarchy between different fundamental rights, and between fundamental rights and other relevant interests, by establishing that some rights or interests are more important than others, such that, in the event of conflicts between them, those that are hierarchically superior should prevail.[19] Thus, for example, it is sometimes suggested that civil and political rights are more important than economic, social, and cultural rights. Notice that if there are absolute rights—meaning rights that can never be sacrificed to some other good—these rights should be hierarchically superior to all other rights and interests, and if several such rights are at stake, they should never conflict with one another, unless we are ready to admit that some conflicts of rights are tragic and can be resolved only by way of completely arbitrary decisions.

While the idea of a hierarchy of fundamental rights can help us make some sense of the controversial idea of absolute rights, hierarchization appears to be of limited utility in resolving conflicts involving fundamental rights. It would be useful only if it were possible to rank fundamental rights and the associated interests under a complete hierarchy, but that seems to be difficult. It is a common view that fundamental rights and their associated interests are not such that, whenever a conflict arises between two of them, the same right or interest should always prevail. Thus, for example, when dealing with conflicts involving the right to privacy and the right to freedom of expression and the right to information, it is only sometimes established that the right to privacy should prevail: other times, the reasoning is that it could be sacrificed.

A second technique for resolving conflicts involving fundamental rights consists in specifying those rights and, in that way, restricting their range of application.[20] A fundamental right can be specified by establishing that it applies only to some particular cases or by establishing that it does not apply to others. A fundamental right can be so specified either after a conflict arises involving that right—making it necessary to resolve that conflict—or before such an occurrence, so as to forestall it, as when drafting the legal provisions by which to guarantee the same right. For example, it may be established that the fundamental right to freedom of expression only applies to private communications, or to oral communications, or to politically significant communications—which would require the interpreter to decide what counts

---

[19]   In a different context, this is the technique that John Rawls employs to avoid conflicts between different principles of justice and the fundamental rights dependent on those principles. See John Rawls, *A Theory of Justice* (Harvard UP 1971; rev edn, Harvard UP 1999).

[20]   For a defence of specification see José Juan Moreso, 'Ways of Solving Conflicts of Fundamental Rights: Proportionalism and Specificationism' (2012) 25 *Ratio Juris* 31.

as 'private', 'oral', or 'politically significant'—or it could be established that the right in question does not apply to libel, false advertising, blasphemy, hate speech, and so on.

However useful the specification of fundamental rights may be in preventing conflicts, this is not always possible. Not all conflicts involving fundamental rights can be anticipated. But even if some potential conflicts could be anticipated, an attempt to specify such rights *ex ante*—while drafting a charter of fundamental rights—would make the drafting much more difficult, because the different actors involved in the process may disagree about the proper way to specify a given fundamental right. Given how much is at stake when fundamental rights are at issue, the disagreements may be very strong. That explains why the provisions included in charters of fundamental rights are typically quite vague: the vague language is what made it possible to reach an agreement on those provisions. This is why the matter of how fundamental rights are to be specified is postponed to the later stage of their political and judicial implementation.

A third technique for resolving conflicts involving fundamental rights is that of balancing fundamental rights against one another (along with the interests they protect) and against general interests so as to decide, for each hypothetical or real case of conflict, which one should prevail.[21] In order to solve a conflict involving fundamental rights by balancing, the costs and possible benefits of sacrificing each of the interests at stake are weighed so as to determine which interest should be sacrificed in order to minimize the overall costs. In that process, it should also be considered how the costs entailed by different solutions to the conflict would be distributed among the different persons involved: sometimes a solution under which costs are shared by different persons may be preferable to one under which all the costs fall on a single person. Balancing may lead to identifying the central or 'core' dimension of a fundamental right, consisting of some subset of the interests protected by that right which deserve special regard and are more resistant to balancing, such that when a conflict involves the core dimension of one fundamental right and a peripheral dimension of another, the first right should prevail.

Balancing is the more useful and frequently used technique for resolving conflicts involving fundamental rights. What differentiates balancing fundamental rights and interests from building a hierarchy of them is that, in different cases of conflict involving the same rights or interests, balancing may result in according priority to one right or interest on one occasion and to another on another occasion: there is no reason to think that the same right or interest should always prevail. Finally, the difference between balancing and specifying fundamental rights comes down to the fact that sometimes, in addressing a conflict, it becomes apparent that some of the interests that may be covered by a fundamental right do not deserve to be protected as fundamental rights: in such cases, it becomes possible to *specify* the right, as opposed to balancing it against the other interests in question. But most often, when a conflict

---

[21] See Robert Alexy, *Theorie der Grundrechte* (Nomos 1985; 2nd edn, Suhrkamp 1994) [English edn, *A Theory of Constitutional Rights* (Julian Rivers tr, OUP 2002)]; Giorgio Pino, *Diritti e interpretazione: Il ragionamento giuridico nello Stato costituzionale* (Il Mulino 2010); Aharon Barak, *Proportionality: Constitutional Rights and Their Limitations* (CUP 2012).

arises between fundamental rights, the interests covered by the conflicting rights all deserve to be protected as fundamental rights, even if these are cases in which some of these interests need to be sacrificed.

6
The justification of fundamental rights

6.1 THE PROBLEM OF THE JUSTIFICATION OF FUNDAMENTAL RIGHTS

6.1.1 Fundamental rights set limits and goals around the exercise of political authority and the use of public resources. In justifying fundamental rights, we therefore need to first justify the idea that some individual or collective interests can only be protected if the exercise of political authority and the use of public resources are limited. But justifying the idea of fundamental rights as a general proposition would be pointless without also specifying which interests are worthy of protection as fundamental rights: once that general idea of fundamental rights is justified, we will have to justify the choice made in selecting some interests as deserving of protection as fundamental rights. The problem of justifying the general idea of fundamental rights can thus be distinguished from the problem of justifying specific fundamental rights. But before we turn to that topic, there is a more basic problem that needs to be addressed in this section: the problem of the kind of validity the justifications offered for fundamental rights partake of. Can claims about fundamental rights in general or about specific fundamental rights be true or false like our claims about states of affairs? Are there objectively valid solutions to such questions as 'Are there fundamental rights?' or 'Which interests are worthy of protection as fundamental rights?' Many persons expend a great deal of effort in reasoning about and discussing these questions. What is the point of such an effort? Would these discussions be pointless if they could not lead to objectively valid conclusions?

6.1.2 According to some fundamental rights theorists, claims about fundamental rights can be true or false, and what makes these claims true or false is institutional facts such as the fact that a declaration of fundamental rights has been signed, or the fact that a list of fundamental rights has been included in a constitution, or the fact that a specific right is included in such a list, or the fact that a court has recognized a specific fundamental right as part of a given legal system. It has been suggested, from this perspective, that the adoption by the United Nations (UN) of the UDHR in 1948 solved once and for all the problem of providing a justification for global fundamental rights: since its adoption, global fundamental rights can be said to have existed as part of a political consensus between governments and organizations that are members of the UN.[1] That claim about the existence of global fundamental rights is true in virtue of institutional facts and historical events: the decision the UN General Assembly made in 1948 to adopt the declaration and the decisions of individual governments and organizations to join the UN. Similar claims can be made with reference to other official documents establishing fundamental rights that have been adopted at national or international levels.

While justifications of fundamental rights based on historically contingent decisions by governments and other organizations may validate some of our assertions about the existence of fundamental rights, they fall short in other respects. On this approach to justification, fundamental rights can be said to exist only if they are set forth in an official document or statement, and only from the time they are set forth in the same document or statement. Furthermore, their validity would be entirely dependent on the validity of that document or statement and internal to the legal system for which that document or statement is considered to be a valid source of law. As a consequence, these justifications are unable to account for the fact that before fundamental rights were laid down in official documents or statements, there were persons who believed in the existence of those rights and in their validity, using them as normative standards by which to criticize governments and advocating their official 'recognition'. The very idea of recognizing rights suggests that they already existed before they were recognized. Justifications based on historically contingent decisions by governments and other organizations would also be unable to account for the fact that ideas about fundamental rights are used as critical tools for evaluating official documents and statements affirming fundamental rights, and for evaluating whether all the rights so affirmed deserve to be considered fundamental and whether there are other rights that ought to be considered fundamental but are not.

All these kinds of external criticism would not make sense if the only justification we had for our belief in the existence and validity of fundamental rights was grounded in the fact that these rights are established in some official document or statement. When we look for a justification of fundamental rights, we are not looking for the official documents or statements that introduced those rights as part of a legal system; rather, we are looking for the reasons that may justify adopting those documents or statements in the first place.

6.1.3 Many fundamental rights theorists believe that there are objectively valid reasons for claiming that some interests must be protected as fundamental rights that do not depend on institutional decisions by governments or other organizations. Let us call these theorists 'objectivists', insofar as they believe in the possibility of an objective justification of fundamental rights, where 'objective' may mean that the justification is either independent of human beliefs and actions or that it should be recognized by all (rational) persons, or both.[2] The most

---

[1] See Norberto Bobbio, 'Sul fondamento dei diritti dell'uomo' in *L'età dei diritti* (Einaudi 1990) 5–16 [English edn, 'On the Fundamental Principles of Human Rights' in *The Age of Rights* (Allan Cameron tr, Polity 1996) 3–11].

[2] For a discussion of objectivist approaches to the justification of fundamental rights see Véronique Champeil-Desplats, *Théorie Générale des droit et libertés: Perspective analytique* (Dalloz 2019) 86–130.

common attempts to defend beliefs in the objective justification of fundamental rights invoke divinity, reason, or nature.[3]

Religious attempts to provide an objective justification of fundamental rights identify the source of these rights in some divine will or prescription, which can be known by human beings either by revelation or by the proper exercise of reason, either divinely inspired or not. This kind of justification for fundamental rights, linking beliefs about these rights to religious beliefs, will not be persuasive to persons who do not share the same religious beliefs, all the more so that some persons do not hold any religious beliefs at all. That makes this kind of justification almost useless within contemporary society, and generally outside the limited boundaries of homogeneous religious communities.

The main alternative to religious attempts to justify the objective validity of fundamental rights lies in the attempt to ground that validity in human reason. The claim here is that if human reason is properly exercised—either individually or collectively (ie through rational discussion)—it may lead human beings to recognize the objective validity of fundamental rights.[4] Different theorists have different ideas about how human reason should be properly exercised, and they disagree about the kinds of truths that human reason properly exercised would lead us to discover: some hold that these truths about fundamental human rights are independent of human reason; others hold that, while these truths are not independent of human reason, they should nonetheless be recognized by all (rational) persons.

Attempts to justify the objective validity of fundamental rights by invoking nature are not real alternatives to attempts that refer to divinity or to reason. Here we cannot discuss the ambiguity of the concept of 'nature',[5] but it should be clear to anyone with a basic under-standing of modern science that nature as the object of the natural sciences cannot provide a justification for fundamental rights. According to modern science, nature is ethically neutral: it cannot be said to be good or right. As a consequence, it is not possible to derive normative standards of goodness and rightness from mere natural facts. When we qualify natural facts or events as good or right, we are presupposing some normative standard which is independent of nature, as when we are evaluating those facts or events in light of their impact on human interests, presupposing a normative standard that identifies those interests as relevant. The idea of nature employed by natural law theories of fundamental (or natural) rights has nothing to do with the idea of nature at work in the natural sciences. The former refers either to some normative standards which are not created by human beings, and may be supposed to have

---

3   See Alan Dershowitz, *Rights from Wrongs: A Secular Theory of the Origins of Rights* (Basic Books 2004) pt 1.

4   See Alan Gewirth, *Reason and Morality* (University of Chicago Press 1978); Alan Gewirth, *The Community of Rights* (University of Chicago Press 1996); Jürgen Habermas, *Faktizität und Geltung: Beiträge zur Diskurstheorie des Rechts und des demokratischen Rechtsstaats* (Suhrkamp 1992; rev edn, Suhrkamp 1994) [English edn, *Between Facts and Norms: Contributions to a Discourse Theory of Law and Democracy* (William Rehg tr, Polity 1996)] ch 3.

5   See John Stuart Mill, 'Nature' (first published 1874, under the title 'On Nature') in *The Collected Works of John Stuart Mill* (John M Robson ed, Routledge and Kegan Paul 1969) vol 10 (*Essays on Ethics, Religion and Society*) 373–401.

been divinely created, or to some set of universally valid prescriptions of human reason, in turn identified with the distinctive nature of human beings.[6]

6.1.4 Other fundamental rights theorists firmly assert the impossibility of an objective justification of fundamental rights. They argue that objectivity pertains only to facts and that only proper factual claims—that is, propositions describing facts—can be true or false. In their view, normative claims—for example, claims about the justice or injustice of some behaviour, practice, or institution—cannot be objectively true or otherwise objectively valid. There is no normative reality independent of human actions and beliefs and there is no common human reason that, if properly exercised, will lead everyone to the same normative conclusions. Normative propositions—including propositions prescribing respect for funda-mental rights—can derive their validity either from human beliefs and preferences, which are ultimately irrational insofar as they cannot be objectively justified, or from human decisions reflecting those beliefs and preferences. In both cases, their validity will not be objective: it could be either subjective, when reflecting the perspective of an individual, or intersubjective, when reflecting the perspective of a collective. Accordingly, we might call these theorists 'subjectivists'.

According to subjectivists, when we claim that governments should respect fundamental rights, either of two things are the case: we are either referring to some human decision man-dating that governments must respect fundamental rights—as when the decision was made in 1948 to adopt the UDHR—or we are expressing a belief in the greater worth of governments that respect fundamental rights or a preference for a world in which such governments are the norm. In the latter case we can back up our claim with reasons, to be sure, but eventually in this process we will land on some basic belief or preference that is not amenable to rational justification. The idea is that only with persons who share our more basic beliefs or preferences can we argue rationally and hope to reach a rational agreement. But when our basic beliefs and preferences differ, all we can do is resign ourselves to the fact that our disagreement is fundamental and that we will not get our interlocutors to reconsider their own position by way of rational argumentation.[7]

It is sometimes argued that if we do not believe in the possibility of an objective justification for fundamental rights, we cannot defend the universalism of global human rights, that is, the idea that these rights apply to all governments and to all human beings. According to this argument, subjectivists could not answer challenges to universalism based on cultural diversity (s 3.2.3), since the idea of human rights applies only to those cultural communities whose basic beliefs and preferences can provide an internal justification for that idea, and since each of those communities may have its own list of human rights, including only those rights that may be justified on the basis of its own basic beliefs and preferences. Subjectivism, it is claimed,

---

[6]   Cf John Finnis, *Natural Law and Natural Rights* (OUP 1980; 2nd edn, OUP 2011).

[7]   Cf Richard Rorty, 'Human Rights, Rationality, and Sentimentality' in *On Human Rights* (Stephen Shute and Susan Hurley eds, Basic Books 1993) 111–34.

would imply a form of 'normative cultural relativism'. According to many fundamental rights theorists this is a reason to reject subjectivism.

There is no reason, however, to think that all subjectivists should accept that form of normative cultural relativism. If subjectivists are confronting a foreign cultural community that according to their subjective normative standards are oppressing some of their members—a predicament in which they feel compelled to take sides, having to decide to stand with either the oppressive community or its oppressed members—why should they make that decision without referring to their own standards, adopting instead the normative standards that are prevalent within the oppressive community? If persons committed to normative standards of gender equality are confronted with the practices of a traditional patriarchal community, why should they judge that community according to standards internal to that community—that is, prevalent among its members—rather than rely on their own standards of gender equality and side with the victims of gender-based oppression and persons that, within that community, are fighting for gender equality against their own cultural tradition?

If subjectivists support fundamental rights because they believe that universal respect for fundamental rights would maximize persons' chances of living long and happy lives and because they think they have reasons to support whatever would maximize such chances for all persons (not just for those who share their basic beliefs and preferences), they would have valid reasons to support whatever would promote universal respect for fundamental rights. Of course, they may be wrong to assume that universal respect for a specific list of fundamental rights would maximize persons' chances of living long and happy lives, because that specific list could be culturally skewed. And it may be argued that they should pay attention to cultural diversity—and possibly engage with persons from different cultures—before deciding that their favoured list of fundamental rights, if implemented globally, would maximize persons' chances of living long and happy lives. They have reasons to do so that are internal to their own view, since these reasons are implied by the factual claim about the impact of universal respect for fundamental rights. But once they determine that a given list of fundamental rights would maximize persons' chances of living long and happy lives if globally implemented, they would have reasons to support whatever could promote universal respect for the rights included in that list, no matter what persons with different beliefs or preferences might think in that regard.

It is sometimes argued that subjectivism must be false because it is unable to account for the strength or intensity of our normative disagreements, including disagreements about fundamental rights. If normative standards were a matter of personal belief and preference, we would not spend so much of our time and energy trying to work out our normative disagreement and convince our interlocutors of the validity of our normative standards. We would treat normative disagreements the way we treat disagreements about matters of taste. This is an incredibly weak argument against subjectivism. Rejecting subjectivism because it is unable to account for the strength or intensity of our normative disagreements would be like rejecting atheism because it is unable to account for the strength and intensity of our religious disagreements. The fact that persons believe their normative standards to have some objective validity does not prove that those standards have that kind of validity, no more than the fact that persons believe in the existence of some god proves that that god, or some god, really exists. In both cases, persons may simply be mistaken. Furthermore, in suggesting that if we were to consider our normative standards as having no more than a subjective validity, we should treat our normative disagreements as disagreements about matters of taste, those who raise this argument against subjectivism reveal themselves to be unclear about the nature of disagreements about such normative standards as fundamental rights, or what those disagreements are about. If we typically do not put a lot of effort into trying to convince our interlocutor that, say, pizza tastes better than ice cream, it is because we can easily live side by side in a nonconflictual way with someone whose tastes are different from our own: one who prefers pizza can have pizza without preventing those who prefer ice cream from having their ice cream. Of course, preferences that may be assimilated to matters of taste can become an object of violent normative disagreement (as has happened in the past and may still happen today): the clearest example, perhaps, is that of disagreement about the permissibility of homo-sexual acts between consenting adults. At the roots of those normative disagreements, though, there are doctrines affirming objective normative standards: while not impossible, it will not be easy to find normative subjectivists expending a great deal of effort in trying to convince their interlocutors that heterosexual acts are normatively superior to homosexual ones. But with normative standards such as fundamental rights things are different. Those standards are ones that frame the basic terms of our cohabitation, establishing what we owe to each other, both negatively (noninterference) and positively (assistance and remuneration). If we want to cohabit peacefully, or at least to reduce our conflicts as much as possible, we need to agree on some common normative standards: if persons were permitted to act on the basis of their own different subjective normative standards, we should expect mutual disappointment, lack of coordination, and, most importantly, all manner of conflicts resulting from mutual interfer-ence. That is why we invest a lot of effort in trying to convince our interlocutors to adopt our preferred normative standards as common standards under which to govern our cohabitation or, if that should prove impossible, to reach a workable compromise between our competing normative standards, one that hews as closely to our preferred standards as is consistent with those that others are committed to.

6.1.5 Besides objectivist and subjectivist theorists, there are sceptical theorists who call into question the capacity of human reason to discover an objective justification of fundamental rights, even if they concede that such a justification may exist. Whatever position we may feel inclined to espouse—objectivism, subjectivism, or scepticism—there is a fact that can hardly be denied: the fact of pervasive disagreement about the justification of fundamental rights.

Confronted with such a fact, we might all conclude that there is not any realistic chance that such a disagreement could be overcome. What would be the implications of such a pessimistic conclusion? That depends on the kind of interest that motivates us to address the question of the justification of fundamental rights. If the interest is purely theoretical, the fact that we will never be able to reach an agreement about the justification of fundamental rights should not stop us from pursuing that interest. The same is true if what motivates us to look for a justifi-cation of fundamental rights is an interest in the subjective reasons that, considering our per-sonal beliefs and preferences, we have for supporting these rights. But if what motivates us is an interest in promoting fundamental rights, then we should not assume that the reasons that may convince us to support those rights are the same ones that will prove convincing to others: rather, we should be asking which reasons are more likely to be convincing to them. We should recognize that, maybe, the best way we can promote fundamental rights is to show others that they can support these rights for reasons rooted in their own beliefs and preferences, even if these beliefs and preferences differ from our own and even if we think them wrong. Even if there is no way to reach an agreement on the justification of fundamental rights, this may not be a problem if the alternative and mutually exclusive justifications we have still converge in supporting the same list or sufficiently similar lists of fundamental rights.[8] To the extent that our interest in fundamental rights is a practical interest, agreeing to support these rights is more important than agreeing about reasons for supporting them. Insisting on an objective or true justification for fundamental rights may not contribute to promoting these rights, and may even backfire. What we should look for, then, is not an agreed set of justifications but different justifications that all point in the same direction.

What has been said about the impossibility of reaching an agreement on the justification of fundamental rights carries some implications concerning the correct way of approaching positive fundamental rights, that is, fundamental rights that are laid down in official documents and statements and are part of positive legal systems. Within each political community recognizing fundamental rights and translating those rights into legal provisions, an agreement has been reached on a list of fundamental rights and on the need to guarantee these rights. And the same holds true at the international level, when a document or a statement affirming fundamental rights is adopted. What we should not assume is that there should be a coherent theory able to account for that list, or for the way in which the rights included in it are implemented. Members of political communities affirming fundamental rights disagree about what justifies these rights and about how they ought to be implemented. This disagreement exists among public officials no less than among lay citizens. Official documents and statements about fundamental rights and the ways in which these rights are to be implemented are not expressive of a single coherent view about the same rights but are rather the result of a compromise between the different views which in that regard are held by the members of the political community involved in the process of drafting those documents and statements, and especially by political actors (members of a constitutional assembly, legislators, representatives of governments, and so on).

6.2   FUNDAMENTAL RIGHTS, LEGITIMACY, AND DEMOCRACY

6.2.1 Justifying the general idea of fundamental rights, as constraints on the exercise of political authority and on the use of public resources means justifying the idea of the limited sovereignty of governments. Justifications of the general idea of fundamental rights can be of two different types: justifications claiming that these rights translate prepolitical or nonpoliti-

---

[8]   Cf Rawls, 'The Idea of an Overlapping Consensus' in *Political Liberalism* (Columbia UP 1993; 3rd edn, Columbia UP 2005) lecture 4.

cal norms into the political order, and justifications claiming that these rights are co-original with the political order. According to both views, once a political order exists, fundamental rights are conditions for its legitimacy, the difference being that, on the second view, the idea of fundamental rights makes sense only if a political order is already in place.

According to the first type of justification of fundamental rights, even in the absence of a political order we are subject to normative standards imposing duties that limit our liberty to secure the interests of others, and according to some views we are also subject to duties that limit our liberty to impose respect for some independent good. Natural law theories provide the best example of this strategy for justifying the general idea of fundamental rights. According to these theories, persons are subject to a normative order even before a political order is established. This normative order may be described as a legal order based not on the positive law enacted by a political authority, but on a natural law deriving its authority either from divinity or from reason (s 1.1). The content of this prepolitical or nonpolitical law may be described in terms of goods and their correlative duties or in term of rights and their correlative duties. Thus, for example, according to medieval catholic theologian Thomas Aquinas (1225–1274), whose doctrine has been and still is extremely influential within the Catholic Church, and to some of his contemporary followers,[9] some absolute goods exist which are basic ingredients of a good human life and which all persons should respect in all of their actions. Furthermore, all persons should try to realize some of these goods in their lives. According to John Locke and contemporary libertarians, each person in the state of nature will instead have some natural rights (which according to contemporary libertarianism may be reduced to a basic right to self-ownership)[10] and the liberties they need to defend themselves against violations of those rights and to punish those violations. According to Immanuel Kant (1724–1804) and to contemporary Kantians, human reason, properly exercised, requires each of us to respect the dignity of persons as rational beings including our own dignity.[11] According to these views, the establishment of a political order does not do away with duties to respect prepolitical goods and rights. On the contrary, these duties apply to governments as well as to individuals, along with other duties that apply specifically to governments. Thus, for instance, according to Locke, when persons exit the 'state of nature' to submit to a political order, they retain their natural rights but transfer to the state their liberty to defend themselves against violations of their rights and to punish such violations, and in exchange the state commits to protecting their fundamental rights and rendering justice.

According to the second type of justification of fundamental rights, these are rights that should be recognized for individuals to make it acceptable to them to submit to a political

---

[9]   See Finnis (n 6) and John Finnis, *Aquinas: Moral, Political, and Legal Theory* (OUP 1998).

[10]   See Robert Nozick, *Anarchy, State, and Utopia* (Basic Books 1974). On self-ownership cf GA Cohen, *Self-Ownership, Freedom, and Equality* (OUP 1995).

[11]   See Immanuel Kant, *Groundwork for the Metaphysics of Morals* (first published in German, under the title *Grundlegung zur Metaphysik der Sitten*, 1785; Mary Gregor ed and tr, CUP 1998); Immanuel Kant, *The Metaphysics of Morals* (first published in German, under the title *Die Metaphysik der Sitten*, 1797; Mary Gregor ed and tr, CUP 1991). Cf Gewirth, *Reason and Morality* (n 4); Gewirth, *The Community of Rights* (n 4).

order. This kind of justification of the general idea of fundamental rights is best exemplified by some social contract theories. According to these views, regardless of whether any normative standards precede the establishment of a political order, no one could rationally accept to submit to a government's political authority without receiving in return some guarantee that their interests will be promoted, rather than frustrated, and that guarantee comes in the form of governments making a commitment to protect fundamental rights. Some of these rights may be grounded in rights that pre-exist the state, but that does not matter. Even if we reject the idea of prepolitical or nonpolitical rights, fundamental rights can be said to originate with the political order as conditions of its legitimacy.[12]

Clearly, this is a normative idea, not a historical truth: political orders have existed before the emergence of the idea of fundamental rights, finding their legitimation in other ideas, such as that of a political order's divine legitimation or that of a natural inequality and hierarchy (paradigmatically expressed in the notion of the great chain of being). At a certain point in history, these ideas lost their capacity to secure legitimacy for political orders: other sources of legitimation thus offered themselves, and it was here that the idea of the guarantee of fundamental rights came into play, along with that of promoting the general interest.

Also brought into play as a condition for the legitimacy of a political order was the idea of the basic equality of all the members of the political community, meaning the idea—dovetailing with that of fundamental rights—that everyone in the political community is accorded the same fundamental status. Thus Thomas Hobbes suggested that nobody would accept to exit the 'state of nature' and unite with other persons—and with them submit to a political sovereign—unless everyone accepted to treat everyone else as an equal.[13] Even if Hobbes thought that this principle was consistent with absolute government, other theorists have suggested that all fundamental rights can be deduced from a fundamental right to equality. That is true of Jeremy Bentham,[14] whose utilitarianism presupposes basic equality, and more recently of Ronald Dworkin, who defends the idea of a fundamental right to equal concern and respect[15] and suggests that this is the basic premise behind the most important contemporary reformulation of the social contract theory, namely, John Rawls' theory of social justice.[16]

---

[12]   See John Rawls, *A Theory of Justice* (Harvard UP 1971; rev edn, Harvard UP 1999); Habermas (n 4); Thomas Nagel, 'The Problem of Global Justice' (2005) 33 *Philosophy & Public Affairs* 113. Cf Dershowitz (n 3).

[13]   See Thomas Hobbes, *Leviathan* (first published 1651; Richard Tuck ed, CUP 1991) pt 1, ch 15, 107: 'If Nature […] have made men equall; that equalitie is to be acknowledged: or if Nature have made men unequall; yet because men that think themselves equall, will not enter into conditions of Peace, but upon Equall terms, such equalitie must be admitted.'

[14]   Jeremy Bentham, *An Introduction to the Principles of Morals and Legislation* (first published 1789; JH Burns and HLA Hart eds, The Athlone Press 1970).

[15]   Ronald Dworkin, 'What Rights Do We Have?' in *Taking Rights Seriously* (Harvard UP 1977; 2nd edn, Harvard UP 1978) 266–78 at 272–4. See also Ronald Dworkin, 'Liberalism' in *A Matter of Principle* (Harvard UP 1985) 181–204.

[16]   See Rawls (n 12). Cf Ronald Dworkin, 'Justice and Rights' (first published 1973) in *Taking Rights Seriously* (n 15) 150–83.

6.2.2 Strictly linked to the problem of justifying the general idea of fundamental rights is the problem of justifying the compatibility of fundamental rights with democracy. This problem has emerged in contemporary debates as the problem of justifying judicial review. As noted, judicial review is the strongest guarantee of constitutional rights and, through those rights, of fundamental rights (s 5.2.4). In exercising judicial review, constitutional courts have the power to interfere in political decisions. This has led some persons—generally dissatisfied with decisions by constitutional courts striking down laws enacted by elected legislative bodies—and some theorists—not necessarily dissatisfied with those decisions—to question the legitimacy of judicial review and to suggest it exists in tension with democracy.[17] Judicial review may result in a decision by a body of unelected judges to invalidate decisions taken by democratically legitimate legislators. While the degree of democratic legitimation of constitutional judges may vary depending on how they are selected and how long their mandate is, there is no doubt that constitutional courts are much less democratically representative than democratically legitimate legislatures. Those courts can invalidate decisions that may have the support of a majority of the population and/or that have been voted for by a majority of the democratically elected members of a parliament, and they would do so on the basis of their interpretation of a text—the constitutional text—that typically cannot be changed with the consensus of a simple majority of the parliament, to the extent that it can be changed at all. And in many cases decisions by constitutional courts can be overturned only by constitutional courts themselves. To someone who identifies democracy with government by the people through its democratically elected representatives, and the will of the people with the will of the majority of the people or of their representatives, constitutional democracies implementing a system of judicial review look like limited democracies.

Proponents of judicial review defend this institution by arguing that constitutional democracies implementing judicial review are the better for it because judicial review makes it possible to make up for the shortcomings of an unlimited majoritarian authority.[18] Some advocates of judicial review contest the idea of constitutional democracies as limited democracies by arguing that, like constitutional democracies, majoritarian democracies are only an approximation of the ideal of democracy. In majoritarian representative democracies, decisions concerning the exercise of political authority and the use of public resources are made not by unanimous vote by all the members of a parliament but by a majority of its members, who can at best represent an absolute majority of the people but more often represent only a relative

---

[17] See Mark Tushnet, *Taking the Constitution away from the Courts* (Harvard UP 1999); Jeremy Waldron, *Law and Disagreement* (OUP 1999) pt 3; Jeremy Waldron, 'The Core of the Case against Judicial Review' (2006) 115 *The Yale Law Journal* 1346; Richard Bellamy, *Political Constitutionalism: A Republican Defence of the Constitutionality of Democracy* (CUP 2007).

[18] See John H Ely, *Democracy and Distrust: A Theory of Judicial Review* (Harvard UP 1980); Ronald Dworkin, 'The Forum of Principle' (first published 1981) in *A Matter of Principle* (n 15) 33–71; Habermas (n 4) ch 6; Ronald Dworkin, 'Introduction: The Moral Reading and the Majoritarian Premise' in *Freedom's Law: The Moral Reading of the American Constitution* (OUP 1996) 1–38; Alessandro Ferrara and Frank I Michelman, *Legitimation by Constitution: A Dialogue on Political Liberalism* (OUP 2021) pt 2.

majority (ie the largest minority): a large part of the population—in some cases the majority of the population—is subject to decisions made by parliamentarians who represent only a part of the population. In a constitutional democracy, judicial review offers a counterweight to the majoritarian dimension of democracy, and by correcting some of the flaws inherent in majoritarian democracies, it more closely approximates the ideal of democracy.

In particular, judicial review can mitigate three risks associated with an unlimited majoritarian authority. First, through judicial review, constitutional courts can protect minorities by securing some relevant interests of their members against the risk of a tyranny of the majority. This can be done by securing the universality of fundamental rights, that is, by foreclosing the possibility of enacting discriminatory provisions under which some classes of persons would not be entitled to fundamental rights or would otherwise be prevented from accessing the guarantees they secure. Second, judicial review would enable constitutional courts to defend democracy from self-destructing: it would do so by making it possible to preserve rights and institutions that exist as conditions of democracy itself and of its proper functioning—a list that includes broad (even if not unlimited) freedom of expression, information, assembly, and association, as well as a free and independent press, political rights, political parties, regular elections, and a system providing for the education of all citizens.[19] Third, and finally, according to some of its proponents, judicial review enables constitutional courts to ensure that political authority and public resources will not be used exclusively to promote the interests of the more politically influential segment of the population, which typically is not its majority but the wealthy and the powerful. This could be done by ensuring that each member of the political community can benefit from social cooperation and receive a fair share of its fruits. Notice that this third argument assumes that constitutional courts are less exposed than parliaments to the potentially distorting political influence of the more politically influential segment of the population. But that is contested by some critics of judicial review who argue that this system may also be used to protect the entrenched interests of dominant social groups by striking down legislation introducing progressive reforms (as happened in the United States with the New Deal legislation when it was first being introduced). But suppose, for the sake of argument, that constitutional courts do tend to promote social progress, rather than holding it back. Even on this assumption, ensuring that each member of the political community can benefit from social cooperation and receive a fair share of its fruits would probably be the most difficult goal that can be achieved through judicial review, in part because it is difficult to establish what should count as a fair share of the fruits of social cooperation, but more importantly because there is only so much that can be accomplished by way of judicial review when it comes to the fundamental rights that matter the most in this respect, namely, economic and social rights, since these are implemented under legislative and policy decisions whose course cannot easily be changed by judicial review.[20]

---

[19] See Robert A Dahl, *On Democracy* (Yale UP 1998).

[20] On the role constitutional courts may play in securing economic and social rights see Cécile Fabre, *Social Rights under the Constitution: Government and the Decent Life* (OUP 2000) ch 5; Katharine G Young, *Constituting Economic and Social Rights* (OUP 2012) pt 2.

6.3   THE JUSTIFICATION OF SPECIFIC FUNDAMENTAL RIGHTS

To conclude on the justification of fundamental rights, we have to address the problem of justifying specific fundamental rights. We cannot here go through all the normative arguments that may be used to justify each fundamental right. The discussion will therefore be confined to some general remarks followed by a quick overview of the normative arguments that can be used, and have been used, to justify each of the classes of fundamental rights that have been distinguished (s 5.1.2): civil rights, political rights, social rights, economic rights, and cultural rights.

6.3.1 A normative argument to support the idea that a specific interest is worth protecting as a fundamental right should combine at least two kinds of claims: claims that securing that right will yield some individual or collective good and claims that securing that right is required under some principle of social justice.

The good that comes from a right can be identified with (a) some individual or collective *freedom*, which, depending on the perspective, may include not only the formal dimensions of freedom—the formal status of liberty (distinguishing a freeman from a slave or a serf, or a sovereign state from a colony)[21] and the formal liberty (or permission) to do something—and its social dimension—the fact nobody would prevent us from doing something or punish us for doing that thing—but also its effective dimensions—the capacities, resources, and opportunity to do something; (b) individual *welfare*, understood as a mental state, a more objective condition of body and mind, or a combination of both; or (c) *security*, that is, an objective condition of low risk to lose one's life, integrity, freedoms, welfare, or some other individual goods one may possess. But the list may also include (d) relational goods such as *respect*, *equality*, and *community*, that is, the fact of belonging to a group united by a common culture and bonds of solidarity.[22] These relational goods may be considered instrumentally valuable, insofar as they promote individual welfare, but are sometimes considered intrinsically valuable.

As for principles of social justice requiring that a right be secured, they could prescribe some form of *respect*, some form of *fairness*, and/or some form of *solidarity*.[23] It is generally assumed

---

[21]   The concept of freedom (or 'liberty') is the object of a vast philosophical literature. The most important contribution to that literature is Isaiah Berlin, 'Two Concepts of Liberty' (first published 1958) in *Liberty: Incorporating Four Essays on Liberty* (Henry Hardy ed, OUP 2002) 166–217. For an overview of the literature see Ian Carter, 'Positive and Negative Liberty', *The Stanford Encyclopedia of Philosophy* (Winter edn 2019) <https://plato.stanford.edu/archives/win2019/entries/liberty-positive-negative/> accessed 14 July 2021; and Ian Carter, Matthew H Kramer, and Hillel Steiner (eds), *Freedom: A Philosophical Anthology* (Blackwell 2007).

[22]   On respect and equality as relational goods see Elizabeth S Anderson, 'What Is the Point of Equality' (1999) 109 *Ethics* 287; Harry G Frankfurt, 'Equality and Respect' (1997) 64 *Social Research* 3.

[23]   In the philosophical literature, the two most influential attempts to articulate principles of equal respect, fairness, and solidarity in a complete theory of social justice are Rawls's and Dworkin's. For Rawls's theory see Rawls (n 12); John Rawls, *Justice as Fairness: A Restatement* (Erin Kelly ed, Harvard UP 2001). As for Dworkin's theory, the

that persons deserve respect because of their agency, that is, their ability and desire to act; their autonomy, that is, their ability and desire to choose their own ends and the means by which to reach them; and/or their dignity, that is, their being 'an end in themselves', meaning that they may not be used as mere instruments with which to pursue ends other than their own. As regards fairness, this principle can be argued to require *impartiality* in considering the interests of different persons, as well as some form of *reciprocity* establishing that all those who contribute to a collective enterprise should receive a fair share of the product of that enterprise, where 'fair share' means a share in some way proportional to their contributions. Finally, solidarity is meant to mitigate the meritocratic character of the principle of reciprocity by providing partial redress for the bad effects on people's life prospects owing to factors that are not, or not entirely, under their control, and by partially compensating the victims of persistent social injustices. Contemporary political communities and principles of social justice that are widely shared within those communities are broadly egalitarian not in the sense that they support some radical form of economic equality—they do not—but in the sense that they assume the *basic equality of all persons*, recognizing them as having an equal fundamental status, which implies that they are owed *equal* respect and that their interests deserve *equal* consideration.[24]

Claims of both kinds are needed for a normative argument in support of a specific fundamental right. In the absence of claims that securing that right is required under some principle of social justice, claiming that securing that right will yield some individual or collective good will only provide reasons to think that it would be good to secure that right, but then it may turn out that this good can only be secured in ways that are unjust and therefore impermissible. A libertarian, for example, may agree that it would be a good thing if all persons could fulfil their basic needs and access healthcare, but will still object to recognizing fundamental rights to those goods insofar as the only ways to enforce those rights would require imposing some unjust taxes, thereby violating fundamental rights to freedom and private property.[25] Furthermore, it seems that—given the special status of fundamental rights as limits on the exercise of political authority by democratically legitimate governments—claims of the second kind need to be especially strong. More to the point, if we want to make the case that a given right needs to be guaranteed as a fundamental right by virtue of the good it sustains, it will not be enough to show that this can be done in ways that are permissible (or not unjust): we will more demandingly have to show that it would be unjust not to secure this right.

With these general remarks as background, let us now turn to the question of how the different classes of fundamental rights may be justified.

---

outline provided in Dworkin, 'Liberalism' (n 15) is developed in Ronald Dworkin, *Sovereign Virtue: The Theory and Practice of Equality* (Harvard UP 2000) and in Ronald Dworkin, *Justice for Hedgehogs* (Harvard UP 2011).

24   On basic equality see Jeremy Waldron, *One Another's Equals: The Basis of Human Equality* (Harvard UP 2017). Cf Peter Singer, *Practical Ethics* (CUP 1980; 3rd edn, CUP 2011) chs 2–3; Ian Carter, 'Respect and the Basis of Equality' (2011) 121 *Ethics* 538.

25   See Nozick (n 10). Cf Liam Murphy and Thomas Nagel, *The Myth of Ownership: Taxes and Justice* (OUP 2002).

6.3.2 As noted, the class of civil rights includes many different rights protecting many different interests (s 5.1.2). Some civil rights secure individual freedoms: that is the case with rights against slavery or forced labour; with basic freedoms,[26] including basic economic freedoms; and also with the right to private property, insofar as possessing private property is a condition of effective freedom.[27] Some other rights would, if guaranteed, ensure security and welfare: that is the case, for example, with rights protecting life and integrity, with rights against torture and other forms of inhumane and degrading treatment, and with rights protecting individuals from abuses and misuses of coercive political authority.

As regards social justice as a basis on which to justify civil rights, the main principles that fall under this heading prescribe respect for human agency, human autonomy, and human dignity. The fundamental right to legal personality may be considered as expressing respect for the dignity of all human beings (or for all the human beings who are recognized as having that status of dignity). Civil rights securing various freedoms reflect respect for human agency, human autonomy, and human dignity all at the same time. Other civil rights reflect principles of fairness, as is the case with the right to equality before the law or with the right to a fair trial and to proportionate punishments.

6.3.3 Political rights are a condition of democracy. A political community cannot be considered democratic if it does not recognize these rights for a majority of its members. In contemporary democracies, it is a common view that that majority should include all adult members of the political community and that their political rights should be equal rights.[28] Political rights, as noted, enable citizens to participate, through their political representatives, in the exercise of political authority and to have a say in the decisions that are made about

---

[26]   Among the fundamental rights to basic freedoms, the fundamental right to freedom of expression (or 'freedom of speech') has been in recent years the object of important debates. Focusing on controversial issues such as pornography and hate speech, some authors have challenged the standard liberal defence of that right, based on the ideal of the 'free market of ideas' often combined with the assumption that words and images may offend but not really harm. For the standard liberal defence of freedom of expression see John Stuart Mill, 'On Liberty' (first published 1859) in *On Liberty: With 'The Subjection of Women' and 'Chapters on Socialism'* (Stefan Collini ed, CUP 1989) 1–116. Among the more recent contributions to the debate on freedom of expression see Dworkin, *A Matter of Principle* (n 15) chs 17–19; Catharine A MacKinnon, *Only Words* (Harvard UP 1993) (on pornography); Dworkin, *Freedom's Law* (n 18) pt 2; Judith Butler, *Excitable Speech: A Politics of the Performative* (Routledge 1997); Jeremy Waldron, *The Harm in Hate Speech* (Harvard UP 2012). For an overview of the literature see David van Mill, 'Freedom of Speech', *The Stanford Encyclopedia of Philosophy* (Spring edn 2021) <https://plato.stanford.edu/archives/spr2021/entries/freedom -speech/> accessed 14 July 2021.

[27]   See Jeremy Waldron, *The Right to Private Property* (OUP 1988).

[28]   See Charles R Beitz, *Political Equality: An Essay on Democratic Theory* (Princeton UP 1989); Iris Marion Young, *Inclusion and Democracy* (OUP 2000); Robert A Dahl, *On Political Equality* (Yale UP 2006); Thomas Christiano, *The Constitution of Equality: Democratic Authority and Its Limits* (OUP 2008); David Estlund, *Democratic Authority: A Philosophical Framework* (Princeton UP 2008). Cf Jason Brennan, *Against Democracy* (Princeton UP 2016).

the use of public resources: in this way political rights realize an ideal of collective freedom as collective self-government. And in the same way they express respect for human autonomy. To a degree, political rights can also function as a guarantee against abuses and misuses of political authority and public resources, for they enable citizens to exercise some control, albeit indirectly, over the way authority is exercised and resources are used. Finally, to the extent that democratic procedures may reveal what the interests are that matter to the members of the political community, and to the extent that governments will pay impartial attention to those interests, political rights may also contribute to a fair exercise of political authority and to a fair use of public resources.

6.3.4 Fundamental social rights impose on governments an obligation to secure some basic opportunities for everyone, citizens and noncitizens alike, by making available the goods and services needed to that end: these can be delivered either directly by the government or indirectly through the market (in which case the government will purchase them and make them available for free or at a price below market value), or again the government can facilitate access to them by regulating the market. These goods and services may include safe food and water, clothes, shelter, healthcare, education, jobs, and income. When governments are effective in providing the opportunities that depend on these goods and services, they can correct for some of the ill effects of market competition, the idea being to secure at least some of the material bases that individuals need to exercise their freedoms, including their political freedoms, all the while promoting individual welfare and security.[29]

To the degree that social rights enable each individual to enjoy the conditions for a minimally decent human life, they can be considered to express respect for human dignity, but the strongest justifications of social rights rest on principles of fairness and solidarity. Fairness is considered to require some form of equality of opportunity.[30] In contemporary liberal communities, the idea is widely shared that social inequalities can be considered legitimate only to the extent that they are the result of individual choices from an initial condition of equality of opportunity and to the extent that they can be considered to be either deserved or to promote the interests of all. Among social rights, it is especially the right to education[31] and the right

---

[29] See Fabre (n 20) ch 1.

[30] The most influential accounts of equality of opportunity in the contemporary philosophical debate on social justice are the Rawlsian account, Dworkin's account (sometimes referred to as 'luck-egalitarianism'), and the 'capability approach'. The Rawlsian account, first elaborated in Rawls (n 12), has been developed by many others: see, eg, Thomas Nagel, *Equality and Partiality* (OUP 1991); Brian Barry, *Why Social Justice Matters* (Polity 2005); Thomas M Scanlon, *Why Does Inequality Matter?* (OUP 2018). For Dworkin's account see especially Ronald Dworkin, 'Equality of Welfare' and 'Equality of Resources' (first published 1981) in *Sovereign Virtue: The Theory and Practice of Equality* (n 23) 11–119; Richard J Arneson, 'Equality and Equal Opportunity for Welfare' (1989) 56 *Philosophical Studies* 77; and, critically Anderson (n 22). Finally, for the 'capability approach' see Amartya Sen, *Inequality Reexamined* (OUP 1995); Amartya Sen, *Development as Freedom* (OUP 1999); Martha C Nussbaum, *Frontiers of Justice: Disability, Nationality, Species Membership* (Harvard UP 2006); Amartya Sen, *The Idea of Justice* (Penguin 2009).

[31] See Amy Gutmann, *Democratic Education* (Princeton UP 1987; 2nd edn, Princeton UP 1999).

to a fair access to jobs and offices that contribute to equality of opportunity. Besides equality of opportunity, fairness requires some form of reciprocity: everyone participating in social cooperation deserves to benefit from that cooperation. As regards the principle of solidarity, it suggests that not all disadvantages give rise to a legitimate claim for compensation: this claim arises only where the disadvantages depend on unfortunate events over which individuals have no control and for which they accordingly cannot be considered responsible. Some of these normative requirements can be met by social rights providing access to the means by which to fulfil one's basic needs[32] and the need for healthcare.[33]

6.3.5 Among economic rights, labour rights protect workers' collective freedom, while other economic rights protect their individual freedoms, welfare, and security by ensuring safe workplaces and conditions, fair wages, and adequate leisure. They may be considered to protect human dignity by establishing that workers cannot be entirely considered as means of production. They try to correct for some of the inequalities that may result from the asymmetry of power between employers and employees, in such a way as to achieve a fairer apportionment of the product of human labour.

6.3.6 Finally, cultural rights protect the collective freedom and survival of cultural minorities and the individual freedom and welfare of their members. In doing so they secure the relational good of community. Justifications for cultural rights point to the fact that a political community's accepted culture and official institutions tend to reflect the culture(s) of the larger or more powerful group(s) within that community. This is thought to be true as well in political communities that tolerate cultural diversity, and even in those that purport to be neutral towards different cultures. Given this set of circumstances, accessing the same opportunities that are open to members of the dominant culture(s) may be more burdensome for members of cultural minorities, who will sometimes be required to set aside their cultural identity in order to access those opportunities. Members of cultural minorities are pressured to integrate into the dominant culture, and this threatens the survival of minority cultures.

Proponents of multiculturalism advocating cultural rights claim that classical civil rights protecting freedoms of religion, expression, and association are not enough to protect the interests of members of cultural minorities.[34] It is certainly possible to rely on traditional rights, such as freedom of religion, in seeking to reform existing institutions by removing some of the obstacles that make it more difficult for members of minority cultures to follow the pre-

---

[32]   It has been suggested that access to the means to fulfil one's basic needs could, and should, be secured by paying persons on a regular basis a 'minimum' or a 'basic' income. See Philippe Van Parijs and Yannick Vanderborght, *Basic Income: A Radical Proposal for a Free Society and a Sane Economy* (Harvard UP 2019). Cf Stuart White, *The Civic Minimum: On the Rights and Obligations of Economic Citizenship* (OUP 2003).

[33]   On the right to healthcare see Norman Daniels, *Just Health Care* (CUP 1985); Sudhir Anand, Fabienne Peter, and Amartya Sen (eds), *Public Health, Ethics, and Equity* (OUP 2004); Norman Daniels, *Just Health: Meeting Health Needs Fairly* (CUP 2008); Allen Buchanan, *Justice and Healthcare: Selected Essays* (OUP 2009); Shlomi Segall, *Health, Luck and Justice* (Princeton UP 2009).

[34]   See references in ch 5, n 11.

scriptions of their religion, but that is hardly enough to ensure that minority cultures have fair chances of survival. That would require institutional support specifically designed to preserve minority cultures, including some form of financial support. This kind of support could be provided by recognizing cultural rights. According to some theorists, cultural rights should also include special collective rights to political participation, consultation, representation, and partial self-government for cultural minorities, but other theorists are concerned that such collective rights may be used to suppress the individual rights of vulnerable and/or dissenting members within minority cultures.[35]

6.3.7 To conclude this overview of the normative arguments that may be used and have been used to support specific fundamental rights, I will offer two remarks that apply to all classes of those rights. First, insofar as fundamental rights are equally recognized for all persons, either as persons or as citizens of a political community, they express equal respect for their human dignity and an impartial consideration of some of their most fundamental interests. And second, insofar as fundamental rights make governments responsible not only for respecting these rights but also for protecting them, all fundamental rights are an expression of solidarity between the members of a political community, and in the case of global fundamental rights, between all persons. In this way they realize the relational goods of respect, equality, and community.

---

[35] See Susan M Okin, *Is Multiculturalism Bad for Women?* (Joshua Cohen and Martha C Nussbaum eds, Princeton UP 1999); Martha C Nussbaum, *Women and Human Development: The Capabilities Approach* (CUP 2000); Ayelet Shachar, *Multicultural Jurisdictions: Cultural Differences and Women's Rights* (CUP 2001). For a radical critique of multiculturalism see Brian Barry, *Culture and Equality: An Egalitarian Critique of Multiculturalism* (Polity 2000).

PART III
CASES

Silvia Falcetta

INTRODUCTION

Part III focuses on the jurisprudence of the European Court of Human Rights (ECtHR) and of the Court of Justice of the European Union (CJEU). The aim of this part is to show how the European regime of fundamental rights protection operates 'in action' and how the ECtHR and the CJEU interpret and apply fundamental rights to specific cases. While not exhaustive of the issues considered by the European courts, the chapters that follow provide an overview of the ways in which the ECtHR and the CJEU evaluate an increasingly diverse body of sociolegal claims through the lens of fundamental rights (s 3.3). As discussed in Chapter 3 and Chapter 5, the multiplication of fundamental rights in contemporary societies creates conflicts between fundamental rights and between the protection of individual rights versus the protection of public interest. Against this background, Part III aims to show how the ECtHR and the CJEU deal with clashes between competing rights and interests.

Part III is divided into chapters that each focus on a different thematic area. Chapter 7 considers the ways in which the ECtHR and the CJEU approach complaints about sexual orientation, sex, and gender differences in areas such as marriage, family, labour policy, and filiation. Chapter 8 examines the jurisprudence of the ECtHR and the CJEU on socioeconomic rights in areas such as employment, access to social security benefits, and protection of the environment. Chapter 9 illustrates how the ECtHR and the CJEU adjudicate complaints on religious freedoms, on racial and ethnic discrimination, and on rights associated with cultural practices.

Before turning our attention to the jurisprudence of the European courts, let us consider some key notions about the ECtHR's and CJEU's functioning.

The ECtHR interprets the ECHR, ensuring that member states of the Council of Europe (CoE) respect the rights set out in the European Convention on Human Rights (ECHR) and its Protocols.[1] Until 1998, the European Commission of Human Rights (ECmHR) decided on the admissibility of applications, and the ECtHR delivered judgments on cases found admissible. With the entry into force of Protocol 11 on 1 November 1998, the ECmHR ceased to function and the ECtHR now examines applications, decides on their admissibility, and delivers judgments. The number of judges sitting in the ECtHR reflects the number of the state parties to the ECHR (47 at present). The ECtHR generally hears complaints either as a Chamber or as

---

[1]   Convention for the Protection of Human Rights and Fundamental Freedoms (4 November 1950, ETS No 005).

a Grand Chamber. After a Chamber delivers a judgment, the parties may request referral of the case to the Grand Chamber.[2]

The ECHR protects mainly civil and political rights, which are derived from the 1948 Universal Declaration of Human Rights (s 3.3). Some articles protect rights that do not admit derogations or exceptions and can never be interfered with—for example, Article 3 (prohibition of torture) and Article 7 (no punishment without law). Other articles identify specific exceptions that fall outside of the scope of the right protected by that provision. For example, Article 2 (right to life) specifies that deprivation of life is not regarded as in contravention of that provision when 'it results from the use of force which is no more than absolutely necessary' in one of the circumstances defined by Article 2(2). Article 15 makes provision for derogating from some of the ECHR rights in time of 'war or other public emergency threatening the life of the nation', but it is not possible to derogate from the rights enshrined in Article 2, except in respect of 'deaths resulting from lawful acts of war', Article 3, Article 4(1) (prohibition of slavery and forced labour), and Article 7. Articles 8–11 set out the conditions under which the rights protected in those provisions may be interfered with. In assessing complaints concerning the alleged violation of Articles 8–11, the ECtHR will consider whether the interference is prescribed by law, whether the aim pursued falls within the ambit of one or more of the legitimate aims stated in the impugned provision, and whether the interference is necessary in a democratic society. Article 14 protects individuals from discrimination in the enjoyment of their ECHR rights. Not all differences in treatment amount to discrimination, and the ECtHR will find a violation of Article 14 if a difference in treatment does not pursue a legitimate aim or if the means employed are not proportionate to the aim pursued.

The ECtHR has established that the ECHR is a 'living instrument' which must be interpreted 'in the light of present-day conditions' and that the ECtHR 'cannot but be influenced by the developments and commonly accepted standards in […] the member States of the Council of Europe'.[3] If comparative analysis shows the existence of common standards in legislation and policy among CoE member states on a particular issue, the ECtHR may evolve the interpretation of the ECHR on that issue and may, for instance, impose new obligations on contracting states. The principle of European consensus is closely related to the concept of 'margin of appreciation'. The notion of margin of appreciation indicates the degree of discretion that is available to national authorities when regulating matters that fall within the ambit of the ECHR. The existence of a European consensus on a certain issue is likely to narrow

---

[2]   Individual applications may also be heard by a single-judge formation or a Committee of three judges. For an overview of the history of ECHR organs, see Jonas Christoffersen and Mikael Rask Madsen (eds), *The European Court of Human Rights between Law and Politics* (OUP 2011). For an overview of the functioning of the ECtHR, see David J Harris, Michael O'Boyle, Ed P Bates, and Carla M Buckley, *Law of the European Convention on Human Rights* (4th edn, OUP 2018) pt 1; Bernadette Rainey, Pamela McCormick, and Clare Ovey, *The European Convention on Human Rights* (8th edn, OUP 2021) pt 1. For a discussion of the challenges faced by the ECtHR, see Spyridon Flogaitis, Tom Zwart, and Julie Fraser (eds), *The European Court of Human Rights and Its Discontents: Turning Criticism into Strength* (Edward Elgar 2013).

[3]   *Tyrer v the United Kingdom* (1978) Series A no 26, para 31.

the margin of appreciation available to the authorities in fulfilling their obligations under the ECHR. The absence of a European consensus on a certain issue is likely to result in a wide margin of appreciation available to national authorities.[4]

The CJEU ensures that the law of the European Union (EU law), which includes the Charter of Fundamental Rights of the European Union (EU Charter),[5] is interpreted and applied consistently by member states of the European Union (EU) and EU institutions and bodies. National courts that are in doubt about how to interpret EU law in a specific case can refer that case to the CJEU and ask for clarification. National courts can also ask for clarification if in doubt about the compatibility of national legislation or practice with EU law. In addition, the CJEU deals with complaints initiated by EU member states, EU institutions, and, under exceptional circumstances, by private individuals and companies who have had their interests harmed by EU institutions. The CJEU is divided into two distinct courts: the Court of Justice and the General Court.

The meaning and scope of EU Charter rights which correspond to ECHR rights is the same as those laid down in the ECHR (Article 52(3)). The EU Charter does not extend the field of application of EU law beyond the powers of the EU, and the EU Charter does not establish any new power or task for the EU (Article 51(2)). Like the ECHR, the EU Charter contains rights that cannot be interfered with—for example, Article 4 (prohibition of torture and inhuman or degrading treatment or punishment)—and rights that admit derogations or exceptions—for example, Article 17 (right to property). Unlike the ECHR, the EU Charter contains express reference to economic and social rights (on economic and social rights, s 5.1.2).[6] For example, the EU Charter secures the 'right to engage in work and to pursue a freely chosen or accepted occupation' (Article 15) and the freedom to 'conduct a business' (Article 16). Similarly, Title IV of the EU Charter (solidarity) enshrines a range of provisions that protect socioeconomic interests, such as: workers' right to information and consultation (Article 27); the right of collective bargaining and action (Article 28); the right to fair and just working conditions (Article 31); the right to social security and assistance (Article 34); the right of access to healthcare (Article 35); and to services of general economic interest (Article 36).

Pursuant to Article 52(1), any limitation on the exercise of EU Charter rights and freedoms must be 'provided for by law' and must respect 'the essence of those rights and freedoms'. Limitations may be made only if they are 'necessary' and 'genuinely meet objectives of general

---

[4]   For an introduction to the doctrine of the margin of appreciation, see Yutaka Arai-Takahashi, *The Margin of Appreciation Doctrine and the Principle of Proportionality in the Jurisprudence of the ECHR* (Intersentia 2002). For an introduction to the doctrine of European consensus, see Kanstantsin Dzehtsiarou, *European Consensus and the Legitimacy of the European Court of Human Rights* (CUP 2015).

[5]   Charter of Fundamental Rights of the European Union [2012] OJ C 326/391.

[6]   For an overview, see Giacomo Di Federico (ed), *The EU Charter of Fundamental Rights* (Springer 2011); Koen Lenaerts, 'Exploring the Limits of the EU Charter of Fundamental Rights' (2012) 8 *European Constitutional Law Review* 375; Marton Varju, *European Union Human Rights Law: The Dynamics of Interpretation and Context* (Edward Elgar 2014). For a discussion of the fundamental values underpinning EU law, and their relationship with the ECHR, see Dirk Ehlers (ed), *European Fundamental Rights and Freedoms* (de Gruyter 2007).

interest recognised by the Union or the need to protect the rights and freedoms of others'. Moreover, any limitation must be in accordance with the principle of proportionality, which establishes that the means employed to interfere with the exercise of EU Charter rights must be proportionate to the aims pursued. When transposing EU directives into national legislation, member states must rely on an interpretation of EU legal instruments which is consistent with the fundamental rights enshrined in the EU Charter and which strikes a fair balance between the various fundamental rights protected by EU law.

7
Sex, gender, sexual orientation

7.1   SEX AND GENDER

7.1.1 The principle of equality between men and women is embedded in EU law.[1] As illustrated below, the notion of equal treatment was originally introduced in EU law purely for economic reasons. However, the CJEU gradually paved the way for mainstreaming the principle of equal treatment in other areas of EU action. Several provisions of the EU Charter enshrine the principle of equal treatment. For example, Article 21 prohibits discrimination based on sex, Article 23 requires member states to ensure equality between men and women in 'all areas', and Article 33 secures the right to paid maternity leave and protects workers from dismissal for a reason connected with maternity.

The principle of 'equal remuneration for equal work' between men and women was first introduced in the Treaty establishing the European Economic Community (EEC) with the aim to ensure fair competition among member states.[2] When the EEC Treaty was adopted, of the states making up the EEC only France had introduced legislation on women's equal pay. As a consequence, the French government supported the introduction of the principle of equal pay in order to avoid unfair competition from other member states. However, the CJEU subsequently established that the principle of equal remuneration also pursues a 'social' aim[3] and that this social aim constitutes 'the expression of a fundamental human right'.[4] The CJEU further established that the principle of equal remuneration also applies to situations in which men and women are not 'contemporaneously' doing equal work for the same employer,[5] and

---

[1]   For an overview, see Roberta Guerrina, 'Gender, Mainstreaming and the EU Charter of Fundamental Rights' (2003) 22 *Policy and Society* 97; Mark Bell, 'The Principle of Equal Treatment: Widening and Deepening' in *The Evolution of EU Law* (Paul Craig and Gráinne de Búrca eds, OUP 2011) 611–39.

[2]   Article 119 of the Treaty establishing the European Economic Community (EEC Treaty) (then Article 141 Treaty establishing the European Community [2002] OJ C 325/1, now Article 157 of the Consolidated Version of the Treaty on the Functioning of the European Union (TFEU) [2012] OJ C 326/47).

[3]   Case 43/75 *Gabrielle Defrenne v Société anonyme belge de navigation aérienne Sabena* [1976] ECR 00455, para 12.

[4]   Joined Cases C-270/97 and C-271/97 *Deutsche Post AG v Elisabeth Sievers and Brunhilde Schrage* [2000] ECR I-00929, para 57.

[5]   Case 129/79 *Macarthys Ltd v Wendy Smith* [1980] ECR 01275, para 13.

it prohibits differences in pay where the 'lower-paid category of workers is engaged in work of higher value'.[6] Moreover, the CJEU held that this principle applies to cases of indirect discrimination and forbids the adoption of criteria in occupational pension schemes that negatively affect a greater number of women than men without any objective justification that is not based on sex.[7]

The CJEU has acknowledged that the 'mere fact that a male candidate and a female candidate are equally qualified does not mean that they have the same chances' in employment,[8] and it has established that positive action measures may be compatible with the principles of EU law.[9] For example, national authorities may give priority to female candidates in sectors of public service in which women are underrepresented or concentrated at the lower end of the scale, unless 'reasons specific to an individual male candidate' tilt the balance in his favour[10] and provided that all applications are subject to an 'objective assessment which takes account of the specific personal situations of all candidates'.[11] Thus, the principle of equal treatment precludes positive actions which for candidates belonging to the underrepresented sex guarantee an 'absolute and unconditional'[12] priority in appointment or promotion.

The CJEU has also developed relevant jurisprudence on the protection of workers on the grounds of pregnancy. For example, the CJEU has determined that a refusal to appoint a pregnant woman, whom the employer considers to be suitable for the job, amounts to 'direct discrimination on grounds of sex',[13] and it has also held that the principle of equal treatment precludes the dismissal of a worker 'at any time' during her pregnancy for absences caused by illness resulting from her pregnancy.[14] Pregnant women and women on maternity leave require special protection, and neither 'financial loss incurred by the employer'[15] nor consid-

---

[6]   Case 157/86 *Mary Murphy and Others v An Bord Telecom Eireann* [1988] ECR 00673, para 9. This case concerned a group of female factory workers that received a lower wage than less skilled male store labourers employed in the same factory.

[7]   Case 170/84 *Bilka-Kaufhaus GmbH v Karin Weber von Hartz* [1986] ECR 01607, para 31. The notion of indirect discrimination describes the effect of policies or measures that are couched in neutral terms but have disproportionately prejudicial effects on a particular group.

[8]   Case C-409/95 *Hellmut Marschall v Land Nordrhein-Westfalen* [1997] ECR I-06363, para 30.

[9]   The term 'positive action' refers to measures undertaken with the aim of achieving substantive equality for members of groups that are disadvantaged or face the consequences of past disadvantage.

[10]   *Hellmut Marschall* (n 8) para 35.

[11]   Case C-158/97 *Georg Badeck and Others* [2000] ECR I-01875, para 38.

[12]   Case C-450/93 *Eckhard Kalanke v Freie Hansestadt Bremen* [1995] ECR I-03051, para 22. See also Case C-407/98 *Katarina Abrahamsson and Leif Anderson v Elisabet Fogelqvist* [2000] ECR I-05539.

[13]   Case C-177/88 *Elisabeth Johanna Pacifica Dekker v Stichting Vormingscentrum voor Jong Volwassenen (VJV-Centrum) Plus* [1990] ECR I-03941, para 12.

[14]   Case C-394/96 *Mary Brown v Rentokil Ltd* [1998] ECR I-04185, para 28. See also Case C-32/93 *Carole Louise Webb v EMO Air Cargo (UK) Ltd* [1994] ECR I-03567; Case C-109/00 *Tele Danmark A/S v Handels- og Kontorfunktionærernes Forbund i Danmark (HK)* [2001] ECR I-06993.

[15]   *Tele Danmark A/S* (n 14) para 23.

erations of 'the proper functioning of the undertaking'[16] justify the dismissal of a pregnant worker on account of her pregnancy. Thus, EU law must be interpreted in such a way as to protect pregnant women and women on maternity leave in cases where 'the legal relationship linking her to another person has been severed on account of her pregnancy'.[17] However, the CJEU has accepted that member states may allow an employer to dismiss a pregnant worker because of a collective redundancy 'without giving any grounds other than those justifying the collective dismissal'.[18]

7.1.2 Women's reproductive choices are a central theme of feminist theory, and feminist movements have long framed access to safe and lawful abortion as an issue concerning women's rights and women's agency over their bodies. The ECtHR has refused to establish *in abstracto* whether the 'unborn child' is a 'person' for the purposes of Article 2 (right to life)[19] but it has held that, even if unborn children have a right to life, this right would be 'implicitly limited by the mother's rights and interests'.[20] However, the ECtHR has not ruled out that 'in certain circumstances' safeguards may be extended to the unborn child.[21]

The ECtHR has accepted that the voluntary termination of pregnancy falls within the scope of a woman's private life, but it has also held that the life of a pregnant woman becomes 'closely connected with the developing foetus', and the woman's right to respect for her private life (Article 8) 'must be weighed against other competing rights and freedoms' that include those of the unborn child.[22] Thus, the introduction of legislation restricting access to lawful abortion does not necessarily amount to a violation of women's rights under Article 8, and national authorities enjoy of a wide margin of appreciation in determining the circumstances under which a voluntary termination of pregnancy will be deemed lawful. However, the legal framework devised for this purpose must be shaped in a coherent manner[23] and be respectful of women's ECHR rights.

First, if abortion is formally allowed under domestic legislation, the state 'must not structure its legal framework in a way which would limit real possibilities to obtain it'.[24] In *Tysiąc v Poland* the ECtHR noted that Polish legislation allowed abortion only under a limited number of exceptions and criminalized physicians who terminate a pregnancy in breach of those exceptions. The ECtHR did not dispute the decision to allow legal abortion only in few exceptions, but it held that the general prohibition on abortion, taken together with the risk of incurring criminal liability and with the lack of clear procedures regulating access to abortion,

---

[16]　*Carole Louise Webb* (n 14) para 26.

[17]　Case C-232/09 *Dita Danosa v LKB Lizings SIA* [2010] ECR I-11405, para 70.

[18]　Case C-103/16 *Jessica Porras Guisado v Bankia SA and Others* EU:C:2018:99, para 75(2).

[19]　*Vo v France* [GC] ECHR 2004-VIII, para 85.

[20]　ibid, para 80.

[21]　ibid.

[22]　*A B and C v Ireland* [GC] ECHR 2010, para 213.

[23]　ibid, para 249.

[24]　*RR v Poland* ECHR 2011 (extracts) para 200. See also *Tysiąc v Poland* ECHR 2007-I, para 116.

had a 'chilling effect' on doctors[25] assessing whether the legal requirements in any individual case were met.

Secondly, national authorities must ensure timely and effective access to 'reliable information' that is necessary to determine whether a woman is eligible for a voluntary termination of pregnancy.[26] In *RR v Poland* the ECtHR heard the complaint of a woman who was denied access to prenatal genetic tests until the legal limit for abortion had expired. Since Polish law permitted abortion in cases of foetal malformation, the ECtHR concluded that national authorities and medical staff had a duty to provide 'relevant' and 'full' information on the foetus's health in a timely manner.[27] Relatedly, the ECtHR rejected the government's argument that genetic testing is closely bound up with access to abortion and that physicians should be allowed to refuse to carry out these tests on grounds of conscience. On the contrary, the ECtHR held that national authorities must ensure that a physician's or health professional's exercise of freedom of conscience does not jeopardize a woman's right to access services to which she is entitled under national law.[28] The ECtHR adopted a similar approach in cases concerning the selling of contraceptives, and it dismissed the complaint of two pharmacists who refused to sell contraceptive pills on religious grounds.[29]

Thirdly, the ECtHR has acknowledged that, in the absence of a coherent and effective legal framework on termination of pregnancy, women may be forced to endure prolonged periods of 'painful uncertainty', 'acute anguish', and humiliation that reach the threshold of severity sufficient to trigger the protection of Article 3 against inhuman and degrading treatment.[30] Thus, the ECtHR enables women to invoke one of the most important principles enshrined in the ECHR—the absolute prohibition of degrading or inhuman treatment—against the systematic failure of national authorities to guarantee effective implementation of domestic legislation regulating the termination of pregnancy.

7.1.3 Victims of domestic violence and relatives of women and children killed by family members have repeatedly complained to the ECtHR about the lack of adequate legal and policy measures for preventing, investigating, and policing episodes of abuse within the family. The ECtHR has defined domestic violence as a form of violence that can take 'various forms'—such as physical violence; verbal, psychological, or economic abuse; and controlling or coercive behaviour[31]—and it has acknowledged that, under certain circumstances, domestic violence amounts to a form of 'gender-based' violence.[32] A failure to prevent and adequately police incidents of domestic violence can result in a violation of some of the most important ECHR pro-

---

[25] *Tysiąc* (n 24) para 116.

[26] *RR* (n 24) para 200.

[27] ibid.

[28] ibid, para 206.

[29] *Pichon and Sajous v France* (dec) ECHR 2001-X.

[30] *RR* (n 24) para 159.

[31] *Opuz v Turkey* ECHR 2009, para 132; *Volodina v Russia* App no 41261/17 (ECHR, 9 July 2019) para 71.

[32] *Opuz* (n 31) para 200.

visions, such as Article 2 and Article 3.[33] ECHR jurisprudence on domestic violence sits within a broader framework of legal instruments adopted by the CoE to tackle domestic abuse.[34] In particular, the Istanbul Convention has introduced an approach against gender-based violence and domestic violence that is based on four pillars—prevention, protection, prosecution, and coordinated policies—and the ECtHR has identified key obligations that national authorities must fulfil in order to prevent domestic violence, protect victims, and prosecute perpetrators.

First, national authorities must devise a legal framework under which domestic violence is singled out and can be prosecuted. The ECtHR has established that member states should adopt 'positive measures in the sphere of criminal-law protection', either by introducing specific criminal sanctions for incidents of domestic violence or by considering domestic abuse an aggravating form of other offences.[35] The ECtHR has also determined that provisions under which the prosecution of charges of domestic violence falls entirely to the victim's private initiative are incompatible with the ECHR.[36] On the contrary, if the offence is serious or if there is a significant risk of future offences, a prosecution should continue even if the victim withdraws her complaint.[37] The ECtHR has further held that refusing to initiate a criminal investigation into injuries that do not meet a certain threshold of severity is incompatible with the ECHR. For example, in *Volodina v Russia* the ECtHR held that Russian legislation failed to adequately capture the offence of domestic violence because it criminalized battery on family members only if committed at least twice within a 12-month period or if, at a minimum, the incident results in minor bodily harm.[38]

Secondly, national authorities must put an effective law enforcement machinery in place in order to protect victims and deter perpetrators from committing further offences. In *Opuz v Turkey* the ECtHR considered the complaint of a woman who had been subjected to repeated assaults by her former husband and whose mother had been killed by the same man. The ECtHR ruled that national authorities had failed to take appropriate measures to protect the two women, and it found a violation of Article 2, in respect of the death of the applicant's mother, and Article 3, in respect of the ill-treatment suffered by the applicant.[39] The ECtHR noted that the applicant had repeatedly reported her former husband to the police before the

---

[33]   Episodes of domestic violence can also amount to a violation of Article 8 (right to respect for private and family life). See David J Harris, Michael O'Boyle, Ed P Bates, and Carla M Buckley, *Law of the European Convention on Human Rights* (4th edn, OUP 2018) 520.

[34]   For example, see Council of Europe, Committee of Ministers, 'Recommendation Rec(2002)5 of the Committee of Ministers to Member States on the Protection of Women Against Violence' (Adopted by the Committee of Ministers on 30 April 2002 at the 794th meeting of the Ministers' Deputies); Council of Europe Convention on Preventing and Combating Violence Against Women and Domestic Violence (Istanbul Convention) ETS No 210.

[35]   *Volodina* (n 31) para 78. See also ibid, para 79.

[36]   *Opuz* (n 31) paras 137–43. See also *Volodina* (n 31) para 82.

[37]   *Opuz* (n 31) para 139.

[38]   *Volodina* (n 31) para 81.

[39]   *Opuz* (n 31) para 153 and para 176 respectively. The ECtHR found also a violation of Article 14 in conjunction with Article 2 and Article 3 (ibid, para 202).

lethal attack. Nevertheless, competent authorities had failed to take 'special measures consonant with the gravity of the situation',[40] and the applicant's former husband had received small fines for causing serious injuries to the applicant and life-threatening injuries to her mother. Moreover, police forces had been reluctant to investigate the applicant's complaints because they saw domestic violence as a private 'family matter'.[41] On this basis, the ECtHR concluded that national authorities had not displayed 'due diligence' in protecting the right to life of the applicant's mother,[42] and they had failed to take 'protective measures in the form of effective deterrence' against 'serious breaches' of the applicant's right to personal integrity.[43] The ECtHR strengthened this approach in subsequent complaints concerning the failure of national authorities to protect women and their children from ill-treatment and/or fatal injuries,[44] and it clearly established that national authorities must address episodes of domestic violence in a way commensurate with the gravity of the violence.

Thirdly, national authorities must address discriminatory attitudes that underpin prosecutorial and judicial passivity towards violence against women. The ECtHR has established that—whether intentionally or unintentionally—failure to prevent and appropriately investigate episodes of domestic violence may amount to a violation of women's right to 'equal protection of the law'.[45] In *Opuz* the ECtHR held that the 'overall unresponsiveness' and passivity of police forces and judicial authorities in protecting victims of domestic violence disproportionately affected women and therefore amounted to a form of gender-based discrimination prohibited under Article 14 (prohibition of discrimination).[46] In *Eremia v the Republic of Moldova* the ECtHR found a violation of the principle of nondiscrimination on the basis that the failures and delays of national authorities reflected a 'discriminatory attitude' towards the applicant 'as a woman'.[47] Likewise, in *Volodina v Russia* the ECtHR held that the continued failure to adopt legislation to combat domestic violence fell short of creating the conditions for 'substantive gender equality',[48] in violation of the principle of nondiscrimination. Thus, national authorities must take appropriate actions to ensure that women 'live free from fear of ill-treatment or attacks on their physical integrity' and 'benefit from the equal protection of the law'.[49]

---

[40]   ibid, para 148.

[41]   ibid, para 143.

[42]   ibid, para 149.

[43]   ibid, para 176.

[44]   For instance, see *MG v Turkey* App no 646/10 (ECtHR, 22 March 2016); *Halime Kılıç v Turkey* App no 63034/11 (ECtHR, 28 June 2016); *Talpis v Italy* App no 41237/14 (ECtHR, 2 March 2017). For an overview of complaints concerning episodes of domestic violence that have resulted in the death of women and/or their children, see European Court of Human Rights, 'Factsheet: Domestic Violence' (December 2021).

[45]   *Opuz* (n 31) para 191.

[46]   ibid, para 200.

[47]   *Eremia v the Republic of Moldova* App no 3564/11 (ECHR, 28 May 2013) para 89.

[48]   *Volodina* (n 31) para 132.

[49]   ibid.

7.2   SEXUAL ORIENTATION AND GENDER IDENTITY

7.2.1 Gay men and lesbians have repeatedly invoked the ECHR to challenge sexual orientation discrimination and demand equal treatment in several realms of private, public, and family life. Until 1981, the ECtHR held the view that the criminalization of same-sex sexual acts was compatible with the ECHR.[50] In *Dudgeon v the United Kingdom* the ECtHR for the first time found that the existence of provisions criminalizing private sexual acts between consenting adult men was incompatible with their fundamental right to respect for their private life (Article 8).[51] In *Dudgeon*, the ECtHR conceptualized homosexuality as an 'essentially private manifestation of the human personality'[52] and concluded that 'moral attitudes' towards homosexuality[53] cannot justify legislation that criminalizes 'a most intimate aspect of private life'.[54]

A key principle of ECHR jurisprudence on sexual orientation discrimination is that negative attitudes that represent 'a predisposed bias on the part of a heterosexual majority against a homosexual minority' do not amount to a sufficient justification for interfering with gay men and lesbians' rights enshrined in the ECHR.[55] Examples of such a predisposed bias include provisions that exclude gay men and lesbians from the army[56] and restrict their right to freedom of expression.[57] The ECtHR has included sexual orientation among the characteristics protected by Article 14, and it has found a violation of the principle of nondiscrimination in cases involving the parental rights of a gay man,[58] the conditions of detention for homosexual prisoners,[59] the restriction of gay men and lesbians' right to freedom of peaceful assembly,[60] the failure to protect gay men and lesbians from bias-motivated violence,[61] the lack of adequate investigations into homophobic physical and verbal attacks,[62] the exclusion of same-sex partners from

---

[50]   For a discussion of early complaints on sexual orientation and ECHR jurisprudence on sexual orientation more generally, see Paul Johnson, *Homosexuality and the European Court of Human Rights* (Routledge 2013).

[51]   *Dudgeon v the United Kingdom* (1981) Series A no 45, para 63.

[52]   ibid, para 60.

[53]   ibid, para 61.

[54]   ibid, para 52.

[55]   *Smith and Grady v the United Kingdom* ECHR 1999-VI, para 97.

[56]   ibid. See also *Lustig-Prean and Beckett v the United Kingdom* App nos 31417/96 and 32377/96 (ECtHR, 27 September 1999).

[57]   *Bayev and Others v Russia* App nos 67667/09, 44092/12, and 56717/12 (ECtHR, 20 June 2017).

[58]   *Salgueiro da Silva Mouta v Portugal* ECHR 1999-IX.

[59]   *X v Turkey* App no 24626/09 (ECtHR, 9 October 2012).

[60]   *Bączkowski and Others v Poland* App no 1543/06 (ECtHR, 3 May 2007); *Alekseyev v Russia* App nos 4916/07, 25924/08, and 14599/09 (ECtHR, 21 October 2010).

[61]   *Identoba and Others v Georgia* App no 73235/12 (ECtHR, 12 May 2015).

[62]   *MC and AC v Romania* App no 12060/12 (ECtHR, 12 April 2016); *Beizaras and Levickas v Lithuania* App no 41288/15 (ECtHR, 14 January 2020). See also *Identoba and Others* (n 61).

a social protection scheme,[63] and the exclusion of the surviving partner of a same-sex couple from the right to succeed to a tenancy.[64]

The principle of nondiscrimination is also embedded in the jurisprudence of the CJEU on sexual orientation. For example, the CJEU has established that statements about the unwillingness to recruit persons of a certain sexual orientation may be indicative of discrimination, even if such statements were made without any legal capacity to represent the employer in recruitment matters[65] or without having opened any recruitment procedure.[66] Moreover, the CJEU has determined that if national legislation does not allow same-sex marriage and the national courts determine that unmarried same-sex couples are in a situation comparable to married different-sex couples, then under the principle of nondiscrimination employees in a same-sex relationship and married employees may not be treated differentially for purposes of recognizing pension benefits[67] and other occupational benefits.[68]

The ECtHR and CJEU have been required to determine whether the ECHR and EU law offer any protection to homosexual asylum seekers who resist being deported to a country of origin that criminalizes same-sex sexual acts. Whereas the ECHR does not recognize a right to asylum, Article 18 of the EU Charter does provide that the right to asylum will be protected with due respect for the rules enshrined in the Geneva Convention, the Treaty on European Union and in the Treaty on the Functioning of the European Union (TFEU). The ECtHR has established that the expulsion of an alien may engage the responsibilities of CoE member states only if there are substantial reasons for believing that the person will be at 'real risk' of death, torture, or other inhuman or degrading treatment in the receiving country. Article 19(2) of the EU Charter transposes this principle into EU law and prohibits any removal, expulsion, or extradition where there is a serious risk of death or other inhuman or degrading treatment or punishment in the receiving country.

The ECtHR has so far maintained that the 'mere existence' of laws that criminalize homosexual acts in a country outside the jurisdiction of the CoE does not constitute a serious ground for believing that homosexual persons would be exposed to inhuman or degrading treatment should they be returned to that country.[69] In order to evaluate complaints lodged by gay and lesbian asylum seekers, the ECtHR will instead consider whether laws criminalizing homo-

---

[63]   *PB and JS v Austria* App no 18984/02 (ECtHR, 22 July 2010).

[64]   *Karner v Austria* ECHR 2003-IX; *Kozak v Poland* App no 13102/02 (ECtHR, 2 March 2010). For a discussion of the principle of nondiscrimination in respect of civil partnerships, see s 7.3.2. For a discussion of the principle of nondiscrimination in respect of adoption, see s 7.3.3.

[65]   Case C-81/12 *Asociaţia Accept v Consiliul Naţional pentru Combaterea Discriminării* EU:C:2013:275.

[66]   Case C-507/18 *NH v Associazione Avvocatura per i Diritti LGBTI – Rete Lenford* EU:C:2020:289.

[67]   Case C-267/06 *Tadao Maruko v Versorgungsanstalt der deutschen Bühnen* [2008] ECR I-01757; Case C-147/08 *Jürgen Römer v Freie und Hansestadt Hamburg* [2011] ECR I-03591.

[68]   Case C-267/12 *Frédéric Hay v Crédit agricole mutuel de Charente-Maritime et des Deux-Sèvres* EU:C:2013:823.

[69]   *B and C v Switzerland* App nos 889/19 and 43987/16 (ECtHR, 17 November 2020) para 59. See also *IIN v the Netherlands* (dec) App no 2035/04 (ECtHR, 9 December 2004); *MKN v Sweden* App no 72413/10 (ECtHR, 27 June 2013); *ME v Sweden* App no 71398/12 (ECtHR, 26 June 2014).

sexuality are 'applied in practice', whether there is a 'real risk' of ill-treatment at the hands of the authorities or 'rogue' officers, and whether individuals who openly express their sexual orientation 'are likely to face discrimination' from state actors.[70]

Similarly, the CJEU has found that the criminalization of homosexual acts does not in itself constitute 'an act of persecution', but the 'term of imprisonment' which accompanies a provision criminalizing homosexual acts does amount to an act of persecution, provided that the provision is actually applied.[71] The CJEU has further determined that in assessing an asylum application, national authorities cannot expect or require applicants to 'conceal' their homosexuality in their country of origin in order to avoid persecution.[72] Moreover, Article 1 (human dignity) and Article 7 of the EU Charter (respect for private and family life) preclude questions that are based solely on 'stereotyped notions' concerning homosexuality[73] and pro- hibit national authorities from accepting evidence such as the performance of homosexual acts by asylum seekers or audio-visual material in which asylum seekers perform homosexual acts in order to prove their sexual orientation.[74] The CJEU has also barred national authorities from assessing asylum seekers' sexual orientation on the basis of contentious 'projective personality tests', whose reliability is disputed by the scientific community.[75]

7.2.2 Transgender men and women have repeatedly complained to the ECtHR about national legislation that prevents them from having their gender identity recognized by law. In *Christine Goodwin v the United Kingdom*, the ECtHR established that the impossibility for a post-operative transgender woman to have her gender reassignment legally recognized for all purposes amounted to a violation of her right to respect for her private life. Indeed, the ECtHR interpreted Article 8 as securing the right of post-operative transgender persons to 'establish details of their identity as individual human beings', and it held that post-operative transgender persons' right to 'personal development' and to 'physical and moral security' could not be regarded as a matter of 'controversy'.[76] Moreover, the ECtHR found that there was no justification for barring post-operative transgender persons from marrying a person of a different sex and denied that Article 12—securing the right to marry—should be interpreted in light of 'purely biological criteria'.[77]

The ECtHR has applied these principles in relation to three key issues concerning gender identity. First, the ECtHR has found a violation of Article 8 in respect of legislation that recog-

---

[70]   *B and C* (n 69) para 59.

[71]   Joined Cases C-199/12 to C-201/12 *Minister voor Immigratie en Asiel v X and Y and Z v Minister voor Immigratie en Asiel* EU:C:2013:720, para 61.

[72]   ibid, para 76.

[73]   Joined Cases C-148/13 to C-150/13 *A and Others v Staatssecretaris van Veiligheid en Justitie* EU:C:2014:2406, para 72.

[74]   ibid.

[75]   Case C-473/16 *F v Bevándorlási és Állampolgársági Hivatal* EU:C:2018:36, para 71.

[76]   *Christine Goodwin v the United Kingdom* [GC] ECHR 2002-VI, para 90.

[77]   ibid, paras 100–104.

nizes transgender persons' right to gender reassignment but fails to regulate access to gender reassignment surgery. If the recognition of the new gender for all legal purposes is conditional on full gender reassignment surgery, the existence of such a legislative gap exposes transgender persons to a situation of 'distressing uncertainty' incompatible with their right to respect for their private life.[78] Secondly, the ECtHR has held that a refusal to allow a transgender person to change her forename during the gender transition process, and before completing her gender reassignment surgery, may amount to a disproportionate interference with her right to respect for her private life.[79]

Thirdly, the ECtHR has established that the criteria regulating gender reassignment must not infringe the right of transgender persons to 'physical integrity'.[80] For instance, the ECtHR found Turkish legislation on gender reassignment in breach of Article 8, because it granted access to gender reassignment surgery only to those who were already unable to procreate, and it subjected individuals to an interference with their private life that could not be deemed necessary in a democratic society.[81] In *AP, Garçon and Nicot v France* the ECtHR heard a complaint against the requirement that, inter alia, transgender persons undergo sterilizing surgery or treatment in order to obtain full legal recognition of their gender identity.[82] The ECtHR held that this requirement infringed the applicants' right to respect for their intimate 'identity' and 'physical integrity'.[83] The ECtHR noted that in subordinating the recognition of the applicants' gender identity to sterilization surgery or treatment, national authorities made 'the full exercise of their right to respect for their private life' dependent on 'their relinquishing full exercise of their right to respect for their physical integrity'.[84] Thus, French legislation presented the applicants with an 'impossible dilemma',[85] in violation of their Article 8 rights. National authorities are allowed to make gender reassignment conditional on a psychiatric or other medical diagnosis but cannot force transgender persons to undergo sterilization surgery or treatment against their wishes in order to obtain full legal recognition of their identity.

The CJEU has established that the principle of equal treatment for men and women also protects transgender men and women from discrimination. Thus, discrimination arising from gender reassignment qualifies as sex discrimination, and the CJEU has noted that to tolerate a similar discrimination would be tantamount to 'a failure to respect the dignity and freedom' to which transgender persons are entitled.[86] In particular, the principle of equal treatment

---

[78]   *L v Lithuania* ECHR 2007-IV, para 59.

[79]   *SV v Italy* App no 55216/08 (ECtHR, 11 October 2018) para 75.

[80]   *YY v Turkey* ECHR 2015 (extracts) para 119.

[81]   ibid, paras 102–22. On the criteria to access gender reassignment surgery, see also *YT v Bulgaria* App no 41701/16 (ECtHR, 9 July 2020).

[82]   *AP, Garçon and Nicot v France* App nos 79885/12, 52471/13, and 52596/13 (ECtHR, 6 April 2017) para 120.

[83]   ibid, para 123.

[84]   ibid, para 131.

[85]   ibid, para 132.

[86]   Case C-13/94 *P v S and Cornwall County Council* [1996] ECR I-02143, para 22.

precludes legislation that requires transgender persons to satisfy additional criteria in order to be able to claim a social security benefit recognized to workers of their acquired gender.[87]

7.3   MARRIAGE AND FAMILY

7.3.1 Article 12 ECHR guarantees '[m]en and women' the 'right to marry and to found a family, according to the national laws governing the exercise of this right'. Over the years the ECtHR has developed jurisprudence on a number of issues concerning the right to marry and has established that there is a 'close affinity' between Article 12 and the right to respect for private and family life secured by Article 8.[88] Although the ECtHR has sometimes engaged in an evolutive interpretation of Article 12, it has maintained a very restrained approach to the issue of whether the ECHR secures the right to divorce.

A key principle shaping ECHR jurisprudence on marriage and divorce is that Article 12 covers only 'the formation of marital relationships' and not their 'dissolution'.[89] In *Johnston and Others v Ireland* the ECtHR noted that the preparatory works to the ECHR did not disclose any intention to include the right to have the ties of marriage dissolved by divorce, and it concluded that Article 12 could not be interpreted as imposing on national authorities an obligation to recognize a right to divorce.[90] Despite acknowledging that divorce is permitted in the majority of CoE member states, the ECtHR recalled the principle that it is not possible to derive from the ECHR 'a right that was not included therein at the outset'.[91] However, the ECtHR has later established that if national legislation allows divorce, Article 12 secures for divorced persons the right to remarry without 'unreasonable restrictions'[92] or insurmountable obstacles.[93] Likewise, if national legislation allows divorce, Article 12 requires national authorities to conduct divorce proceedings efficiently and within a reasonable time.[94]

In *Babiarz v Poland* the ECtHR reiterated the principle that the ECHR does not enshrine a right to divorce. The applicant complained about his inability to obtain a divorce from his wife and to marry his current partner, who was also the mother of his child. Under Polish legislation in force at that time, a divorce could not be granted if it had been requested by the

---

[87]   Case C-451/16 *MB v Secretary of State for Work and Pensions* EU:C:2018:492. On social security benefits, see also Case C-117/01 *KB v National Health Service Pensions Agency and Secretary of State for Health* [2004] ECR I-00541; Case C-423/04 *Sarah Margaret Richards v Secretary of State for Work and Pensions* [2006] ECR I-03585.

[88]   *Jaremowicz v Poland* App no 24023/03 (ECtHR, 5 January 2010) para 50. For an overview of ECHR jurisprudence on Article 12, see European Court of Human Rights, 'Guide on Article 12 of the European Convention on Human Rights' (31 August 2021).

[89]   *Johnston and Others v Ireland* (1986) Series A no 112, para 52.

[90]   ibid, paras 51–4.

[91]   ibid, para 53.

[92]   *F v Switzerland* (1987) Series A no 128, para 38.

[93]   *Ivanov and Petrova v Bulgaria* App no 15001/04 (ECtHR, 14 June 2011) para 61.

[94]   See, for instance, *VK v Croatia* App no 38380/08 (ECtHR, 27 November 2012); *Chernetskiy v Ukraine* App no 44316/07 (ECtHR, 8 December 2016).

party whose fault it was that the marriage had broken down and the other party refused to consent, unless a court decided to override the refusal of the 'innocent' party.[95] In *Babiarz* the applicant's wife had refused to consent and the national courts had decided to not override her refusal. The ECtHR accepted that the applicant was in a 'stable relationship' with his child's mother and noted that even domestic courts had acknowledged the 'complete and irretrievable' breakdown of his marriage with his wife.[96] However, the ECtHR denied that the requirement of consent from the 'innocent' party represented an insurmountable obstacle to obtaining a divorce and it noted that the applicant was not prevented from submitting a fresh petition for divorce to the national courts, asking them to override his wife's refusal. Thus, the ECtHR ruled that the ECHR could not be interpreted as guaranteeing a 'favourable outcome in divorce proceedings' and concluded that the applicant could not claim a violation of his ECHR rights.[97]

The ECtHR reasoning in *Babiarz* attracted considerable criticism, and two judges filed dissenting opinions which identify key shortcomings in the ECtHR judgment. According to the dissenting judges, the ECtHR can be seen as taking a 'one-sided' approach, which fails to achieve a balance between the rights of the applicant and the interests of the applicant's wife.[98] Moreover, the ECtHR arguably recognized a 'right to family life with a specific person against that person's will'[99] and completely disregarded the 'autonomy-based' demands of the other person to be free and move on with his own life.[100] As a consequence, this judgment arguably allows national authorities to favour the enforcement of morals over the protection of individuals' rights and to enforce a legal fiction which bears no resemblance to the spouses' lived reality. As Judge Sajó pointed out, forcing people to live in a broken marriage can be seen as an 'impermissible intrusion' into individuals' private lives.[101] Thus, in *Babiarz* the ECtHR espoused a restrained interpretation of the ECHR which arguably does not offer substantive safeguards to spouses who are trapped in a marriage gone wrong.

7.3.2 In *Schalk and Kopf v Austria* the ECtHR considered whether Article 12 protects the right to marry a partner of the same sex, and it developed a number of principles that still orient ECHR jurisprudence on same-sex marriage. The ECtHR held that Article 12 must be interpreted in light of the historical context in which the ECHR was adopted, and it concluded that the reference to 'men and women' in Article 12 is 'deliberate' and aimed at securing marriage 'in the traditional sense of being a union between partners of different sex'.[102] Despite acknowledging that over the years the institution of marriage had undergone 'major social

---

[95] *Babiarz v Poland* App no 1955/10 (ECtHR, 10 January 2017) para 17.

[96] ibid, para 54.

[97] ibid, para 56.

[98] ibid, dissenting opinion of Judge Pinto de Albuquerque, para 34.

[99] ibid, dissenting opinion of Judge Sajó, para 6.

[100] ibid, para 7.

[101] ibid, para 23.

[102] *Schalk and Kopf v Austria* ECHR 2010, para 55.

changes',[103] the ECtHR noted that there was no European consensus on same-sex marriage, and it further recalled that marriage has 'deep-rooted social and cultural connotations which may differ largely from one society to another'.[104] On this basis, the ECtHR concluded that Article 12 could not be interpreted as granting same-sex couples access to marriage.[105] The ECtHR strengthened the principles developed in *Schalk and Kopf* in subsequent judgments.[106] For example, in *Hämäläinen v Finland* the ECtHR reiterated that Article 12 enshrines the 'traditional concept of marriage as being between a man and a woman',[107] and in *Orlandi and Others v Italy* it found that member states are 'still free […] to restrict access to marriage to different-sex couples'.[108]

Although Article 12 does not enshrine a right to marry a same-sex partner, same-sex couples living in a stable *de facto* partnership fall within the notion of private and family life protected under Article 8,[109] and, admittedly, they are 'in need of legal recognition and protection of their relationship'.[110] For example, in *Oliari and Others v Italy* the ECtHR ruled that the failure of Italian authorities to recognize and protect same-sex relationships through a 'specific legal framework'—as through civil partnerships—amounted to a violation of the applicants' right to respect for their family life.[111] In *Taddeucci and McCall v Italy*, the second applicant complained about the fact that national authorities had refused to grant him a residence permit for family reasons on the ground that he was not married to the first applicant and that an unmarried partner could not qualify as a 'family member'. The ECtHR acknowledged that the applicants had been treated in the same way as unmarried different-sex couples and that there was no direct discrimination against them. However, the ECtHR recalled that, at the time the events unfolded, Italian legislation did not provide for any form of legal recognition of same-sex relationships and the second applicant had 'no legal means' of being recognized as a 'family member' in relation to the first applicant.[112] On this basis, the ECtHR concluded that Italian legislation on residency rights amounted to indirect discrimination on grounds of sexual orientation.[113]

---

[103]   ibid, para 58.

[104]   ibid, para 62.

[105]   ibid, paras 63–4.

[106]   See *Oliari and Others v Italy* App nos 18766/11 and 36030/11 (ECtHR, 21 July 2015); *Chapin and Charpentier v France* App no 40183/07 (ECtHR, 9 June 2016).

[107]   *Hämäläinen v Finland* [GC] ECHR 2014, para 96.

[108]   *Orlandi and Others v Italy* App nos 26431/12, 26742/12, 44057/12, and 60088/12 (ECtHR, 14 December 2017) para 192.

[109]   *Schalk and Kopf* (n 102) para 94.

[110]   *Oliari and Others* (n 106) para 165.

[111]   ibid, para 185. See also *Orlandi and Others* (n 108) paras 210–11.

[112]   *Taddeucci and McCall v Italy* App no 51362/09 (ECtHR, 30 June 2016) para 95.

[113]   ibid, paras 96–9.

7.3.3 The ECtHR has established key principles in relation to the use and regulation of techniques of medically assisted procreation. The ECtHR has acknowledged that the notion of private and family life incorporates the right to respect for the 'decision to become genetic parents'.[114] However, the ECtHR has also found that national authorities enjoy a wide margin of appreciation in regulating *in vitro* fertilization techniques, which give rise to 'sensitive moral and ethical issues against a background of fast-moving medical and scientific developments'.[115] As a consequence, the ECtHR is very cautious in imposing negative and positive obligations in respect of medically assisted procreation.

In *Evans v the United Kingdom* the ECtHR held that, in the absence of European consensus on this issue, national authorities could legitimately allow either partner in a couple to withdraw their consent to the storage and use of embryos before these are implanted in the uterus.[116] The applicant had been diagnosed with ovarian tumour and before undergoing surgery to remove her ovaries she and her former partner had created six embryos. However, after the surgery their relationship fell apart and the applicant's former partner withdrew his consent to the continued storage and implantation of the embryos. Before the ECtHR, the applicant argued that the requirement that these embryos be destroyed violated her right to respect for her private and family life and deprived her of the chance to have a child to whom she is biologically related.[117] The ECtHR acknowledged that this case entailed a 'conflict' between the Article 8 rights of two individuals, whose interests are 'irreconcilable'.[118] The ECtHR expressed 'great sympathy' for the applicant's desire to have a child to whom she is genetically related, but it concluded that 'the applicant's right to respect for the decision to become a parent in the genetic sense' should not prevail over her former partner's right 'to respect for his decision not to have a genetically related child with her'.[119] On this basis, the ECtHR concluded that there was no violation of the applicant's rights under Article 8.

The ECtHR has established that, in the absence of a clear European consensus, national legislation prohibiting heterologous techniques of artificial procreation does not amount to a violation of the ECHR.[120] In *SH and Others v Austria* two different-sex couples challenged the existence of a total ban on using gametes external to the couple for the purposes of *in vitro* fertilization, and they claimed a violation of their right to respect for their private and family life.[121] The ECtHR held that the solution chosen by the Austrian legislature was extremely

---

[114] *Dickson v the United Kingdom* [GC] ECHR 2007-V, para 66.

[115] *SH and Others v Austria* [GC] ECHR 2011, para 97.

[116] *Evans v the United Kingdom* [GC] ECHR 2007-I, para 92. The Grand Chamber confirmed the findings of the Chamber. See *Evans v the United Kingdom* App no 6339/05 (ECtHR, 7 March 2006).

[117] The applicant also invoked Article 2, but the Court concluded that there was no violation of that provision.

[118] *Evans* [GC] (n 116) para 73.

[119] ibid, para 90.

[120] *SH and Others* (n 115) paras 115–16. The Grand Chamber reversed the findings of the Chamber, which had found a violation of Article 14 taken in conjunction with Article 8. See *SH and Others v Austria* App no 57813/00 (ECtHR, 1 April 2010).

[121] *SH and Others* (n 115) para 49.

cautious, noting that a number of CoE member states allowed ovum and sperm donation for *in vitro* fertilization. Nevertheless, the ECtHR determined that there was no 'sufficiently established European consensus',[122] and it concluded that the legal framework regulating *in vitro* fertilization in Austria did not exceed the margin of appreciation available to national authorities.[123] In reaching this conclusion, the ECtHR attached great importance to the fact that Austrian legislation reflected the then 'current state of medical science and the consensus in society',[124] and it invited Austrian authorities to take medical and social developments into account in any future assessment of the criteria regulating *in vitro* fertilization. Moreover, the ECtHR reiterated the well-established principles that the ECHR must be interpreted 'in the light of current circumstances' and that CoE member states need to keep under review areas in which 'the law appears to be continuously evolving' and which are 'subject to a particularly dynamic development in science and law'.[125] Such remarks indicate that ECHR jurisprudence in this area is still evolving and that, in the future, the ECtHR may interpret the right to respect for private and family life as imposing an obligation on national authorities to not interfere with the right of infertile couples to avail themselves of heterologous techniques of artificial procreation.

The principle of nondiscrimination enshrined in Article 14 applies to additional rights 'falling within the general scope of any Convention Article, for which the State has voluntarily decided to provide'.[126] The right to adopt or access adoption is not included among the rights protected by the ECHR, but the ECtHR has accepted that 'the right to establish and develop relationships with other human beings' falls within the ambit of Article 8.[127] Thus, the ECtHR has interpreted Article 14, taken in conjunction with Article 8, as prohibiting differences in treatment on the grounds of sexual orientation as regards the conditions to access adoption.[128] Once a state decides to allow adoption by single persons, access to adoption must become accessible to both heterosexual persons and homosexual persons.[129] Once a state decides to allow adoption by unmarried couples, national authorities may not discriminate between unmarried different-sex couples and unmarried same-sex couples who are in a relevantly similar situation.[130] However, if a state prohibits same-sex marriage and allows certain types of adoption only by married couples, the principle of nondiscrimination does not forbid a difference in treatment between unmarried same-sex couples and married different-sex couples.[131]

---

[122]   ibid, para 106.

[123]   ibid, para 115.

[124]   ibid, para 117.

[125]   ibid, para 118.

[126]   *EB v France* [GC] App no 43546/02 (ECtHR, 22 January 2008) para 48.

[127]   ibid, para 43.

[128]   For an overview of ECHR jurisprudence on adoption, see Bernadette Rainey, Pamela McCormick, and Clare Ovey, *The European Convention on Human Rights* (8th edn, OUP 2021) 391–3.

[129]   *EB* (n 126) paras 85–98.

[130]   *X and Others v Austria* [GC] ECHR 2013, paras 152–3.

[131]   *Gas and Dubois v France* ECHR 2012, paras 61–73.

8
Employment, social protection, the environment

8.1   EMPLOYMENT

8.1.1 The EU Charter protects employers' freedoms and workers' rights in the context of industrial relations. On the one hand, Article 16 protects the 'freedom to conduct a business' and the EU Charter's preamble enshrines 'freedom of establishment' and the principle of 'free movement of persons, services, goods and capital'.[1] On the other hand, Article 12 recognizes 'the right of everyone to form and to join trade unions for the protection of his or her interests', Article 27 protects workers' right to 'information and consultation within the undertaking', and Article 28 secures the right of 'collective bargaining and action' between employers and workers or their respective organizations. Economic integration stands at the heart of the EU project and EU law has generally sought to balance different economic interests and rights. As a consequence, over the years the CJEU has been repeatedly called on to strike a balance between the protection of workers' fundamental rights and the protection of employers' economic freedoms secured by the EU Charter and EU law.

In the *International Transport Workers' Federation and Finnish Seamen's Union* case the CJEU was asked to balance the protection of workers' right to undertake collective actions with the protection of employers' freedom of establishment. In this case a Finnish ferry operator decided to reflag one of its ferries by registering it in Estonia, where crew wages were lower. As a result, the Finnish Seamen's Union and the International Transport Workers' Federation undertook boycott actions against the company and the CJEU was called on to determine whether these industrial actions were compatible with the principle of free movement of persons, services, and capital.[2] Although this case did not concern the interpretation of the EU Charter, the CJEU recalled that the right to take collective action is a 'fundamental right' and the protection of workers is a 'legitimate interest' which may justify an interference with the

---

[1]   Freedom of establishment and freedom to provide services within the EU are also protected by Article 49 and Article 63 TFEU, respectively. For an overview of economic issues in EU law, see Damian Chalmers and Anthony Arnull (eds), *The Oxford Handbook of European Union Law* (OUP 2015) part IV.

[2]   Case C-438/05 *International Transport Workers' Federation and Finnish Seamen's Union v Viking Line ABP and OÜ Viking Line Eesti* [2007] ECR I-10779.

principle of free movement of goods and services.[3] However, restrictions on the principle of free movement will be justified only insofar as the restriction is 'suitable' to achieve a 'legitimate objective' and 'does not go beyond what is necessary to achieve that objective'.[4] Trade unions must therefore satisfy three conditions when undertaking collective actions. First, collective actions must pursue a legitimate interest under EU and national law. Second, the choice of collective action must be suitable for the aim pursued. Third, trade unions must adopt means that are proportionate to the aim pursued, and it is up to the domestic courts to determine whether there are other appropriate and suitable means at the trade unions' disposal which are less restrictive of employers' freedom of establishment.[5] Thus, in this case the CJEU identified substantial limitations on the lawfulness of collective actions with a view to protecting employers' fundamental economic freedoms.[6]

In *AGET Iraklis* the CJEU developed key criteria on the circumstances under which national authorities may interfere with employers' freedom to conduct their business in the context of collective redundancies.[7] The CJEU reiterated that the notion of freedom to conduct a business 'must be viewed in relation to its social function'[8] and may be subject to a broad range of interventions that pursue 'the public interest'.[9] In particular, the protection of workers and the 'maintenance of employment' are legitimate reasons for interfering with employers' freedoms,[10] and the CJEU noted that the introduction of legislation regulating collective redundancies cannot, in principle, be considered to affect the 'essence' of the freedom to conduct a business.[11] However, the CJEU recalled that the 'promotion of the national economy or its proper functioning' cannot justify restrictions on the freedom of establishment and on the freedom to conduct a business,[12] not even in times of acute economic crisis and high unemployment. Moreover, the legal framework regulating collective redundancies must be founded on 'precise', 'objective', and 'verifiable' conditions[13] that clearly identify under what circumstances national authorities may use their power to interfere with employers' freedoms.

8.1.2 Article 31(1) of the EU Charter establishes that every worker has 'the right to working conditions which respect his or her health, safety and dignity' and Article 31(2) of the EU

---

[3] ibid, paras 44–5.

[4] ibid, para 90.

[5] ibid, para 87.

[6] See also Case C-341/05 *Laval un Partneri Ltd v Svenska Byggnadsarbetareförbundet and Others* [2007] ECR I-11767.

[7] Case C-201/15 *Anonymi Geniki Etairia Tsimenton Iraklis (AGET Iraklis) v Ypourgos Ergasias, Koinonikis Asfalisis kai Koinonikis Allilengyis* EU:C:2016:972.

[8] ibid, para 85.

[9] ibid, para 86.

[10] ibid, para 75.

[11] ibid, para 84.

[12] ibid, para 72. See also ibid, para 97.

[13] ibid, para 100.

Charter protects 'the right to limitation of maximum working hours, to daily and weekly rest periods and to an annual period of paid leave'. As is the case with other EU Charter provisions, EU legal instruments on health and safety, and the jurisprudence the CJEU had developed in this regard before the EU Charter entered into force, underpin the content of Article 31.[14]

In the *United Kingdom v Council* case the CJEU denied that the concept of 'health and safety' refers exclusively to physical conditions and risks in the workplace. On the contrary, the CJEU held that the notion of health and safety includes 'certain aspects of the organization of working time' and must be interpreted in accordance with the World Health Organization's definition of health as a 'state of complete physical, mental and social well-being'.[15] The effective protection of workers' health and safety requires that workers be entitled to 'actual rest', and the CJEU has determined that the minimum period of paid annual leave cannot be replaced by an allowance in lieu, except upon termination of the employment relationship.[16]

In *Robinson-Steele* the CJEU established that workers must receive their normal remuneration during periods of leave, so that they are in a position 'comparable to periods of work'.[17] In *Williams and Others* the CJEU strengthened this principle and determined that the remuneration received during leave must take into account 'any inconvenient aspect which is linked intrinsically to the performance of the tasks which the worker is required to carry out under his contract of employment and in respect of which a monetary amount is provided'.[18] By contrast, the remuneration received during leave will not take into account the components of the total remuneration which exclusively cover 'occasional or ancillary costs' arising at the time of the worker's performance.[19] It is up to national courts to determine which components of the worker's total remuneration are intrinsically linked to the performance of the tasks that she or he is required to carry out, but the criteria identified by the CJEU provide an essential guideline for adjudicating disputes on the level of remuneration for periods of rest and leave.

The right of every worker to paid leave must be regarded as a 'particularly important principle' that admits no derogations,[20] and the CJEU has established that the right to annual leave

---

[14]   In particular, see Council Directive 89/391/EEC of 12 June 1989 on the introduction of measures to encourage improvements in the safety and health of workers at work [1989] OJ L 183/1; Council Directive 93/104/EC of 23 November 1993 concerning certain aspects of the organization of working time [1993] OJ L 307/18 (no longer in force); Directive 2003/88/EC of the European Parliament and of the Council of 4 November 2003 concerning certain aspects of the organisation of working time [2003] OJ L 299/9. See also Explanations relating to the Charter of Fundamental Rights [2007] OJ C 303/17, Article 31.

[15]   Case C-84/94 *United Kingdom of Great Britain and Northern Ireland v Council of the European Union* [1996] ECR I-05755, para 15.

[16]   Joined Cases C-131/04 and C-257/04 *CD Robinson-Steele v RD Retail Services Ltd and Others* [2006] ECR I-02531, para 60.

[17]   ibid, para 59.

[18]   Case C-155/10 *Williams and Others v British Airways plc* [2011] ECR I-08409, para 24.

[19]   ibid, para 25.

[20]   Case C-118/13 *Gülay Bollacke v K + K Klaas & Kock BV & Co KG* EU:C:2014:1755, para 15; see also Joined Cases C-569/16 and C-570/16 *Stadt Wuppertal v Maria Elisabeth Bauer and Volker Willmeroth v Martina Broßonn* EU:C:2018:871, para 38.

includes the right to receive an allowance in lieu of annual leave not taken upon termination of the employment relationship.[21] For instance, if a worker dies, his or her legal heirs have the right to receive a monetary allowance in lieu of the right to paid annual leave the worker acquired before dying.[22] Moreover, if the worker has been unable to take his or her leave due to reasons beyond his or her control, the right to paid annual leave cannot be forfeited at the end of the leave year or at the end of a carryover period fixed by national law.[23]

8.2   SOCIAL PROTECTION

8.2.1 ECHR organs have adjudicated complaints on a wide range of issues concerning social security benefits.[24] The applicants in these cases often invoked Article 1 of Protocol 1 ECHR (protection of property, P1-1), taken alone or in conjunction with other provisions. P1-1 secures for every natural or juristic person the right to 'peaceful enjoyment of his possessions', and the concept of possessions has been interpreted to cover both 'existing possessions' and claims in respect of which the applicant can argue a 'legitimate expectation' under domestic law.[25] The ECtHR is aware that many individuals in contemporary societies are 'completely dependent for survival on social security and welfare benefits'.[26] Nevertheless, the ECHR has a subsidiary role, and national authorities are in principle 'better placed' to determine what is in the public interest on social or economic grounds.[27] As a consequence, the ECtHR is likely to apply strict scrutiny only in circumstances in which the applicants are left with hardly any type of social security coverage or in which national authorities impose particularly harsh policies that lack any objective and reasonable justification.

The ECtHR's approach to complaints about social security benefits under P1-1 is based on three key principles. First, insofar as an individual has 'an assertable right under domestic law' to a welfare benefit, that interest will amount to a pecuniary right within the meaning of P1-1.[28] P1-1 does not include 'a right to acquire property' and places 'no restriction' on the freedom of national authorities to decide 'whether or not to have in place any form of social security

---

[21]   *Stadt Wuppertal* (n 20) para 58.

[22]   ibid, para 62. See also *Gülay Bollacke* (n 20).

[23]   Case C-214/16 *Conley King v The Sash Window Workshop Ltd and Richard Dollar* EU:C:2017:914, para 56. See also Joined Cases C-350/06 and C-520/06 *Gerhard Schultz-Hoff v Deutsche Rentenversicherung Bund* [2009] ECR I-00179.

[24]   For an overview of early complaints, see Ana Gómez Heredero, 'Social Security as a Human Right' (Council of Europe Publishing 2007) Council of Europe Human Rights Files no 23.

[25]   *Slivenko and Others v Latvia* (dec) [GC] ECHR 2002-II (extracts) para 121.

[26]   *Stec and Others v the United Kingdom* (dec) [GC] ECHR 2005-X, para 51.

[27]   *Stec and Others v the United Kingdom* [GC] ECHR 2006-VI, para 52; *Valkov and Others v Bulgaria* App nos 2033/04, 19125/04, 19475/04, 19490/04, 19495/04, 19497/04, 24729/04, 171/05, and 2041/05 (ECtHR, 25 October 2011) para 91.

[28]   *Stec and Others* (n 26) para 51.

scheme'.[29] However, if national authorities introduce legislation providing for the payment of welfare benefits, that legislation will generate a proprietary interest that falls within the scope of P1-1.[30] In this context, P1-1 applies to social security benefits, 'whether conditional or not on the prior payment of contributions',[31] and it prohibits inequalities of treatment based on distinctions which appear 'illogical or unsustainable'.[32]

Second, P1-1 cannot be interpreted as securing the right to a benefit of 'a particular amount' or type.[33] On this basis, the ECtHR dismissed complaints challenging reductions in public-sector wages[34] and public pension benefits.[35] In doing this, the ECtHR reiterated that public pension systems are based on 'the principle of solidarity between contributors and beneficiaries',[36] and it accepted that national authorities may, in order to achieve the redistributive function of pension schemes, impose a 'reasonable and commensurate' reduction of certain pension benefits.[37] However, reductions of benefits must not infringe 'the essence' of individuals' rights under P1-1, and national authorities must strike a fair balance between 'the general interest of the community' and 'the protection of the individual's fundamental rights'.[38] For instance, in *Kjartan Ásmundsson v Iceland* the ECtHR upheld the complaint of a disabled man against the discontinuation of his disability pension on the basis that the decision to interrupt the payment of this pension 'totally deprived' him of a benefit that he had been receiving for 20 years,[39] and it placed on him an 'excessive and disproportionate burden' which could not be justified by the legitimate interests of the community.[40]

Third, social security and welfare schemes must operate in a manner which does not give rise to discriminatory treatment. The ECtHR has repeatedly held that differences in the enjoy-

---

[29]   *Stec and Others* (n 27) para 53.

[30]   *Stec and Others* (n 26) para 54.

[31]   ibid.

[32]   ibid, para 49.

[33]   *Kjartan Ásmundsson v Iceland* ECHR 2004-IX, para 39. See also *Stec and Others* (n 27) para 53.

[34]   *Koufaki and Adedy v Greece* (dec) App nos 57665/12 and 57657/12 (ECtHR, 7 May 2013).

[35]   For example, see *Goudswaard-van der Lans v the Netherlands* (dec) ECHR 2005-XI; *Valkov and Others* (n 27); *da Conceição Mateus and Santos Januário v Portugal* (dec) App nos 62235/12 and 57725/12 (ECtHR, 8 October 2013).

[36]   *Valkov and Others* (n 27) para 98.

[37]   ibid, para 97.

[38]   *Kjartan Ásmundsson* (n 33) paras 39–40. See also *Bélané Nagy v Hungary* [GC] App no 53080/13 (ECtHR, 13 December 2016); *Baczúr v Hungary* App no 8263/15 (ECtHR, 7 March 2017). For a discussion, see Ingrid Leijten, 'The Right to Minimum Subsistence and Property Protection under the ECHR: Never the Twain Shall Meet?' (2019) 21 *European Journal of Social Security* 307; Bernadette Rainey, Pamela McCormick, and Clare Ovey, *The European Convention on Human Rights* (8th edn, OUP 2021) 566–8 and 583.

[39]   *Kjartan Ásmundsson* (n 33) para 44.

[40]   ibid, para 45.

ment or entitlement of social security benefits that are exclusively based on nationality[41] or sex[42] are likely to amount to a violation of Article 14 (prohibition of discrimination). However, the ECtHR has also established that in measures of 'economic or social strategy' national authorities enjoy a wide margin of appreciation in assessing whether differences in otherwise similar situations justify a difference in treatment, and the ECtHR will respect the legislature's assessment unless it is 'manifestly without reasonable foundation'.[43] On this basis, in *Stec and Others v the United Kingdom* the ECtHR dismissed a complaint against differences in state pensionable age between men and women. The ECtHR noted that such a difference had been originally introduced with the legitimate aim to 'correct the disadvantaged economic position of women', and it ultimately concluded that a state's decision on when to remove an inequality and by what means fell within the margin of appreciation available to national authorities.[44]

8.2.2 The ECtHR has established that Article 8 (right to respect for private and family life) does not recognize a right 'to be provided with a home', and whether national authorities provide for housing benefits is a matter for political decision.[45] National authorities are entitled to adopt policies and legal measures that seek to achieve 'greater social justice' in the sphere of housing, and the ECtHR has acknowledged that eliminating social injustices is a function of democratic societies.[46]

Article 8 protects the right of individuals to respect for their 'existing' homes.[47] The ECtHR has established that the definition of 'home' is 'a question of fact' that 'does not depend on the lawfulness of the occupation under domestic law'.[48] In accordance with ECHR jurisprudence on Article 8, any interference with individuals' right to respect for their home must be in accordance with the law, must pursue a legitimate aim, and must be necessary in a democratic society.[49] The discretion available to national authorities on housing policies is generally wide, but it will be narrower in cases where the interference encroaches on the individual's 'effective enjoyment of intimate or key rights' or seriously affects 'rights of central importance to the individual's identity, self-determination, physical and moral integrity, maintenance of relationships with others and a settled and secure place in the community'.[50] Individuals who are

---

[41]   For example, see *Gaygusuz v Austria* ECHR 1996-IV; *Koua Poirrez v France* ECHR 2003-X; *Luczak v Poland* App no 77782/01 (ECtHR, 27 November 2007); *Andrejeva v Latvia* [GC] ECHR 2009.

[42]   For example, see *Wessels-Bergervoet v the Netherlands* ECHR 2002-IV; *Willis v the United Kingdom* ECHR 2002-IV.

[43]   *Stec and Others* (n 27) para 52.

[44]   ibid, para 66.

[45]   *Chapman v the United Kingdom* [GC] ECHR 2001-I, para 99.

[46]   *James and Others v the United Kingdom* (1986) Series A no 98, para 47.

[47]   Laurens Lavrysen, 'Strengthening the Protection of Human Rights of Persons Living in Poverty under the ECHR' (2015) 33 *Netherlands Quarterly of Human Rights* 293, 300.

[48]   *McCann v the United Kingdom* ECHR 2008, para 46.

[49]   ibid, paras 48–9.

[50]   *Yordanova and Others v Bulgaria* App no 25446/06 (ECtHR, 24 April 2012) para 118.

at risk of eviction as a consequence of measures adopted by national authorities should be able to have the proportionality and reasonableness of these measures reviewed by an independent tribunal.[51] In the absence of convincing arguments justifying the actions of national authorities, the ECtHR may infer that the state's interest in controlling its property should 'come second' to the applicant's right to respect for his or her home.[52]

In *Yordanova and Others v Bulgaria* the ECtHR considered a complaint concerning a removal order served on a group of applicants of Roma origin who, without authorization, had built their homes on land owned by the municipality.[53] The ECtHR deemed Article 8 to be applicable and developed general considerations on the obligations of national authorities to protect marginalized minorities from extreme economic deprivation. The ECtHR noted, in the first place, that national authorities had tolerated that specific settlement for decades, and it held that situations where a 'whole community and a long period' are concerned must be treated as being 'entirely different' from cases of removal of an individual from unlawfully occupied property.[54] In the second place, the ECtHR held that the authorities' refusal to take into account the specific needs of the Roma community was problematic because it failed to recognize the applicants as a socially disadvantaged group that required assistance in order to effectively enjoy their ECHR rights in the same way as the majority population.[55] In the third place, the ECtHR confirmed that Article 8 does not protect a right to be provided with a home and does not impose an obligation to 'tolerate unlawful land occupation indefinitely'[56] but imposes 'an obligation to secure shelter to particularly vulnerable individuals' in exceptional cases.[57] In the absence of reliable and adequate plans to provide the applicants with alternative accommodation or housing, the ECtHR concluded that the enforcement of the removal order would amount to a violation of the applicants' ECHR rights.[58]

In conclusion, national authorities enjoy a wide margin of appreciation in matters concerning housing policy, and they have discretion in setting out the criteria according to which housing benefits are allocated.[59] However, in exceptional cases Article 8 imposes on national authorities an obligation to provide shelter and appropriate assistance to disadvantaged groups and individuals who are at risk of extreme vulnerability due to their socioeconomic status.

8.2.3 Another key issue considered by the ECtHR in the realm of social protection is whether aliens can claim a right to not be removed to countries that do not meet basic socio-

---

[51]   *McCann* (n 48) para 50.

[52]   *Yordanova and Others* (n 50) para 118.

[53]   ibid, paras 10–11.

[54]   ibid, para 121.

[55]   ibid, para 129.

[56]   ibid, para 131.

[57]   ibid, para 130.

[58]   On the eviction of travellers, see also *Chapman* (n 45); *Winterstein and Others v France* App no 27013/07 (ECtHR, 17 October 2013). For a discussion, see Rainey, McCormick, and Ovey (n 38) 430–33.

[59]   See *Bah v the United Kingdom* ECHR 2011, para 49.

economic and humanitarian standards. Two general principles underpin ECHR jurisprudence on this complex matter. Firstly, migrants cannot, in principle, claim any entitlement to remain in the territory of a CoE member state in order to benefit from 'medical, social or other forms of assistance and services' provided by that state.[60] Secondly, in circumstances where there are 'compelling' humanitarian grounds against the removal, a state's obligations under Article 3 (prohibition of torture) may be engaged.[61] Article 3 prohibits torture, inhuman or degrading treatment or punishment, and a form of ill-treatment must attain a minimum level of severity in order to fall within the scope of this provision.[62] Thus, the ECHR may prevent the expulsion of an alien on the basis of humanitarian concerns only in 'very exceptional cases'.[63]

In respect of the expulsion of terminally ill migrants, the ECtHR in *D v the United Kingdom* heard the case of a man who was dying of AIDS and was challenging an order to remove him to his country of origin, where he would lack any form of social, moral, or medical support. The ECtHR took into account the fact that the applicant's illness was at a critical stage and concluded that his proposed removal disclosed a violation of Article 3.[64] In respect of the expulsion of seriously ill migrants, the ECtHR initially established that a state's obligations under Article 3 are not engaged if that illness is not at a terminal stage and adequate treatments exist in the receiving country, even if at considerable cost and with limited availability. In *N v the United Kingdom* the ECtHR did not dispute that if the applicant, a Ugandan HIV-positive woman, were to be deprived of her medication, she would suffer 'discomfort, pain and death within a few years'.[65] The ECtHR also accepted that in Uganda appropriate medication is generally received only by half of those in need.[66] Nevertheless, the applicant was not yet critically ill and the ECtHR ultimately rejected her complaint.[67] However, In *Paposhvili v Belgium* the ECtHR lowered the threshold to trigger the protection of Article 3 and held that a state's obligations under Article 3 may be engaged if there are substantial reasons to believe that the applicant 'although not at imminent risk of dying' would face a

> real risk, on account of the absence of appropriate treatment in the receiving country or the lack of access to such treatment, of being exposed to a serious, rapid and irreversible decline in his or her state of health resulting in intense suffering or to a significant reduction in life expectancy.[68]

The ECtHR has established a number of criteria in order to establish whether dire economic and humanitarian circumstances meet the threshold to trigger Article 3. In *MSS v Belgium and*

---

[60]   *N v the United Kingdom* [GC] ECHR 2008, para 42.

[61]   *D v the United Kingdom* ECHR 1997-III, para 54. See also *N* (n 60) para 43.

[62]   *N* (n 60) para 29.

[63]   ibid, para 44.

[64]   *D* (n 61) para 54.

[65]   *N* (n 60) para 47.

[66]   ibid, para 48.

[67]   ibid, paras 50–51.

[68]   *Paposhvili v Belgium* [GC] App no 41738/10 (13 December 2016) para 183.

Greece the ECtHR accepted that conditions of 'most extreme poverty' may engage a state's responsibilities under Article 3.[69] In this case the ECtHR upheld an asylum seeker's complaint about the detention conditions in Greek facilities for asylum seekers and found that the applicant had been forced by national authorities to live in alarming conditions, exposed to the risk of 'being attacked and robbed' and 'unable to cater for his most basic needs: food, hygiene and a place to live'.[70]

In subsequent cases, the ECtHR considered whether expelling an alien may trigger the protection of Article 3 on the basis that this person would be forced to live in conditions of 'most extreme poverty' in the receiving country. In doing so, the ECtHR narrowed the scope of the principles developed in *MSS*.[71] The obligations of national authorities under Article 3 will be engaged if in the receiving country an 'exceptional and extreme'[72] humanitarian crisis is underway that is the result of ongoing conflicts and causes 'serious deprivation' and a 'breakdown of social, political and economic infrastructures'.[73] However, a higher threshold may apply if dire humanitarian conditions are mainly attributable to 'poverty or to the State's lack of resources'.[74] Moreover, it may be possible to implement a deportation order to a country with ongoing conflicts if, inter alia, there is a significant presence of international aid agencies, if there is a functioning central government, and if ongoing difficulties are not the result of 'deliberate actions or omissions'[75] by national authorities. Furthermore, the ECtHR emphasized that in *MSS* Greek authorities had failed to comply with positive obligations under European and domestic legislation on asylum seekers. States outside the CoE are not bound by such similar obligations and, as a consequence, Article 3 cannot be interpreted as establishing a general prohibition on deporting migrants to countries outside the CoE on the ground that these countries do not guarantee the minimum living conditions required under the ECHR.[76] Thus, the threshold for demonstrating that the living conditions in a country outside the CoE engage Article 3 remains very high.

---

[69]   *MSS v Belgium and Greece* [GC] ECHR 2011, para 254.

[70]   ibid.

[71]   For a discussion, see Veronika Flegar, 'Vulnerability and the Principle of Non-Refoulement in the European Court of Human Rights: Towards an Increased Scope of Protection for Persons Fleeing from Extreme Poverty?' (2016) 8 *Contemporary Readings in Law and Social Justice* 148.

[72]   *SHH v the United Kingdom* App no 60367/10 (ECtHR, 29 January 2013) para 91.

[73]   *Sufi and Elmi v the United Kingdom* App nos 8319/07 and 11449/07 (ECtHR, 28 June 2011) para 282.

[74]   ibid.

[75]   *SHH* (n 72) para 91.

[76]   ibid, para 90.

8.3   THE ENVIRONMENT

8.3.1   Article 37 of the EU Charter establishes that a 'high level of environmental protection and the improvement of the quality of the environment must be integrated into the policies of the Union and ensured in accordance with the principle of sustainable development'.[77]

The principle of environmental protection has shaped the outcome of a recent key case concerning the use of certain substances in the production of insecticides. In *Bayer CropScience AG* the CJEU considered whether the ban adopted by the European Commission on the use of three pesticides alleged to be harmful to bees was legitimate and proportionate.[78] The company claimed that the ban constituted, inter alia, a disproportionate interference with the right to property (Article 17 of the EU Charter) and the freedom to conduct a business (Article 16 of the EU Charter) enjoyed by the companies that used these substances in their insecticides. In response to this claim, the CJEU recalled that the right to property and freedom to conduct a business are not absolute and must be viewed 'in relation to their social purpose'.[79] Moreover, the CJEU held that the principle of environmental protection enshrined in Article 37 'takes precedence over economic considerations' and may justify 'adverse economic consequences' for certain companies.[80] This approach is consistent with the precautionary principle governing EU environmental law. The precautionary principle enables authorities to prioritize the protection of 'public health, safety and the environment' over economic interests.[81] In the event of 'scientific uncertainty' as to the existence or extent of risks to human health or to the environment, authorities are allowed to take protective measures 'without having to wait until the reality and seriousness of those risks become fully apparent or until the adverse health effects materialise'.[82] The level of risk deemed unacceptable must be assessed by the competent public authority in each individual case and in light of several factors, which include the 'severity of the impact on public health, safety and the environment were the risk to occur', the 'persistency or reversibility of those effects', the 'possibility of delayed effects', and 'the more or less concrete perception of the risk based on available scientific knowledge'.[83] On the basis of these principles, the CJEU upheld the ban imposed by the European Commission.[84]

On the other hand, the outcome of the recent '*People's Climate Case*' suggests that the margin for pursuing climate change litigation under the EU Charter is narrow. The applicants

---

[77]   For an overview, see Eloise Scotford, 'Environmental Rights and Principles: Investigating Article 37 of the EU Charter of Fundamental Rights' in *Environmental Rights in Europe and Beyond* (Sanja Bogojevic and Rosemary Rayfuse eds, Hart Publishing 2018) 133–54.

[78]   Cases T-429/13 and T-451/13 *Bayer CropScience AG and Others v European Commission* EU:T:2018:280.

[79]   ibid, para 586.

[80]   ibid, para 587.

[81]   ibid, para 109.

[82]   ibid, para 110.

[83]   ibid, para 124.

[84]   The CJEU confirmed this finding on appeal, see Case C-499/18 P *Bayer CropScience AG and Bayer AG v European Commission* EU:C:2021:367.

in this case sought to directly challenge a package introduced in EU law to reduce greenhouse emissions,[85] and they alleged a violation of their EU Charter rights.[86] Under EU law, natural or juristic persons can petition the CJEU against acts of EU institutions that affect them directly and individually. Despite acknowledging that 'every individual is likely to be affected one way or another by climate change',[87] the CJEU ultimately held that the applicants could not be considered directly and individually concerned by the EU legislative package being impugned, and it accordingly dismissed the action.[88] Thus, the CJEU strengthened an approach which arguably leads to the paradoxical effect whereby 'the more serious the damage and the higher the number of affected persons, the less judicial protection is available'.[89]

8.3.2 The ECHR and its additional Protocols do not enshrine a right to the enjoyment of a clean environment. However, the ECtHR has developed jurisprudence that is relevant in assessing disputes on a number of environment-related issues, and it has accepted that serious harms to the environment may undermine the exercise of certain ECHR rights. Although the ECtHR has not established a general duty of environmental protection, it has developed from the ECHR—mainly from Article 2 (right to life) and Article 8 (right to respect for private and family life)—a number of substantive and procedural obligations that national authorities must fulfil in matters relating to the environment.[90]

States' responsibilities under Article 2 can be engaged in the event of natural disasters that are provoked by industrial operations or human negligence and that result in unintentional deaths. National authorities should take adequate regulatory measures on the 'licensing, setting up, operation, security and supervision' of dangerous industrial activities and make it compulsory for everyone concerned to 'ensure the effective protection of citizens'.[91] Moreover, it is crucial that national authorities inform the public about any life-threatening risk due to industrial operations,[92] and that they implement procedures for identifying mistakes commit-

---

[85]   Case T-330/18 *Armando Carvalho and Others v European Parliament and Council of the European Union* EU: T:2019:324 (*People's Climate Case*).

[86]   ibid, para 30. The applicants alleged a violation of Article 2 (right to life), Article 3 (right to the integrity of the person), Article 24 (the rights of the child), Article 15 (freedom to choose an occupation and right to engage in work), Article 16 (freedom to conduct a business), Article 17 (right to property), Article 20 (equality before the law), and Article 21 (nondiscrimination).

[87]   ibid, para 50.

[88]   The CJEU confirmed this approach on appeal, see Case C-565/19 P *Armando Carvalho and Others v European Parliament and Council of the European Union* EU:C:2021:252.

[89]   *People's Climate Case* (n 85) para 32.

[90]   For an overview, see European Court of Human Rights, 'Factsheet: Environment and the European Convention on Human Rights' (December 2021).

[91]   *Öneryildiz v Turkey* [GC] ECHR 2004-XII, para 90. See also *Budayeva and Others v Russia* ECHR 2008 (extracts) para 132.

[92]   *Öneryildiz* (n 91) para 108.

ted by those responsible at different levels.[93] Competent authorities are required to adopt a 'clear legislative and administrative framework', implement a 'coherent supervisory system', and foster 'sufficient coordination and cooperation' between the various actors involved in industrial operations.[94] National authorities are also required to conduct appropriate investigations and judicial enquiries into incidents in which the state's responsibility is potentially engaged.[95] Although these principles are not explicitly concerned with environmental protection, the ECtHR has found substantive and procedural violations of Article 2 in respect of disasters which have a serious impact on the environment. For instance, in *Öneryildiz v Turkey* the ECtHR upheld a complaint about the failure of national authorities to prevent an explosion at a public rubbish tip which caused the death of several civilians. Similarly, the ECtHR found a violation of Article 2 in cases concerning the lack of land-planning and emergency relief policies for preventing mudslides,[96] the lack of adequate maintenance of a river channel,[97] and the failure to protect workers from the risks associated with the exposure to asbestos in state-run industrial facilities.[98]

The ECtHR has accepted that 'severe environmental pollution'—whether directly caused by the state or arising from the state's failure to regulate private industry—may affect individuals' private and family life in such a way as to fall within the scope of Article 8.[99] The scope of protection against environmental pollution varies depending on a range of circumstances. Firstly, the detriment complained of must attain a 'certain minimum level' exceeding 'the environmental hazards inherent to life in every modern city'.[100] Secondly, states enjoy a wide margin of appreciation in matters concerning environmental disputes, and regard must be had to the 'fair balance that has to be struck between the competing interests of the individual and of the community as a whole'.[101] Thirdly, national authorities must ensure that the 'procedural aspects' of the process for making decisions about environmental issues adequately protect the interests safeguarded by Article 8.[102] This means that the ECtHR will review elements such as, for example, the type of policy or decision involved, the procedural safeguards available in the domestic system, and the extent to which the views of individuals were taken into account in the decision-making process.

---

[93]   ibid, para 90; see also *Budayeva and Others* (n 91) para 132.

[94]   *Kolyadenko and Others v Russia* App nos 17423/05, 20534/05, 20678/05, 23263/05, 24283/05, and 35673/05 (ECtHR, 28 February 2012) para 185.

[95]   *Öneryildiz* (n 91) para 91.

[96]   *Budayeva and Others* (n 91).

[97]   *Kolyadenko and Others* (n 94).

[98]   *Brincat and Others v Malta* App nos 60908/11, 62110/11, 62129/11, 62312/11, and 62338/11 (ECtHR, 24 July 2014).

[99]   *López Ostra v Spain* (1994) Series A no 303-C, para 51; *Guerra and Others v Italy* ECHR 1998-I, para 60.

[100]   *Fadeyeva v Russia* ECHR 2005-IV, para 69.

[101]   *Powell and Rayner v the United Kingdom* (1990) Series A no 172, para 41. See also *Hatton and Others v the United Kingdom* [GC] ECHR 2003-VIII, para 98.

[102]   *Hatton and Others* (n 101) para 104.

In *Hatton and Others v the United Kingdom* the ECtHR acknowledged that the noise generated by aircraft at night-time affected the quality of the applicants' private life within the meaning of Article 8.[103] However, the ECtHR noted that, inter alia, night flights contributed to the well-being of the country, and it further pointed out that national authorities had implemented general measures to mitigate the impact of aircraft noise. Thus, the ECtHR concluded that the government had struck a fair balance between the competing interests of the applicants and of the community.[104] Conversely, in *López Ostra v Spain* the ECtHR held that the chemical fumes given off by a waste-collection plant at a level exceeding the legal limit, combined with the failure of national authorities to reduce such emissions or to promptly relocate those who lived near the plant, gave rise to a violation of Article 8.[105] Similarly, in *Fadeyeva v Russia* the ECtHR held that prolonged exposure to toxic emissions beyond legal limits made the applicant 'more vulnerable to various illnesses' and engaged her rights under Article 8,[106] even if it was not possible to establish a causal link between the deterioration in the applicant's health and the high levels of pollution in the area.[107] In both *López Ostra* and *Fadeyeva*, the ECtHR did accept that the operation of industrial implants was beneficial to the economic well-being of the population, but it ultimately concluded that national authorities had failed to balance the interests of the community against the rights of the applicants.

The recent *Cordella and Others v Italy* highlights key shortcomings in the ECtHR's approach to environmental issues. In this case the applicants complained under Article 2 and Article 8 against the failure of Italian authorities to reduce polluting emissions from a steelworks plant that had caused serious detriment to the local population's health.[108] The ECtHR chose to consider only the applicants' complaint under Article 8 and, in doing so, it arguably missed an opportunity to strengthen the protections against pollution under one of the most important provisions enshrined in the ECHR (Article 2). The ECtHR did find a violation of Article 8, but it refused to follow the pilot-judgment procedure[109] and identify ways to eliminate the systemic

---

[103] On noise pollution, see *Balzarini and 435 Others v Italy* (dec) App no 3717/03 (ECtHR, 28 October 2004); *Moreno Gómez v Spain* ECHR 2004-X.

[104] *Hatton and Others* (n 101) para 129.

[105] *López Ostra v Spain* (n 99) para 58. On pollution caused by the operation of a gold mine, see *Taşkın and Others v Turkey* ECHR 2004-X. On pollution provoked by a chemical plant, see *Guerra and Others* (n 99). On waste treatment, see *Giacomelli v Italy* ECHR 2006-XII.

[106] *Fadeyeva v Russia* (n 100) para 88.

[107] The ECtHR made similar considerations about the applicant's health in *Dubetska and Others v Ukraine* App no 30499/03 (ECtHR, 10 February 2011) and *Grimkovskaya v Ukraine* App no 38182/03 (ECtHR, 21 July 2011).

[108] *Cordella and Others v Italy* App nos 54414/13 and 54264/15 (ECtHR, 24 January 2019) para 93. The applicants invoked also Article 13 and the ECtHR found a violation of this provision.

[109] The ECtHR developed the pilot-judgment procedure as a way to deal with large numbers of repetitive cases that are rooted in the same problem at domestic level. Under the pilot-judgment procedure, the ECtHR will generally aim to, inter alia, 'give clear indications to the Government as to how it can eliminate [a] dysfunction' and to 'bring about the creation of a domestic remedy capable of dealing with similar cases' (Registrar of the European Court of Human Rights, 'The Pilot-Judgment Procedure' (Information note, entered into force 1 April 2011)).

and structural failures which had allowed ongoing high levels of toxic emissions for over four decades.[110]

Despite these shortcomings, individuals and groups keep petitioning the ECtHR to obtain legal remedies against the lack of appropriate environmental policies. In November 2020 the ECtHR communicated the case of *Duarte Agostinho and Others v Portugal and Others*, in which the applicants complain about the failure of 33 CoE member states to honour their commitments under the 2015 Paris Agreement.[111] Likewise, a group of senior women recently lodged an application against the environmental policies adopted by the Swiss government.[112] Thus, there are ongoing attempts to approach climate change litigation from the perspective of human rights, and a growing number of individuals and groups are arguing that environmental protection is a precondition for the effective enjoyment of their ECHR rights. It is unclear how the ECtHR will respond to these complaints, but climate change litigation is likely to intensify at national and international level.

---

[110]   See also *Smaltini v Italy* (dec) App no 43961/09 (ECtHR, 24 March 2015). For a discussion of *Cordella and Others*, see Roberta Greco, '*Cordella et al v Italy* and the Effectiveness of Human Rights Law Remedies in Cases of Environmental Pollution' (2020) 29 RECIEL 491.

[111]   *Duarte Agostinho and Others v Portugal and Others* App no 39371/20 (communicated on 13 November 2020).

[112]   The group 'Senior Women for Climate Protection' filed a complaint with the ECtHR in December 2020, which has been accepted but has yet to be communicated.

9
Religion, 'race' and ethnicity, culture

9.1 RELIGION

9.1.1 Article 9 ECHR enshrines the 'right to freedom of thought, conscience and religion'. The right to hold any religious or nonreligious belief is absolute. Under Article 9(2), freedom to manifest one's religion or beliefs may be subject to limitations, but only insofar as they are 'prescribed by law' and 'necessary in a democratic society in the interests of public safety, for the protection of public order, health or morals, or for the protection of the rights and freedoms of others'.

The ECtHR has adjudicated several complaints concerning the wearing of religious symbols/clothing in public spaces[1] and legislation that restricts Muslim women's freedom to manifest their religious beliefs by wearing the Islamic veil in public places.[2] The ECtHR has determined that restrictions on wearing the Islamic headscarf and full-face veil can pursue legitimate aims, such as protecting public order and the rights of others,[3] and may be necessary in order to promote equality between men and women.[4] For example, in *Leyla Şahin v Turkey* the ECtHR accepted that limitations on wearing the Islamic headscarf in higher-education institutions were necessary in order to protect the public order and the rights of others in a society in which the majority of the population adheres to Islam but professes a 'strong attachment to the rights of women and a secular way of life'.[5]

---

[1] For an overview of the ECtHR jurisprudence on religious clothing, see European Court of Human Rights, 'Guide on Article 9 of the European Convention on Human Rights' (31 August 2021) paras 94–111.

[2] In many of these cases, the ECtHR does not identify the type of Islamic veil worn by the applicants. The ECtHR refers to types of veil that do not conceal the face as 'headscarf'/'veil' and it indicates types of veil that conceal the face as 'full-face veil'. Whenever possible, I will indicate the type of veil worn by the applicant.

[3] *Leyla Şahin v Turkey* App no 44774/98 (ECtHR, 29 June 2004) paras 82–4. See also *Ebrahimian v France* ECHR 2015, para 53.

[4] *Leyla Şahin* (n 3) paras 107–8.

[5] ibid, para 108.

The ECtHR has also determined that restrictions on wearing the headscarf may be necessary in order to protect the principles of secularism and neutrality.[6] For example, in *Ebrahimian v France* the ECtHR held that the protection of the principles of secularism and neutrality requires 'impartiality towards all religious beliefs on the basis of respect for pluralism and diversity' and may justify the obligation for civil servants to refrain from manifesting their religious beliefs in the exercise of their professional duties.[7]

The ECtHR's approach is still evolving, and in *Lachiri v Belgium* the ECtHR found that the decision to expel the applicant from a courtroom on account of her refusal to remove her hijab amounted to a violation of her fundamental right to express her religious beliefs.[8] The outcome of this case suggests that there may be some scope to develop stronger protections for women who assert a right to wear the Islamic headscarf in public. However, the ECtHR's approach to this complaint is deeply rooted in the peculiarities of the case, and it does not completely overturn the principles developed in *Ebrahimian* and *Leyla Şahin*. The obligation to appear before a judge without a head covering was aimed at preventing behaviours that are disrespectful towards the judiciary or disruptive of the smooth running of hearings.[9] Thus, the ECtHR confined itself to assessing whether the prohibition on wearing the Islamic veil in the courtroom was justified for the purpose of maintaining order, and it did not examine whether the same prohibition could be justified with a view to protecting the principle of secularism and neutrality of the judiciary and of public spaces.[10]

The ECtHR has further established that prohibitions on wearing religious clothing that conceals the face are ECHR-compliant. In *SAS v France* the applicant argued that the prohibition on the public wearing of clothing designed to conceal the face violated her right to express her religious beliefs, culture, and personal convictions by wearing a burqa and niqab. French authorities replied that the ban on full-face veils in public places was necessary to ensure 'respect for the minimum set of values of an open and democratic society'.[11] French authorities notably claimed that in social interactions the face 'expresses the existence of the individual as a unique person' and reflects 'one's shared humanity with the interlocutor, at the same time as one's otherness'.[12] On this basis, the act of concealing one's face in public places would amount to a refusal of the principle of 'living together' in society and would breach 'the right of others

---

[6]   *Ebrahimian* (n 3) para 53. See also *Leyla Şahin* (n 3) paras 104–6. On the relevance of the principle of neutrality, see *Dahlab v Switzerland* (dec) ECHR 2001-V. On the relevance of the principle of secularism in complaints concerning the refusal of pupils to remove their headscarf on school premises, see *Köse and Others v Turkey* (dec) App no 26625/02 ECHR 2006-II; *Kervanci v France* App no 31645/04 (ECtHR, 4 December 2008); *Dogru v France* App no 27058/05 (ECtHR, 4 December 2008).

[7]   *Ebrahimian* (n 3) para 67. For a discussion of neutrality policies in the workplace, s 9.1.2.

[8]   *Lachiri v Belgium* App no 3413/09 (ECtHR, 18 September 2018).

[9]   ibid, para 38.

[10]   ibid, para 46.

[11]   *SAS v France* [GC] ECHR 2014 (extracts) para 82.

[12]   ibid.

to live in a space of socialisation which makes living together easier'.[13] The ECtHR agreed with the French government and accepted that the impugned prohibition sought to protect a principle of interaction between individuals which is 'essential for the expression not only of pluralism, but also of tolerance and broadmindedness without which there is no democratic society'.[14]

9.1.2 Both the ECtHR and the CJEU have developed jurisprudence about workers being sanctioned by their employers for wearing religious symbols in the workplace.

In *Eweida and Others v the United Kingdom* the first and second applicant were sanctioned by their employers for wearing a visible cross at work.[15] The first applicant was employed by an airline company and the ECtHR accepted that the company's interest in preserving a 'certain corporate image' was legitimate.[16] However, the ECtHR recalled that the wearing of religious symbols in the workplace falls within the ambit of Article 9, and it reiterated that the protection of the right of individuals to manifest their religious beliefs is essential to sustaining 'pluralism and diversity' in a healthy democratic society.[17] In the absence of any 'real encroachment' on the interests of others,[18] the ECtHR found that the restrictions impugned amounted to a violation of Article 9.[19] The second applicant was employed as a nurse in a geriatric ward and the ECtHR accepted that hospital managers had imposed restrictions on jewellery and necklaces in order to reduce the risk of injury when handling patients. The ECtHR concluded that these restrictions were proportionate to the aim sought and did not amount to a violation of Article 9.

In *G4S Secure Solutions* the CJEU considered the case of a woman who had been dismissed after she had disclosed her intention to wear an Islamic headscarf, in breach of an internal policy that prohibited the wearing of any visible signs of political, philosophical, or religious beliefs in the workplace.[20] The CJEU left it to the referring court to determine whether the policy pursued a legitimate aim and whether it was necessary and proportionate.[21] However,

---

[13]   ibid, para 122.

[14]   ibid, para 153. In respect of similar prohibitions introduced in Belgian legislation, see *Dakir v Belgium* App no 4619/12 (ECtHR, 11 July 2017); *Belcacemi and Oussar v Belgium* App no 37798/13 (ECtHR, 11 July 2017). For a discussion, see Jill Marshall, 'S.A.S. v France: Burqa Bans and the Control or Empowerment of Identities' (2015) 15 *Human Rights Law Review* 377; Ilias Trispiotis, 'Two Interpretations of "Living Together" in European Human Rights Law' (2016) 75 *Cambridge Law Journal* 580. For a critical analysis of veiling laws introduced in Europe, see Neville Cox, *Behind the Veil: A Critical Analysis of European Veiling Laws* (Edward Elgar 2019).

[15]   *Eweida and Others v the United Kingdom* ECHR 2013 (extracts) paras 9–17 and paras 18–22.

[16]   ibid, para 94.

[17]   ibid.

[18]   ibid, para 95.

[19]   ibid.

[20]   Case C-157/15 *Samira Achbita and Centrum voor gelijkheid van kansen en voor racismebestrijding v G4S Secure Solutions NV* EU:C:2017:203, paras 10–6.

[21]   ibid, paras 35–6.

the CJEU pointed out that the 'desire to display, in relations with both public and private sector customers, a policy of political, philosophical or religious neutrality' falls within the ambit of Article 16 of the EU Charter (freedom to conduct a business) and must be considered legitimate, especially where this policy applies only to workers who are required to come into contact with the public.[22] In *Micropole SA* the CJEU confirmed the general framework developed in *G4S Secure Solutions* but it also held that absent a general internal rule prohibiting visible signs of political, philosophical, or religious beliefs, an employer cannot require a Muslim employee to remove her headscarf solely to satisfy the particular wishes of any one customer.[23]

In *G4S Secure Solutions* and *Micropole SA* the CJEU developed general principles on how to balance employers' freedom to conduct a business and employees' fundamental right to manifest their religious beliefs. First, any prohibition should apply to any religious, philosophical, and political symbols. Second, a more stringent scrutiny may apply to prohibitions restricting the religious freedom of employees who are not required to come into contact with the public. Third, prohibitions which are not based on internal rules or policies are likely to fall foul of the principle of nondiscrimination. However, employers enjoy considerable discretion in framing neutrality policies for their employees, especially for those who are required to interact with the public.[24]

9.1.3   Article 2 of Protocol 1 to the ECHR (P1-2) protects the fundamental right to education, and the second sentence of P1-2 prescribes that 'in the exercise of any functions which it assumes in relation to education and to teaching', the state shall 'respect the right of parents to ensure such education and teaching in conformity with their own religious and philosophical convictions'. The ECtHR has determined that the setting and planning of the school curriculum falls in principle within the competence of national authorities. However, information or knowledge in the curriculum must be conveyed in an 'objective, critical and pluralistic manner', and national authorities are forbidden to pursue an 'aim of indoctrination that might be considered as not respecting parents' religious and philosophical convictions'.[25]

The ECtHR has developed jurisprudence addressing complaints from parents arguing that certain subjects in the school curriculum infringe their fundamental right to educate their children in accordance with their own religious and philosophical convictions. For instance, the ECtHR has established key criteria to determine what amounts to 'indoctrination' in the

---

[22]   ibid, paras 37–8.

[23]   Case C-188/15 *Asma Bougnaoui and Association de défense des droits de l'homme (ADDH) v Micropole SA* EU: C:2017:204, para 41.

[24]   For a discussion, see Saïla Ouald-Chaib and Valeska David, 'European Court of Justice Keeps the Door to Religious Discrimination in the Private Workplace Opened: The European Court of Human Rights Could Close It' (*Strasbourg Observers*, 27 March 2017) <https://strasbourgobservers.com/2017/03/27/european-court-of-justice -keeps-the-door-to-religious-discrimination-in-the-private-workplace-opened-the-european-court-of-human -rights-could-close-it/> accessed 10 January 2022.

[25]   *Folgerø and Others v Norway* [GC] ECHR 2007-III, para 84.

context of compulsory sex education.[26] Firstly, the ECtHR has determined that the introduction of compulsory sex education can pursue legitimate aims that do not amount to indoctrination, such as providing pupils with objective and factual knowledge about sexual life,[27] promoting tolerance between human beings,[28] and preventing sexual violence and exploitation of minors.[29] Secondly, teaching about sexuality may be in accordance with the principles of objectivity and pluralism if it is age-appropriate and not characterized by 'carelessness, lack of judgment or misplaced proselytism'[30] and if pupils are not encouraged to 'put into question' their parents' convictions[31] or to 'indulge precociously in practices that [...] many parents consider reprehensible'.[32] Thirdly, national authorities must not restrict the right of parents to 'enlighten and advise their children' outside school hours in conformity with their religious convictions.[33] So far, the ECtHR has never upheld a complaint brought by parents claiming a fundamental right to have their children exempted from sex education lessons on the basis that it contradicts their religious or philosophical beliefs.

The ECtHR has also considered whether the display of religious symbols in state schools violates the fundamental right to respect for parents' and pupils' religious and philosophical convictions. In *Lautsi v Italy*, the applicants complained about the presence of crucifixes in the classrooms of state schools.[34] The Chamber found a violation of P1-2 and Article 9 on the basis of the following considerations. First, it noted that in the context of public education crucifixes are 'powerful external symbols'[35] that may easily be interpreted by pupils as indicating that the school environment is marked by a particular religion. Second, the Chamber held that in states where the majority of the population profess one religion, the display of symbols of that religion 'without restriction as to place and manner'[36] may be 'emotionally disturbing' to pupils of other religions or to pupils who profess no religion at all.[37] Third, judges reiterated that the state has a duty to 'uphold confessional neutrality' in public and compulsory education.[38] On this basis, the Chamber concluded that the display of crucifixes in state school classrooms

[26] For a discussion of ECHR jurisprudence on parental objections to compulsory sex education lessons, see Paul Johnson and Silvia Falcetta, 'The Inclusion of Sexual Orientation and Gender Identity in Relationships Education: Faith-Based Objections and the European Convention on Human Rights' (2021) ECHR Law Review (advance publication online).

[27] *Kjeldsen, Busk Madsen and Pedersen v Denmark* (1976) Series A no 23, para 54.

[28] *Dojan and Others v Germany* (dec) App no 319/08 (ECtHR, 13 September 2011) 'The Law' para 2.

[29] *AR and LR v Switzerland* (dec) App no 22338/15 (ECtHR, 19 December 2017) para 35.

[30] *Kjeldsen, Busk Madsen and Pedersen* (n 27) para 54.

[31] *Dojan and Others* (n 28) 'The Law' para 2.

[32] *Kjeldsen, Busk Madsen and Pedersen* (n 27) para 54.

[33] ibid.

[34] *Lautsi v Italy* App no 30814/06 (ECtHR, 3 November 2009) para 27.

[35] ibid, para 54.

[36] ibid, para 50.

[37] ibid, para 55.

[38] ibid, para 56.

violated the fundamental right of parents to 'educate their children in conformity with their convictions', and it infringed the fundamental right of pupils to 'believe or not believe'.[39]

This case was referred to the Grand Chamber, which reversed the Chamber's judgment and found no violation of the ECHR.[40] The Grand Chamber granted that the presence of crucifixes in state classrooms confers 'preponderant visibility' on the country's majority religion,[41] but it held that a crucifix on a wall is an 'essentially passive symbol'[42] that cannot lead to indoctrination. The Grand Chamber further observed that the presence of crucifixes was not associated with compulsory teaching about Christianity or with the marginalization of pupils who held different religious or nonreligious convictions. Thus, the Grand Chamber ultimately held that national authorities had not exceeded the margin of appreciation available to them in the realm of education.[43]

9.2   'RACE' AND ETHNICITY

9.2.1 Article 14 ECHR enshrines the principle of nondiscrimination in the enjoyment of the rights set forth in the ECHR, stating that there can be no discrimination on the basis of, inter alia, 'race', 'colour', 'national or social origin', 'birth', or 'association with a national minority'.

The ECtHR considers ethnicity and 'race' as 'related concepts',[44] and its jurisprudence on racial and ethnic discrimination is guided by the following general principles. The ECtHR uses the notion of 'race' to refer to 'the idea of biological classification of human beings into subspecies on the basis of morphological features such as skin colour or facial characteristics', whereas the notion of ethnicity is rooted in the idea of 'societal groups marked in particular by common nationality, religious faith, shared language, or cultural and traditional origins and backgrounds'.[45] The ECtHR has established that discrimination on account of a person's ethnic origin is a form of racial discrimination,[46] and that differences in treatment based 'exclusively or to a decisive extent' on a person's ethnic origin are incompatible with a democratic society.[47] The ECtHR has also determined that measures couched in neutral terms may amount to racial discrimination if they have 'disproportionately prejudicial effects' on a particular group, even if the measure is not specifically aimed at that group and there is no discriminatory intent.[48]

---

[39]   ibid, para 57.

[40]   *Lautsi and Others v Italy* [GC] ECHR 2011 (extracts).

[41]   ibid, para 71.

[42]   ibid, para 72.

[43]   ibid, para 77.

[44]   *Sejdić and Finci v Bosnia and Herzegovina* [GC] ECHR 2009, para 43.

[45]   ibid.

[46]   *DH and Others v the Czech Republic* [GC] ECHR 2007-IV, para 176.

[47]   ibid.

[48]   ibid, para 184.

However, the principle of nondiscrimination does not prohibit national authorities from treating groups differently in order to correct 'factual inequalities' between them.[49]

Racial violence is a 'particular affront to human dignity',[50] and national authorities must combat racial and ethnic discrimination in order to promote a vision of society in which 'diversity is not perceived as a threat but as a source of enrichment'.[51] Authorities must not discriminate—directly or indirectly, *de jure* or *de facto*—against individuals on the basis of their actual or perceived ethnic origin. Moreover, authorities have the obligation to pursue official investigations into acts supposedly motivated by racial or ethnic hatred with 'vigour and impartiality' and having regard to the need to 'maintain the confidence of minorities in the ability of the authorities to protect them from the threat of racist violence'.[52] Notably, authorities must 'explore all practical means of discovering the truth', 'deliver fully reasoned, impartial and objective decisions', and take into account 'suspicious facts that may be indicative of racially induced violence'.[53] In respect of violent episodes at the hands of state agents, authorities have the additional duty to take all reasonable steps to establish whether racial and ethnic hatred or prejudice played a role in the incidents.

9.2.2 The ECtHR has applied the foregoing principles in addressing discrimination and violence that private individuals and state agents have perpetrated against Roma communities and individuals of Roma ethnicity.[54] According to ECHR jurisprudence, Roma are a 'specific type of disadvantaged and vulnerable minority',[55] and authorities should accordingly give 'special consideration' to their needs and their different lifestyle, with a view to protecting their fundamental rights and preserving 'a cultural diversity' that is of value to the whole community.[56]

In *Škorjanec v Croatia* the applicant's partner had been assaulted by two men on account of his Roma origin and the applicant herself had been physically injured during the attack. During the investigations, the authorities emphasized that the applicant was not of Roma ethnicity and concluded that she could not be considered a victim of a hate crime. The ECtHR instead held that national authorities have a duty to take into account any evidence of anti-Roma abuse even in respect of crimes where the victims have been targeted because of their association with another person who is actually or presumably of Roma origin.[57] Thus, the ECtHR relied on the principle that everyone has a right to enjoy the 'fundamental values' enshrined in the

---

[49]   ibid, para 175.

[50]   *Nachova and Others v Bulgaria* [GC] ECHR 2005-VII, para 145.

[51]   ibid. See also *Sejdić and Finci* (n 44) para 43.

[52]   *Nachova and Others v Bulgaria* App nos 43577/98 and 43579/98 (ECtHR, 26 February 2004) para 157.

[53]   *Škorjanec v Croatia* App no 25536/14 (ECtHR, 28 March 2017) para 57.

[54]   For an overview of ECHR jurisprudence on anti-Roma discrimination, see European Court of Human Rights, 'Factsheet: Roma and Travellers' (April 2021).

[55]   *DH and Others* (n 46) para 182.

[56]   ibid, paras 181.

[57]   *Škorjanec* (n 53) para 66.

ECHR without discrimination,[58] and it established that in determining what counts as an act of violence motivated by racial hatred, national authorities need to also include acts of violence that are based on a victim's 'actual or presumed association or affiliation with another person who actually or presumably possesses a particular status or protected characteristic'.[59]

The ECtHR has also found a violation of the principle of nondiscrimination in a number of complaints concerning Roma children's right to education. In *DH and Others v the Czech Republic* the applicants claimed that they had been placed in schools for children with special needs on account of their 'race or ethnic origin', and they alleged a violation of Article 14 taken together with P1-2.[60] The ECtHR accepted that the relevant provisions concerning the placement of children in special schools were couched in neutral terms and that children were assigned to special schools on the basis of psychological tests carried out at specialized centres. In order to assess whether the application of the relevant provisions resulted in indirect discrimination against Roma pupils, the ECtHR took into account international reports and statistical data concerning the educational system in the Czech Republic.[61] These data clearly indicated that the percentage of Roma students in special schools was disproportionately high.[62] The ECtHR further noted that the tests used to assess children's learning challenges were controversial, and there was a danger that the final evaluation did not take into account the 'particularities and special characteristics' of the Roma children who sat them.[63] Thus, the ECtHR concluded that the Czech educational system infringed the fundamental right to education of Roma children. First, it did not take into account the special needs of Roma children but rather 'compounded their difficulties' and 'compromised their subsequent personal development' by placing them in schools with a more basic curriculum.[64] Second, Roma children remained isolated from students from the wider population, and the educational system failed to help these children to 'develop the skills that would facilitate life among the majority population'.[65]

9.2.3 The prohibition on discrimination on the basis of 'race', ethnic origin, and nationality is enshrined in several instruments of EU law.[66] Notably, Council Directive 2000/43/EC gives

---

[58]   ibid, para 37.

[59]   ibid, para 56.

[60]   *DH and Others* (n 46) para 124. The first sentence of P1-2 reads '[n]o person shall be denied the right to education'.

[61]   ibid, paras 190–92.

[62]   ibid, para 193.

[63]   ibid, para 201.

[64]   ibid, para 207.

[65]   ibid. See also *Oršuš and Others v Croatia* [GC] ECHR 2010; *Horváth and Kiss v Hungary* App no 11146/11 (ECtHR, 29 January 2013). For a discussion, see David J Harris, Michael O'Boyle, Ed P Bates, and Carla M Buckley, *Law of the European Convention on Human Rights* (4th edn, OUP 2018) 797–9.

[66]   For example, see Council Directive 2000/43/EC of 29 June 2000 implementing the principle of equal treatment between persons irrespective of racial or ethnic origin [2000] OJ L 180/22; Article 19 TFEU.

specific expression to the principle of nondiscrimination on the grounds of racial and ethnic origin in the fields of employment, education, training, and supply of goods and services. Article 21 of the EU Charter elevates the principle of equal treatment to a fundamental right and forbids any discrimination based on, inter alia, 'race', 'colour', 'ethnic or social origin', 'membership of a national minority', 'birth' and, within the scope of application of the EU Treaties, 'nationality'.[67]

In *Firma Feryn* the CJEU considered the case of an employer who had publicly declared that his company was not willing to recruit 'immigrants'. The company was seeking to recruit personnel, but in interviews with newspapers and on TV programmes, one of the company's directors said that the company would not recruit immigrants because 'customers don't want them'.[68] As a result, an organization promoting equal treatment brought proceedings against the company. The CJEU established that an employer publicly declaring that it will not recruit 'immigrants' falls within the notion of direct discrimination on the basis of racial and ethnic origin, even if no individual has been effectively denied employment on the basis of his or her ethnic origin. The CJEU denied that the lack of an identifiable complainant implies that there is no discrimination, and it held that similar statements are likely to dissuade candidates from certain backgrounds from even applying, thereby hindering their access to the labour market.[69] In reaching this conclusion, the CJEU adopted a broad definition of the principle of nondiscrimination with the aim to 'foster conditions for a socially inclusive labour market'.[70]

In *CHEZ Razpredelenie Bulgaria* the CJEU interpreted the principle of nondiscrimination in a way that is consistent with the approach the ECtHR adopted in *Škorjanec*. This case concerned an energy supplier's practice of installing electricity meters at a greater height in districts mainly inhabited by persons of Roma origin. The woman who had initiated the proceedings at national level was not of Roma ethnicity and alleged that she was subject to indirect discrimination because she was in a disadvantaged position compared to the customers of the company whose meters were installed at accessible locations.[71] Like the ECtHR, the CJEU held that the concept of discrimination on grounds of ethnic origin must be interpreted as also applying to measures that affect 'persons who, without possessing that origin, suffer, together with the former, the less favourable treatment or particular disadvantage resulting from that

---

[67]   For an overview, see Angela Ward, 'The Impact of the EU Charter of Fundamental Rights on Anti-Discrimination Law: More a Whimper than a Bang?' (2018) 20 *Cambridge Yearbook of European Legal Studies* 32.

[68]   Case C-54/07 *Centrum voor gelijkheid van kansen en voor racismebestrijding v Firma Feryn NV* [2008] I-05187, Opinion of AG Poiares Maduro, para 3.

[69]   Case C-54/07 *Centrum voor gelijkheid van kansen en voor racismebestrijding v Firma Feryn NV* [2008] ECR I-05187, para 25.

[70]   ibid, para 23.

[71]   Case C-83/14 *'CHEZ Razpredelenie Bulgaria' AD v Komisia za zashtita ot diskriminatsia* EU:C:2015:480, paras 21–3.

measure'.[72] Thus, the principle of equal treatment enshrined in Article 21 of the EU Charter protects individuals from 'discrimination by association'.[73]

9.3   CULTURE

9.3.1 The ECHR does not explicitly protect the language rights of linguistic minorities. Still, individuals belonging to linguistic minorities have repeatedly argued that restrictions on their ability to communicate with others, correspond with authorities, and receive education in their own language amount to a violation of their ECHR rights.[74]

A key issue considered by the ECtHR is whether linguistic minorities have a right to receive state or subsidized education in their own language. In the *Belgian Linguistic Case* the applicants were French-speaking parents of school-aged children who lived in a region considered by law as Dutch-speaking.[75] The law on the use of languages in education in Belgium followed the principle of territoriality, and Dutch was the language of education in the Dutch-unilingual region. The applicants claimed that the imposition of linguistic homogeneity in education in unilingual regions infringed their right to have their children educated in their mother tongue.[76]

Whereas P1-2 does not specify the language in which education must be offered, the ECtHR conceded that the right to education would be 'meaningless' if it did not imply 'the right to be educated in the national language or in one of the national languages'.[77] The ECtHR noted that children in unilingual regions had access to public or subsidized education in the national language that was also the language of the region.[78] On this basis, the ECtHR concluded that Belgian authorities had not infringed the right to be educated in one of the national languages and had acted within the margin of appreciation available to them under P1-2. Similarly, the ECtHR held that the right to respect for 'family life' under Article 8 could not be constructed as guaranteeing 'the right to be educated in the language of one's parents'.[79]

---

[72]   ibid, para 50.

[73]   Case C-83/14 'CHEZ Razpredelenie Bulgaria' AD v Komisia za zashtita ot diskriminatsia EU:C:2015:170, Opinion of AG Kokott, paras 107–8.

[74]   For an overview of ECHR jurisprudence on linguistic issues, see European Court of Human Rights, 'Cultural Rights in the Case-Law of the European Court of Human Rights' (Research report, Council of Europe Publishing, 17 January 2017) paras 57–67.

[75]   Case 'relating to certain aspects of the laws on the use of languages in education in Belgium' (merits) (1968) Series A no 6.

[76]   ibid, 'The Facts' para 4.

[77]   ibid, 'Interpretation adopted by the Court' para 3.

[78]   ibid, 'The six questions referred to the Court' para 7.

[79]   ibid. The ECtHR found a violation of Article 14 and P1-2 in respect of legislation preventing certain children, solely on the basis of their parents' place of residence, from having access to French-language schools in the outskirts of Brussels.

The ECtHR further determined that the legal framework regulating the use of languages in education in Belgium did not discriminate against linguistic minorities. In the first place, the principle of territoriality was applied in an 'objective' way to promote the language of the majority of the population in each region, and language policies pursued the legitimate aim to ensure that all state and subsidized schools teach in the language of the region.[80] In the second place, the measures adopted by Belgian authorities were proportionate to the aim sought and achieved a fair balance between the protection of the community's interests and respect for individual rights. Notably, the law did not prevent French-speaking parents from enrolling their children in independent French-language schools in the Dutch-unilingual region or from sending them to school in the unilingual French region. In conclusion, the ECtHR established that the ECHR cannot be interpreted as imposing a general positive obligation to provide linguistic minorities with public or subsidized education in their own language.[81]

In subsequent cases, the ECtHR found that certain restrictions on the languages used in education may amount to a violation of the right to education. In *Cyprus v Turkey* the ECtHR held that the decision of the authorities of the Turkish Republic of Northern Cyprus to abolish secondary-school facilities that offered education in Greek amounted to a violation of P1-2.[82] The ECtHR found a violation of the same provision in respect of restrictions on the use of the Latin alphabet in certain schools located in a separatist region of the Republic of Moldova.[83] In these cases, the ECtHR did not introduce general principles that substantially reverse the approach to linguistic rights developed in the *Belgian Linguistic Case*. However, the ECtHR did accept that the use of a particular language in education may be linked to parents' 'legitimate wish' to have their children educated in accordance with their 'cultural and ethnic tradition',[84] and it strengthened the principle that authorities must not impair the right to receive education in the national language.[85]

9.3.2 The relationship between intellectual property rights (IP rights) and notions such as culture and cultural heritage is contentious.[86] On the one hand, it has been argued that IP rights are based on 'author-centered and mercantilist premises' that may result as inadequate

---

[80]   ibid.

[81]   For a comparison with the approach the Supreme Court of Canada has taken to complaints about the linguistic rights of the Anglophone minority in Quebec, see *Ford v Quebec* (AG) [1988] 2 SCR 712.

[82]   *Cyprus v Turkey* [GC] ECHR 2001-IV, paras 273–80.

[83]   *Catan and Others v the Republic of Moldova and Russia* [GC] ECHR 2012 (extracts) para 150.

[84]   *Cyprus* (n 82) para 275.

[85]   *Catan and Others* (n 83) para 143.

[86]   For a discussion, see Mira Burri, 'Cultural Heritage and Intellectual Property' in *The Oxford Handbook of International Cultural Heritage Law* (Francesco Francioni and Ana Filipa Vrdoljak eds, OUP 2020) 459–82. On the relationship between IP rights and human rights, see Christophe Geiger (ed), *Research Handbook on Human Rights and Intellectual Property* (Edward Elgar 2015); Laurence R Helfer, 'Intellectual Property and Human Rights' in *The Oxford Handbook of Intellectual Property Law* (Rochelle Dreyfuss and Justine Pila eds, OUP 2018) 117–43.

in protecting and promoting traditional forms of knowledge and cultural expression.[87] On the other hand, IP rights aim to protect intellectual, artistic, and economic creativity, and the legal framework regulating IP rights has a crucial impact on the ways in which creative works are circulated, shared, and used in society. The principle of IP rights protection is enshrined in the EU Charter, and Article 17(2) of the EU Charter provides that '[i]ntellectual property shall be protected'. The CJEU has developed key principles for balancing the protection of the interests of IP rights-holders with the public interest in accessing or distributing creative works. Indeed, the CJEU has established that there is 'nothing' in the wording of Article 17(2) or in its general jurisprudence to suggest that IP rights are 'inviolable' and must therefore be 'absolutely pro-tected'.[88] On the contrary, the protection of IP rights must be balanced against the protection of other fundamental rights.

In the electronic communications sector, the CJEU has developed key criteria for balancing the protection of IP rights with the protection of the fundamental right to respect for private life (Article 7 of the EU Charter) and personal data (Article 8 of the EU Charter). In *Promusicae*, an organization of producers and publishers of musical and audio-visual recordings asked for an Internet service provider (ISP) to disclose the identities and physical addresses of certain persons who were exchanging files and were providing online access to phonograms in which the members of Promusicae held exploitation rights.[89] Whereas Promusicae argued that this measure was essential to guaranteeing an effective remedy against the violation of its members' IP rights, the CJEU held that it was necessary to 'reconcile' the protection of IP rights with the fundamental right to respect for the personal data and private lives of ISP customers.[90] On this basis, the CJEU concluded that companies providing online services should not be obliged to communicate personal data about their customers in the context of civil proceedings.[91]

Authorities must also balance the protection of IP rights with the protection of the fun-damental freedom to conduct a business (Article 16 of the EU Charter). In *Scarlet Extended SA* a management company sought an order requiring an ISP to introduce blocking filters that prevent its customers from sharing content without the rights-holders' permission. The CJEU noted that the order sought by the management company would result in a 'serious infringement' of the ISP's fundamental freedoms under Article 16 of the EU Charter, since it would require the ISP to install a 'complicated, costly, permanent' computer system at its own expense, in breach of the principle whereby measures for enforcing IP rights should not be 'unnecessarily complicated or costly'.[92] Similarly, in *UPC Telekabel Wien* the CJEU held that an ISP could be required to block access to a website that infringed copyrights but only insofar

---

[87]   Burri (n 86) 481.

[88]   Case C-70/10 *Scarlet Extended SA v Société belge des auteurs, compositeurs et éditeurs SCRL (SABAM)* [2011] ECR 00000, para 43.

[89]   Case C-275/06 *Productores de Música de España (Promusicae) v Telefónica de España SAU* [2008] ECR I-00271, paras 29–30.

[90]   ibid, para 65.

[91]   ibid, para 70. See also *Scarlet Extended SA* (n 88).

[92]   *Scarlet Extended SA* (n 88) para 48.

as this restriction did not completely deprive the ISP of 'the right for any business to be able to freely use, within the limits of its liability for its own acts, the economic, technical and financial resources available to it'.[93]

Another fundamental right that may be affected by measures designed to protect IP rights is the right to freedom of information (Article 11 of the EU Charter). For instance, the CJEU has repeatedly indicated that an ISP cannot be required to install filters or other systems that might not distinguish between unlawful and lawful content and may thereby lead to the blocking of lawful communications, in breach of an ISP customers' rights under Article 11 of the EU Charter.[94] However, the protection of the right to information under Article 11 does not always override the protection of IP rights under Article 17(2). For example, in *Funke Medien NRW* the CJEU held that freedom of information and freedom of the press can justify a derogation from the author's exclusive IP rights 'only in certain special cases which do not conflict with a normal exploitation of the work' and do not 'unreasonably prejudice the legitimate interests of the rightholder'.[95]

9.3.3 Female genital mutilation (FGM) is practised in several countries around the world for a mix of social and cultural reasons, and it is internationally regarded as one of the most serious human rights violations against women and girls.[96]

The ECtHR has established that FGM amounts to inhuman or degrading treatment within the meaning of Article 3 (prohibition of torture) and has accepted that, in principle, CoE member states may not deport a woman or girl where substantial grounds have been shown for believing that, if deported, she would be at a 'real and concrete risk' of being subjected to FGM in the receiving country.[97] The ECtHR has considered several complaints lodged by asylum seekers claiming that, if deported, they and/or their daughters would be at real risk of FGM. In assessing these complaints, the ECtHR has developed criteria for establishing whether the general legal, social, and cultural conditions in the receiving country indicate a situation where women and girls are routinely forced to undergo FGM. So far, the ECtHR has never found that the conditions in the receiving country or the applicants' personal circumstances put them at a real risk for FGM in the receiving country.

---

[93]   Case C-314/12 *UPC Telekabel Wien GmbH v Constantin Film Verleih GmbH and Wega Filmproduktionsgesellschaft mbH* EU:C:2014:192, para 49.

[94]   *Scarlet Extended SA* (n 88) paras 52–3; *UPC Telekabel Wien* (n 93) para 47 and paras 56–7.

[95]   Case C-469/17 *Funke Medien NRW GmbH v Bundesrepublik Deutschland* EU:C:2019:623, para 61.

[96]   For an overview of the instruments adopted to prevent and tackle FGM in the Council of Europe, see Council of Europe, Steering Committee for Human Rights (CDDH), 'Analysis of the Legal Situation at International Level and in Council of Europe Member States on Combating and Preventing Female Genital Mutilation and Forced Marriage' CDDH(2016)R85 Addendum II (adopted by the CDDH at its 85th meeting, 15–17 June 2016). For an overview of the actions adopted at the level of the EU, see European Commission, 'EU Gender Action Plan III' JOIN(2020) 17 final (25 November 2020).

[97]   *Collins and Akaziebie v Sweden* (dec) App no 23944/05 (ECtHR, 8 March 2007) 'The Law'.

First, the ECtHR considers the existence of laws criminalizing FGM in the receiving country as a sign of the willingness of state authorities to provide appropriate protection against this practice. Relatedly, the presence of projects sponsored by the state or nongovernmental organizations supporting victims of FGM and educating communities about the hazards of FGM is likely to strengthen the conclusion that there are adequate state and nonstate protections in the receiving country. For instance, in *Izevbekhai and Others v Ireland* the ECtHR noted that several Nigerian states criminalize FGM and sponsor projects to help women escape FGM. The ECtHR granted that FGM is still practised in some Nigerian states and that in several parts of the country there is a low level of legal action to enforce the legal prohibition on FGM. Still, it concluded that the general situation in Nigeria did not reveal the existence of a real risk.[98]

Second, if data indicate a decline in the prevalence of FGM in some regions within the receiving country, the ECtHR is likely to find that women can safely relocate to one of these areas. For instance, in *Collins and Akaziebie v Sweden* the applicants pointed out that 80 to 90 per cent of all women had been subjected to FGM in the Nigerian state they came from. The ECtHR did not dispute this figure but noted that the FGM rate for Nigeria as a whole had steadily declined in recent years, and it concluded that the applicants could relocate to another Nigerian state where FGM is less widespread.[99]

Third, the ECtHR often considers whether the applicants have the economic and personal resources needed to avoid FGM in the receiving country. For instance, in *Collins and Akaziebie* the ECtHR noted that the first applicant had shown great 'strength and independence': it therefore saw no reason why she could not succeed in protecting her daughter from being subjected to FGM in Nigeria.[100] Similarly, in *Omeredo v Austria* the ECtHR accepted that it may be difficult to live in Nigeria 'as an unmarried woman without support of her family', but it concluded that, owing to her education and professional experience, the applicant was able to avoid FGM and build a life independently of her family in the receiving country.[101]

These criteria arguably set a high threshold for what will be accepted as evidence that women and girls in the receiving country are at a real risk of being subjected to FGM.[102]

Conversely, in respect of complaints that do not concern FGM, the ECtHR has sometimes adopted a lower threshold for what it will accept as evidence that a woman in the receiving country is at risk of violence and ill-treatment from her family members. In *N v Sweden* the applicant, an Afghan woman, was challenging a deportation order issued by Swedish authorities. She had separated from her Afghan husband in Sweden and had started an extramarital affair with a Swedish man. Thus, the applicant argued that, if deported, she would be exposed

---

[98]   *Izevbekhai and Others v Ireland* (dec) App no 43408/08 (ECtHR, 17 May 2011) para 75.

[99]   *Collins and Akaziebie* (n 97) 'The Law'. See also *Izevbekhai and Others* (n 98) para 80.

[100]   *Collins and Akaziebie* (n 97) 'The Law'.

[101]   *Omeredo v Austria* (dec) App no 8969/10 (ECtHR, 20 September 2011) 'The Law' para 1. For a similar approach in respect of the applicants' economic and social status, see *Izevbekhai and Others* (n 98) paras 80–81; *Sow v Belgium* App no 27081/13 (ECtHR, 19 January 2016) para 68.

[102]   For a discussion, see Annemarie Middelburg and Alina Balta, 'Female Genital Mutilation/Cutting as a Ground for Asylum in Europe' (2016) 28 *International Journal of Refugee Law* 416.

to a real risk of ill-treatment contrary to Article 3. The ECtHR upheld her complaint and observed that women are at risk of ill-treatment in Afghanistan 'if perceived as not conforming to the gender roles ascribed to them by society, tradition and even the legal system'.[103] The ECtHR further indicated that, according to international statistics and reports, the authorities in Afghanistan are likely to condone violence against women.[104] Against this background the ECtHR concluded that, if deported, the applicant would face 'various cumulative risks of reprisals' from her husband, 'his family, her own family and from the Afghan society'.[105]

The ECtHR has also refused to recognize cultural practices associated with marriage that do not comply with national legislation regulating the institution of marriage. For instance, in *ZH and RH v Switzerland* the ECtHR held that the ECHR cannot be interpreted as imposing an obligation to recognize a marriage contracted by a child. In this case, the applicants—two Afghan nationals seeking asylum in Switzerland—had been married at a religious ceremony when the first applicant was 14 years old and the second applicant was 18 years old. Swiss authorities rejected their request on the ground that, inter alia, the applicants' marriage was incompatible with public order because sexual intercourse with a child under the age of 16 is a criminal offence under Swiss law.[106] The ECtHR upheld the decision of Swiss authorities and noted that, owing to the 'sensitive moral choices concerned and the importance to be attached to the protection of children and the fostering of secure family environments', national authorities enjoy a wide margin of appreciation to determine the circumstances under which a marriage will be deemed valid.[107]

---

[103] *N v Sweden* App no 23505/09 (ECtHR, 20 July 2010) para 55.

[104] ibid, para 57.

[105] ibid, para 62. See also *Jabari v Turkey* ECHR 2000-VIII; *RD v France* App no 34648/14 (ECtHR, 16 June 2016).

[106] *ZH and RH v Switzerland* App no 60119/12 (ECtHR, 8 December 2015). On the validity of a religious marriage with a girl who is underage, see also *Khan v the United Kingdom* (dec) (1986) 48 DR 253.

[107] *ZH and RH* (n 106) para 44.

INDEX